INSIDE

WOMEN IN THE ACADEMY SPEAK OUT

INSIDE

CORPORATE U

WOMEN IN THE ACADEMY

SPEAK OUT

Edited by

MARILEE REIMER

SUMACH
PRESS

WOMEN'S ISSUES PUBLISHING PROGRAM

SERIES EDITOR: BETH MCAULEY

*To the women faculty working in quiet desperation
to achieve academic careers in corporatized universities.*

NATIONAL LIBRARY OF CANADA CATALOGUING IN PUBLICATION

Inside Corporate U: women in the academy speak out /
edited by Marilee Reimer.

Includes bibliographical references.
ISBN 1-894549-31-7

1. Universities and colleges—Administration. 2. Academic-industrial
collaboration. 3. Academic freedom. 4. Women college teachers.
5. Women's studies. I. Reimer, Marilee

LB2332.3.I57 2004   378.1   C2004-900027-6

Edited by Beth McAuley
Cover and design by Elizabeth Martin

*Sumach Press acknowledges the support of the Canada Council for the Arts
and the Ontario Arts Council for our publishing program. We acknowledge
the financial support of the Government of Canada through the Book Publishing
Industry Development Program (BPIDP) for our publishing activities.*

ONTARIO ARTS COUNCIL
CONSEIL DES ARTS DE L'ONTARIO

Printed and bound in Canada

Published by
SUMACH PRESS
1415 Bathurst Street Suite #202
Toronto Ontario Canada
M5R 3H8
sumachpress@on.aibn.com
www.sumachpress.com

CONTENTS

INTRODUCTION:
Does My University Include a Woman's Voice?
Marilee Reimer *11*

SECTION I:
WORKING IN CORPORATE U

Chapter 1
Despoiling Professional Autonomy: A Women's Perspective
Dorothy E. Smith *31*

Chapter 2
Corporate Challenges to Academic Freedom and Gender Equity
Jennie M. Hornosty *43*

Chapter 3
Teacher Education or Market Lottery?
A Look at Recent Shifts in Knowledge,
Curriculum and Pedagogy in a Faculty of Education
Linda Eyre *67*

Chapter 4
The "Captive Scientist":
Corporate Influence over Scientific Research
Ella Haley *87*

SECTION II:

WOMEN'S CAREERS IN THE GENDERED STREAM

Chapter 5
Shifting Programs or Undercutting Equity?
A Preliminary Study Using Three University Academic Calendars
Jane Gordon and Ilya Blum *103*

Chapter 6
Will Women's Studies Programs Survive the Corporate University?
Marilee Reimer *118*

Chapter 7
Intellectual Property, Higher Education and Women's Inequality:
Exploring Connections/Proposing Solutions
Claire Polster *138*

Chapter 8
Gender and Herding Cats:
Women and Men in Academic Administration
A. Marguerite Cassin *153*

SECTION III:

EMPLOYMENT AND EDUCATIONAL EQUITY IN THE CORPORATE
UNIVERSITY

Chapter 9
College "Equity" Centres and Women's Studies Faculty:
Regulation of Feminism?
Diane Meaghan *177*

Chapter 10
Agents of Change?
A Study of Equity Practitioners in Canadian Universities
Carol Agocs, Reem Attieh & Martin Cooke *198*

Chapter 11
The Untenured Female Academic in the Corporate University
Linda Joan Paul *226*

SECTION IV:
THE STUDENT EXPERIENCE OF CONSUMERISM,
HIGH TECHNOLOGY AND LIFE IN RESIDENCE

Chapter 12
Going to Market:
Neo-Liberalism and the Social Construction
of the University Student as an Autonomous Consumer
Elizabeth Brulé *247*

Chapter 13
Living on Campus:
Reframing the Residence as a Corporate Business
Elizabeth Blaney and Judy Piers-Kavanaugh *265*

Chapter 14
Control, Alt, Delete? Feminist Pedagogy and the Digital Academy
Cynthia Jacqueline Alexander *286*

Contributors *309*

ACKNOWLEDGEMENTS

I want to thank my colleague Marguerite Cassin whose long-term interest in the issues addressed in this collection and whose extensive professional expertise in organizations and work generated a collaborative dialogue that began between us and gradually came to include a larger group of women academics. I am also greatly indebted to the editorial committee who read and commented on the early drafts: Jane Gordon, Linda Eyre, Marguerite Cassin, Linda Paul and Ella Haley, with a special debt of gratitude to Adele Mueller. Their assistance has been invaluable. I owe a special thanks to my research assistant Monique Bourgeois for her steady and excellent work. Her shared interest in the corporate university and unique contribution from the standpoint of a student has been an inspiration to delve further into the privatization juggernaut. Dorothy E. Smith deserves a round of thanks. Her pioneering work on institutional ethnography and women's place in the professions has inspired many of us to tackle some of the more difficult analytical questions. Beth McAuley, the editor of the Women's Issues Publishing Program at Sumach Press, provided supportive encouragement for this project from the outset and has patiently worked with all of us through the editing of our essays. Thank you ever so much. My appreciation to Anita Saunders, the administrative assistant in my department, for her careful work on different aspects of this project.

I am most grateful to my family, Chris Adam and Meili Adam-Reimer, whose very real labour involved living with an academic spouse and mother during the writing and editing of a book, not to mention their encouragement and, at times, technical support. Meili, my eight-year-old daughter, just told me last night that she wants to be a sociologist, and I hope very much that this book contributes to a dialogue on the conditions necessary for the university to truly promote careers and academic freedom for both women and men.

DOES MY UNIVERSITY INCLUDE
A WOMAN'S VOICE?

Marilee Reimer

IN 1997 I WROTE A RESEARCH ARTICLE about the application of pay
equity in federal government clerical work. I wrote it from a critical and
feminist perspective to assess a universal job-evaluation system then
being proposed by the Treasury Board of Canada. I submitted the article to *Optimum: The Journal of Public Sector Management,* which had
been set up as a public–private partnership under the Publishing
Partnership Agreement.[1] In early 1998, Gilles Paquette, the journal's
editor-in-chief, notified me that the editing and peer-review processes
had been completed and that my article had been accepted for publication in June of that year. However, unbeknownst to the editor, officials
of the Treasury Board and managers of Consulting and Audit Canada
were attempting to stop the publication of my article as well as an article written by John Kervin, who had been solicited to provide a
commentary on my work.[2]

Gilles Paquet wrote a "Memorandum" in which he described these
events. He presented it to the Association of Public Service Executives at
the 2001 Conference on Collaborative Governance and circulated it in
the House of Commons. In one excerpt he wrote:

> It is my view that the issues discussed in this memorandum do not
> pertain only to interference with the editorial process in the publication

of a dossier on the Universal Classification System in a minor public management journal in which the Canadian government happens to be a partner. They reveal the profound difficulties that some federal public servants have in understanding the very meaning of the notion of partnership and the cavalier way in which some members of the bureaucracy feel empowered and authorized to suppress public debate in forums under their control.[3]

In the end, both Kervin's and my article were published in the April 2001 issue of the journal, almost three years after the original commitment to publish. In a much publicized move to address the unworkability of the public–private partnership, the University of Ottawa's Centre for Governance broke the Publishing Partnership Agreement with the government and began publishing *Optimum* as an independent electronic journal.

Beyond the immediate consequences of a greatly delayed publication — I was applying for a SSHRC grant in the ensuing period and central to the granting criteria was having a publishing record in a related area of research — I began to wonder whether the suppression of critical and feminist research was a common occurrence in the university and wondered if the changes within the financial organization of universities were affecting the support and recognition of feminist researchers in the academy. My colleague, Marguerite Cassin, and I began a dialogue on the subject and over a number of years discussed the many different ways the corporate presence in the university was affecting women academics. We decided to invite a larger group of academics doing research in the area to join us in an attempt to broaden the dialogue on these issues. The essays in this collection are the outgrowth of this group's efforts to address and debate these questions.

THE CORPORATE UNIVERSITY

It is important to say at the outset that the essays in *Inside Corporate U* voice the experiences of women who are witnessing the dramatic effects of restructuring within the corporate university. These essays draw on the unique experiences of women who, as a group, are seriously underrepresented in the upper echelons of power and privilege in the university setting.[4] Being socially located somewhat differently than the prototypical male academic, many women have a strong incentive to question the increasing concentration of power and privilege in male hands. These essays also draw on alternative methodological approaches that are more expressive of women's experiences.[5]

Other critical approaches used to anlayze the corporatization of universities in existing literature is useful to mention here. For example, Jan Currie and Janice Newson identify globalization as one of the main factors behind the corporate restructuring of universities. They conceptualize globalization as a process that combines "a market ideology with a corresponding material set of practices drawn from the world of business."[6] Janice Drakich, Karen Grant and Penni Stewart argue that in the past thirty years academics have seen the introduction of hiring freezes and budget cutbacks — initiatives strongly tied to government objectives.[7] This has meant an onslaught of "rationalizing" by corporate management and the "objective proletarianization," or downgrading, of academic work. With major cuts to federal funding in the last decade, universities have seen their per-capita funding and operating expenses decline by 17 percent and 7 percent, respectively.[8] Lisa McCoy identifies two key trends in the restructuring process: the reorganization of universities to fulfill government and business expectations for the "knowledge economy," and the emergence of the "accountability movement," which is imposing systems of accountability on academic work.[9]

As Neil Tudiver points out, this new commercial outlook is based on the notion of entrepreneurialism — students are encouraged to see themselves as consumers; faculty are to treat teaching and research as part of the university's cost-recovery program; and administration is to operate as a form of managerial control. According to Tudiver,

> Where universities have traditionally operated from a professional model, the corporate university follows a business model: capitalizing on research as an investment, seeking profit from its ventures, and forming partnerships with corporations through equity financing and licensing.[10]

In this volume, Elizabeth Brulé links the changing forms of accountability in university financing to the concomitant rise in tuition and the rise in students' view that their education is a commodity that needs to provide them with greater access to the job market. In the name of business prosperity, new regulations in the university are leading to diminished professional autonomy and professional judgement for academics. According to Dorothy Smith, these new "regimes of accountability" are key to maintaining corporate control over the universities. Smith defines these regimes as new forms of regulation that undermine the autonomy of the professions and increasingly subordinate the practices of the professions either directly to the original forms of capital or, in the public sector, to the demands of capital accumulation for lower taxation, reduced government deficits and extended privatization.[11]

One of the key regimes of accountability that affects women is the growing set of regulations that determine where faculty and institutions will be located as differentiation increases between university research and teaching.[12] For example, Claire Polster analyzes how new regimes affecting the dispensing of federal research monies are reorganizing relationships between Canadian universities. The funding of $3.15 billion for the Canada Foundation for Innovation and $900 million for the Canada Research Chairs Program are federal government initiatives intended to promote changes that will make Canada a key player in the global knowledge-based economy.[13] Given that the allocation of funds through these two programs is based on an institution's extant funding records, Polster points to the possibility that the allocation of funds to larger universities with stronger records may preclude some of the smaller universities from ever receiving funds of this sort. These smaller universities may be compromised by these programs and converted into primarily teaching institutions, thus losing their capacity to offer scholars research incentives.[14] Furthermore, at the end of the 2002–03 academic year, the gender distribution of Canada Research Chairs' funding revealed further inequality: a mere 16 percent of the Chairs had been given to women, even after different rounds of program competition had been completed.[15] The first three rounds were carried out without administrators being asked basic questions about whether the program was representative of the full-time academics now employed in Canadian universities.

If we look at the number of allocated Chairs as well as at the number of Chairs that have been projected for the third to fifth years of the program for the top six universities, we can see that the Canada Research Chairs Program helps to establish a "two-tiered" university system. Almost half of the Chairs in the country (48 percent) have been granted to six universities — these were Laval University, University of Montreal, McGill University, University of Toronto, University of Alberta and University of British Columbia.[16] Fifty-six percent of male faculty in Canada work on these six campuses, compared with only 36 percent of female faculty, therefore the concentration of Chairs in these universities has a notable gender bias. In her report, "Gender-Based Analysis for the Canada Research Chair Secretariat," Christine Begin-Heick recommends that a more equitable distribution could be achieved by instituting pro-active gender equity measures for administrators.[17] This and other recommendations have been ignored for the last two years, the proportion of women appointed has remained constant, and the program is now the focus of a class-action suit by a group of women professors.[18]

A report on the status of women in Ontario universities, released less than fifteen years ago, displays how corporatization can affect gender relations. In 1990 the Ontario government established a commission in an effort to analyze women's progress in provincial universities. Its *Final Report on the Status of Women in Ontario Universities* concluded that "women were a minority group receiving a small proportion of full-time university appointments, concentrated in the lower academic ranks, absent from senior administrative positions and paid less than men at equivalent ranks."[19] The report also stated that women were generally allocated the responsibilities for undergraduate teaching and the "house-keeping" aspects of administrative work, rather than the work of the discipline or profession.

The apparent gains of women faculty to the university can only be understood in light of the structural shifts in faculty retirements and funding freezes in the last decade. While women held only 13 percent of faculty positions in 1973–74, women's share of faculty positions increased to 29 percent by 2003,[20] including an increased representation of 13.7 percent for full professors, 29.1 percent for associate professors and 43.8 percent for assistant professors and lecturers.[21] Even though women made up well over half (57 percent) of university students between 1992 and 1997, women were appointed to a mere three hundred faculty positions across Canada.[22] For that same period, over 4,500 male faculty retired, thus inflating the actual gains women made. From 1992–98, full-time positions decreased on average by 9.6 percent and were replaced with part-time positions in most regions in Canada.[23] Progress in hiring continues to be slow, partly as a result of the decreases in funding levels to universities, yet the fact remains that in 1998 alone 35.5 percent of doctorates and 49 percent of doctoral students were women. If the present rate of increase continues (.91 percent from the academic years 1997–98 to 1998–99), it will take over twenty years for women to be hired as faculty in proportion to the annual number of doctorates they are granted.

With ongoing restructuring of universities, where the government and administration decide to concentrate resources becomes a central concern. Under the current corporatist strategy, governments fund corporate-sponsored research, which benefits Canada's largest and most research-intensive universities.[24] With the establishment of this "two-tiered" university system, teaching is no longer a priority for public investment, meanwhile the less research-focused institutions become more "service" and job-oriented in their focus. In addition, teaching workloads are intensified, particularly in the teaching universities and among the ranks of part-time faculty, who are numerically approaching the number of full-time faculty (27,983 part-time to 33,665 full-time for 1998–99).[25] One of the obvious effects of this work intensification on gender is suggested in the national statistics on full-time faculty, which cite that women faculty's average workload averages 64.5 hours weekly compared with their male colleagues' average of 59 hours.[26] If women are working longer hours, primarily in the classroom, it means they have less time to dedicate to their independent research.

The two-tiered system that locates more women in work-intensive teaching universities reflects federal funding cutbacks and disparities in core funding even within a region such as Atlantic Canada. For example, in New Brunswick, the most poorly funded university received $2,448 in operating grant per student, while the average for all other provincial university operating grants was $3,787, with the lowest receiving under 65 percent of the other university's average.[27] Because core funding is not allocated to post-secondary research as it is to health, primary and secondary education, public and private wealth continues to flow to the established, research-based institutions. The disparities in research funding between the economically disadvantaged region of Atlantic Canada and the rest of Canada underlies the "tiering" effect of many universities in the region. With 7.7 percent of the population base, major federal funding agencies (CFI, SSHRC, NSERC and NCE) respectively allocated to the region the following portions of funding: 3.6 percent, 4.7 percent, 6.2 percent and 1.6 percent (NSERC figures for 1998, all the others for 2000–01).[28]

These are some of the issues discussed in this collection. Together, these essays demonstrate that women in the academy are analyzing how they fit into the new corporate university, reflecting on their positions in these changing structures and questioning how they can resist the corporate agenda. In the following sections, I briefly introduce these authors and the topics they are addressing.

SECTION I: WORKING IN CORPORATE U

The authors in this section outline the ways in which women's entry into the hallowed halls of academe signal the beginning of an era of increasing restrictions on scholars in the name of commercial enhancement. In chapter 1, "Despoiling Professional Autonomy: A Women's Perspective," Dorothy E. Smith anchors an analysis of corporatization in the larger organizational processes as a way to frame the discussion of gender relations in academia. By placing universities in relation to the wider managerial hierarchies of government, media and business, Smith helps us to see the "progressive disappearance in society of bases from which voices and influence representing other interests and concerns can be effective." That is, the disappearance of professional autonomy in health, social work and education — professional realms into which many women have entered. Smith describes how American business corporations have created a series of new institutions — right-wing think tanks and institutes that train right-wing journalists, for example — which are being used to organize an ideological campaign against liberal higher education and affirmative action and as a means to establish the hegemony of neo-liberalism. As a neighbour that is highly integrated into the American economy, Canadian society and its post-secondary institutions are subject to the same ideological onslaught and disenfranchisement. The analysis of how women are disenfranchised in the corporatized university lifts a veil on a more general process of de-professionalization. Smith describes this as one of eliminating professional autonomy in favour of managerial systems that reorder the objectives and practices of institutions to better serve the commercial system.

In chapter 2, "Corporate Challenges to Academic Freedom and Gender Equity," Jennie Hornosty focuses on the effects of corporatization on academic freedom and the specific impact on women's scholarship. She reflects on how the corporate agenda is both eroding academic freedom and threatening the concrete gains academic women have made in the last three decades in terms of women's scholarship and improving the infamous "climate" of universities. By examining some of the practices and values of corporatization in the academy, she demonstrates how these are undermining a feminist agenda for transforming the university into a more inclusive place. Alternatively, Hornosty envisions the very minimum requirements for reversing the damage to academic freedom and intellectual inquiry: an academic context which is open, transparent, free from external forces, democratic and pluralistic. Thus, she makes a fundamental connection between what threatens feminist scholarship, Women's Studies programs and equity gains, and the eroding foundations of academic freedom in a commercialized era.

In chapter 3, "Teacher Education or Market Lottery? A Look at Recent Shifts in Knowledge, Curriculum and Pedagogy in a Faculty of Education," Linda Eyre provides a compelling story of how successive Liberal and Conservative governments in New Brunswick influenced the Department of Education to pressure education faculty to accept corporatist values and discourses. One is especially shocked to discover just how the educational policy has shifted towards a for-profit market model and the impact this has had on teacher training. Eyre examines three instances where pressure from the Department of Education (which was transmitted through the faculty's administration) undermined the work of faculty in the areas of literacy, health and alcohol education. Responding to national testing results ranking New Brunswick in literacy, science and math the lowest in Canada, the Department of Education sought to impose a skills-based, assessment-driven approach to literacy. The implementation required faculty to ignore contemporary approaches in these areas of education and to bypass the ordinary collegial consultation policies. Eyre reveals the very active role that faculty who incorporate feminist and critical approaches in their teaching took in speaking out and responding critically to these approaches, which could damage professional autonomy, academic freedom and academic collegiality. Eyre concludes that resistance is possible and demonstrates how critical and feminist scholars can work collaboratively to challenge the dominant relations of power.

In chapter 4, "'The Captive Scientist': Corporate Influence over Scientific Research," Ella Haley address the traditional gender networks and corporate–university ties that go back to the early twentieth century. She takes a close look at a premier "research" university, the

University of Toronto, and its long history of corporate-funded research. She reviews the most recent controversies sparked by the undue influence of pharmaceutical companies on researchers such as Drs. Nancy Olivieri and David Healy, and shows how controversies like these are linked to recent controversies in Health Canada, where corporations present research on new products (e.g., bovine growth hormone) in order to gain approval to market them.

Haley's key argument is that corporate influence over researchers, especially through "gag clauses," is not new. As early as 1915, Harvard University's Department of Industrial Hygiene was totally reliant upon business contributions. Researchers funded by the very company that they were investigating failed to go public after they found that the "jaw rot" of young women in the radium dialpainting factories was due to the radiation in the paint. As a result of "gag" clauses tied to the research contract provided by the radium company, the researchers delayed the diagnosis of this occupational illness, leaving many young women unnecessarily exposed to radiation and, in many cases, to illness and early death. This chapter also illustrates how, from the 1930s onwards, "captive scientists" funded by fluoride emitting industries produced research to counter complaints and lawsuits from southwestern Ontario farmers for damage to their crops, livestock and health from the fluoride emissions. Rather than considering this merely an aberrant instance of how the old boy's network went wrong, Haley's example is a beacon of light shining on what we can expect to see even more frequently in a future where the keys to the castle are turned over to a very self-interested band of intruders.

SECTION II: WOMEN'S CAREERS IN THE GENDERED STREAM

In this section, we see the inextricable links between the manner in which women are being incorporated into academe and the more undemocratic, seamier side of a hierarchical system that is progressively undermining the basis for socially oriented scholarship and programming. Jane Gordon and Ilya Blum examine four key issues affecting women's employment in chapter 5, "Shifting Programs or Undercutting Equity? A Preliminary Study Using Three University Academic Calendars." These include the gender composition of the faculty, the length of faculty attachment to the university, the highest rank achieved by faculty at three universities and the changes in the distribution of disciplines over time with the commercial emphasis on professional programs. They analyze three university calendars to access data in the early years of corporatization (the 1980s to the mid-1990s), which leads them to ask if the shifts to professional programs and marginal employment will nullify the gains women have made in the last two decades. They find that women are making employment inroads, but not always into the best positions. Their data reveal that women are vastly underrepresented in the ranks of full professor as of the mid-1990s, while their representation in part-time and contractually limited positions grew substantially. They make the crucial point that equity gains of the last two decades may be undercut as women are disproportionately located in low-attachment academic employment and barriers to advancement to full professor diminish the career opportunities of women faculty.

In chapter 6, "Will Women's Studies Programs Survive the Corporate University?" Marilee Reimer takes a look at the Women's Studies programs at four central and Atlantic Canadian universities. In many ways a bellwether for new programming in a system overflowing with women students, we see that this is not always the case. For, university programs require administrative backing in not only the course offerings but also in relation to the ways in which research is supported and workloads are distributed within departments. With a strong emphasis on attracting commercially oriented grants and programming, both university administrators and politicians contribute to a context where a focus on human concerns as in feminist scholarship becomes peripheral and a volunteer effort. In effect, what we see is the slow demise of progressive programming where administrators see no commercial incentive to invest. Yet this is taking place at a time when government initiatives in health and law, the labour force and human-service delivery are concerned with issues of diversity and maximizing labour-force utilization that are completely relevant to the kind of programming housed in Women's Studies.[29] However, when short-term commercial gains become the bottom line of university mandates, the fabric of Women's Studies programming and of feminist scholarship that benefits social ends begins to unravel.

Claire Polster raises fundamental questions in chapter 7, "Intellectual Property, Higher Education and Women's Inequality: Exploring Connections/Proposing Solutions." She asks whether it is possible for the university to serve the "public good" while servicing its corporate masters and what might happen to feminist research that addresses human concerns if it doesn't make any contribution to short-term profits. Polster argues that perhaps more than any other group, it is women who have the most to lose from the development and extension of intellectual property regimes (IPRs). Women's already limited control over the conditions of our lives is further threatened as various forms of knowledge are converted into the private property of individuals and corporations. She explores the implications of IPRs on women's and feminists' ability to work in and through the university as a way to advance women's interests and needs, and concludes with a strategy of how to resist the privatization of knowledge in and through the university as a means of protecting the feminist project and the public interest more generally.

Chapter 8, "Gender and Herding Cats: Women and Men in University Administration" by Marguerite Cassin addresses the possibility of there being what she refers to as a "dual collegiality," which includes women as well as men in the project of shaping and creating the university. However, as Ann Oakley puts it, the fundamentally gendered character of corporate restructuring in universities in the U.S. (and elsewhere) precludes such an outcome. She writes that "when the culture of bureaucracy and commodification is combined with a disregard — flagrant in its implications — for the way power operates, the result is bound to be discriminatory."[30] Similarly, Cassin finds that the restructured university promotes a culture of male dominance in administration, and particularly in the development of a knowledge-based culture. By focusing on the culture of knowledge development and its relation to women's faculty involvement in research and administration, this chapter goes a long way in explaining how women are excluded from political power in the corporate university.

SECTION III: EMPLOYMENT AND EDUCATIONAL EQUITY IN THE CORPORATE UNIVERSITY

More than ever before, the equity gains of the twentieth-century university are being eroded and countered with a new order of hierarchical social relations. In the first chapter of this section, "College 'Equity' Centres and Women's Studies Faculty: Regulation of Feminism?" Diane Meaghan profiles a case study of how one community college's Equity

Centre operated as an arm of the administration to attack feminist teaching and attempted to remove feminists and other high-profile advocates of equity. She states that "free speech is a necessary qualification and one of the highest purposes of the college in a democratic society." While community college administrators began addressing equity and inclusion issues a decade ago as a part of the educational mission of colleges, some administrators subverted the intent of these policies and the "charter of rights of professors" ceased to exist. The goal of stemming systematic discrimination and harassment made way for a new concept of harassment, that of a violation merely of individuals by individuals, as some administrators relentlessly scrutinized and censored every facet of educational experience. Meaghan illustrates how vulnerable Women's Studies professors are to such regimes of intimidation and demonstrates how academic freedom is essential if Women's Studies programming is to move forward within the community college.

Then, in chapter 10, "Agents of Change? A Study of Equity Practitioners in Canadian Universities," Carol Agocs, Reem Attieh and Martin Cooke present the outcome of an extensive inquiry into the role and efficacy of equity practitioners across the country. Drawing on a 1998–99 nationwide survey of equity practitioners, they examine whether or not these managers will be able to function effectively as agents of transformative change on behalf of marginalized groups within the university as an organization. Not surprisingly, there are three keys factors to equity outcomes: (1) the personal commitment that equity practitioners make to change, (2) whether or not the university mandates the practitioners to address organizational issues and (3) whether the practitioners are in a structural position to influence change within universities. Their study clearly points out that equity, too, has a price that organizations are becoming less and less willing to pay.

When we realize that an equal number of women academics are working in untenured and part-time positions as there are in tenured positions or positions leading to tenure, it is time to assess the trend towards locating women in what Gordon and Blum call "low attachment" positions within academia. In chapter 11, "The Untenured Female Academic in the Corporate University," Linda Paul astutely outlines the key labour strategy used in the corporate university to exploit this permanent underclass of academic labour, of which women are the growing component. Paul contextualizes the practice of hiring increasing proportions of untenured and contracted labour that in turn displaces more costly tenured faculty. She points out that while "profit derived from intellectual property is central to the corporate university's drive for short-term profits," it is in large part the marginal, untenured academics who are freeing up the elite researchers from teaching. Paul also lays out the gendered contours of government funding practices, which grant male-dominated sciences and engineering disciplines the lion's share of funding. This results in only 20 percent of funding for Canada Research Chairs being granted to the Humanities and Social Sciences, disciplines "where women make up more than 50 per cent of the researchers."

SECTION IV: THE STUDENT EXPERIENCE OF CONSUMERISM, HIGH TECHNOLOGY AND LIFE IN RESIDENCE

In the name of the students, major transformations are occurring on university and college campuses. Yet with close to two-thirds of undergraduate students being female, how realistic are these claims to further the interests of the average student?

In chapter 12, "Going to Market: Neo-Liberalism and the Social Construction of the University Student as an *Autonomous Consumer,*" Elizabeth Brulé addresses the transformation of education into a consumer product. Her overview of the changes in university financing and the related shifts in student, faculty and administration constituencies that accompany them provides a fascinating glimpse into how this transition is taking place. She analyzes how universities have been restructured according to the logic of the market, with increasing emphasis on education as a consumable product and students as *autonomous consumers.* This shift takes curriculum development and teaching practices away from the humanist liberal ideal of fostering active *learning* or *citizenship* to one focused on delivering quantifiable services and satisfying consumers in measurable terms. She demonstrates how common-sense notions of consumer relations provide students with increased opportunities to challenge course curriculum and the social relations and organization of post-secondary teaching, and concludes that "collaborative resistance with our students in identifying restrictive accountability practices and redefining the terms of what constitutes a 'quality' post-secondary education may help in establishing an educational system that is based on social contribution rather than economic gain."

Elizabeth Blaney and Judy Piers-Kavanaugh give us a glimpse of their experiences of working as residence dons during their graduate studies in chapter 13, "Living on Campus: Reframing the Residence as a Corporate Business." In their depiction of the day-to-day lives of female dons, they reveal the corporate discourse of "community" and "leadership" and illustrate how the university administration uses the dominant discourse to implement a gendered division of labour among dons, to silence feminist opposition to physical and verbal forms of violence and abuse of women and to reinforce the old regimes of "patriarchy, racism, classism, heterosexism and elitism." They have creatively structured their chapter as a conversation, making use of their own roles in order to "reveal the resistances and complexities" of striving to achieve their independent identities while living inside the "corporate residence."

In chapter 14, "Control, Alt, Delete? Feminist Pedagogy and the Digital Academy," Cynthia Jacqueline Alexander takes us to one of the country's most wired campuses — Acadia University, an IBM ThinkPad campus in which IBM puts laptop computers into the hands of students and faculty members. Discussions about the role of universities in the twenty first century have tended to ignore the value-laden choices that accompany the adoption of computer-based learning networks, considering them to be value-neutral. She reminds us that in the midst of the major shifts that are accompanying technological change, the gender dimensions of the computer revolution should not be overlooked. She poses two key questions for our consideration: Will our technological future be characterized by further loss of control over feminist-based intellectual activities and an inability to institute alternative gender relations in our classrooms or to include the most vulnerable groups in the academic system? Dare we envision a scenario where we gain control over our own intellectual paths, where alternative gender relationships are realized and valued and where the old gendered power relationships within the academy are rewritten?

*

As we have been discussing these issues over the past years, the corporate agenda has become a daily reality of university life. I feel that much more needs to be written on this subject, because when it is all said and done, women have very little political power in universities and the ones who achieve positions of power are thoroughly aware that they have very little latitude. The fact that women have so little political power in universities intrigues me, as does the way larger and larger groups of both women and men are being disenfranchised as privatization of the university proceeds. It is important that we think about why this is the case, and it is important that we critically and openly challenge what we see as a threat to the higher education we have come to value. We hope that *Inside Corporate U* will voice some of our concerns to a broader audience, which in turn will encourage women in the academy to continue speaking out against what we perceive to be a real danger to all that we have struggled to achieve.

NOTES

1. The Publishing Partnership Agreement was set up between Consulting and Audit Canada (Government of Canada), Prospectus (a private partner), the Centre on Governance at the University of Ottawa (civic sector partner) and the Partnership Board. The Agreement separated editorial authority, vested in the Centre on Governance's designated editor-in-chief, from the physical production process, which was completed by the federal department of Supply and Services.

2. See Marilee Reimer, "Searching for Gender Neutrality in the UCS" and John Kervin, "Helping Find Gender Neutrality: A Theoretical Framework," *Optimum: The Journal of Public Sector Management* 30, nos. 3/4 (April 2001), 29–42 and 43–49.

3. Gilles Paquet, "Memorandum" (paper presented to the Association of Public Service Executives, Conference on Collaborative Governance, Ottawa, 2001), 1.

4. A growing Canadian literature attests to the essentially gendered character of university careers: Sandra Bell and Jane Gordon, "Scholarship — the New Dimension to Equity Issues for Academic Women," *Women's Studies International Forum* 22, no. 6 (1999), 645–658; Chilly Climate Collective, eds., *Breaking Anonymity* (Waterloo: Wilfrid Laurier University Press, 1995); Linda Eyre, "No Strings Attached? Corporate Involvement in Curriculum,"

Canadian Journal of Education (in press). Sheila McIntyre, "Gender Bias within the Law School: 'The Memo' and Its Impact," *Canadian Journal of Women and the Law* 2 (1987–88); Leslie Roman and Linda Eyre, eds., *Dangerous Territories: Struggles for Difference and Equality in Education* (New York: Routledge, 1999); and Jackie Stalker and Susan Prentice, *The Illusion of Inclusion: Women and Post-Secondary Education* (Halifax: Fernwood Publishing, 1998).

5. Many of the authors in this collection draw upon the social organization of knowledge methodology developed by Dorothy E. Smith, and upon feminist methodology more generally. For more on these methodologies, see Dorothy E. Smith, *Writing the Social: Critique, Theory and Investigations* (Toronto: University of Toronto Press, 1999), and Marie Campbell and Fran Gregor, *Mapping Social Relations: A Primer in Doing Institutional Ethnography* (Aurora, ON: Garamond Press, 2002).

6. Jan Currie and Janice Newson, eds., *Universities and Globalisation: Critical Perspectives* (Thousand Oaks, CA: Sage Publications, 1998), 1.

7. Janice Drakich, Karen R. Grant and Penni Stewart, "Editors' Introduction: The Academy in the Twenty-First Century," *The Canadian Review of Sociology and Anthropology* 39, no. 3 (2002), 261–299.

8. Ibid.

9. For a discussion of how accounting practices bring the relevance of the market into all levels of university activity, see Lisa McCoy, "Producing 'What the Deans Know': Cost Accounting and the Restructuring of Post-Secondary Education," *Human Studies* 21 (1998), 395–418. Alison Griffith examines the impact of such restructuring in Ontario public education with the introduction of *The Educational Quality Improvement Act* in "Educational Re-structuring in Ontario: A Textual Analysis" (paper presented at The Restructuring and Transformation of Institutional Processes in Canada: Applications of Institutional Ethnography Conference, Toronto, York University, 1998), 3. See also, Alison Griffith and Cecilia Reynolds, *Equity and Globalization in Education* (Calgary: Detselig Enterprises, 2002).

10. Neil Tudiver, *Universities for Sale: Resisting Corporate Control over Canadian Higher Education* (Toronto: James Lorimer, 1999), 5.

11. See Dorothy E. Smith, "Despoiling Professional Autonomy: A Women's Perspective," in this volume.

12. Donald Fisher and Kjell Rubenson, "The Changing Political Economy: The Private and Public Lives of Canadian Universities," in Currie and Newson, eds., *Universities and Globalisation*, 94.

13. Claire Polster, "A Break from the Past: Impacts and Implications of the Canada Foundation for Innovation and the Canada Research Chairs Initiatives," *The Canadian Review of Sociology and Anthropology* 39, no. 3 (2002), 279.

14. See William Graham, "Academic Freedom or Commercial License?" in James Turk, ed., *The Corporate Campus: Commercialization and the Dangers to Canada's Colleges and Universities* (Toronto: James Lorimer, 2000).

15. See Industry Canada, Canada Research Chairs at <www.chairs.gc.ca/english/ Media/Statistics/gender.html>. June 25, 2003.

16. The number of women in full-time positions and the percentage share for all full-time positions at each of these universities is extrapolated from data in *Status of Women Bulletin 2001; CAUT Bulletin* 8 (October 2001); and the Canada Research Chair Program Web site <www.chairs.gc/english/program/ chair/breakdown.pdf>.

17. Christine Begin-Heick, "Preliminary Gender-based Analysis of the Canada Research Chairs Program," a report prepared for the Canada Research Chair Secretariat (Ottawa, 2001). The working assumption for Tier II, where women in social sciences were underrepresented, was that these nominees were mostly at the associate professor and assistant professor level. In fact, full professors were highly represented as nominees, especially in the SSHRC disciplines, where the majority (almost 50 percent) of nominees were full professors. Only a small proportion was drawn from the assistant professor pool, where the pool of faculty is much larger. The weighting of Tier II nominations towards the higher academic ranks has a discriminatory effect against the nomination of women.

18. The following statement was issued on the PAR-L server in November 2003: "The eight university professors who initiated the human rights complaint against Industry Canada over discrimination in the Canada Research Chairs Program reported in November 2003 that mediation by the Canadian Human Rights Commission to resolve the complaint had failed. The complaints, filed by eight faculty members from universities across Canada, point to the very small allocation of the 2,000 chairs to people from groups protected by human rights legislation. For example, the latest figures on the Canada Research Chairs Web site show that 1,035 Chairs have been awarded to date; of these only 175 (17 percent) have been awarded to women. Complete data are not available for any other equity-seeking group. Industry Canada is responsible for the design and implementation of the $900 million program. The complainants hope that the complaint process will result in the kinds of changes that will make the hiring of the Chairs transparent and fair in all cases, and will avoid secretive, single-candidate searches. The complainants also challenge the small allocation to the humanities and social sciences, disciplines which involve the majority of Canadian students and professors. Although mediation has failed, the eight complainants will continue to pursue the issues with the Human Rights Commission. They feel strongly that federal government programs should be in conformity with Canadian law and the international agreements that Canada has signed to protect individuals from discrimination. The eight faculty members who filed complaints are Marjorie Griffin Cohen (Simon Fraser University), Louise Forsyth (Emerita,

University of Saskatchewan), Glenis Joyce (University of Saskatchewan), Audrey Kobayashi (Queen's University), Shree Mulay (McGill University), Michèle Ollivier (University of Ottawa), Susan Prentice (University of Manitoba) and Wendy Robbins (University of New Brunswick)." Background information is available on the PAR-L Web site <www.unb.ca/PAR-L/CRCcomplaint.htm>; on the Web site of the Canadian Federation for the Humanities and Social Sciences <www.fedcan.ca/english/policyandadvocacy/win/researchchairs.cfm#background>; and from the Canada Research Chairs Secretariat, under Media, <www.chairs.gc.ca/web/media/stats/ gender_e.asp>. You can search for your own (or any other) university's complete list of Chairholders at <www.chairs.gc.ca/web/chairholders/index_e.asp>.

19. Janice Drakich, Dorothy E. Smith, Penni Stewart, Bonnie Fox and Alison Griffith, *Final Report on the Status of Women in Ontario Universities* (Toronto: Ontario Ministries of Colleges and Universities, 1991).

20. Janice Drakich and Penni Stewart, "A Profile of Women Faculty in Canada: Rank, Discipline and Age, 1957–1994," in *CAUT Bulletin, Status of Women Supplement* (April 1998); Statistics Canada data cited in Canadian Association of University Teachers, *CAUT Almanac of Post-Secondary Education in Canada* (2003), 24–25.

21. Statistics Canada data cited in *CAUT Almanac of Post-Secondary Education in Canada*, 24–25.

22. Statistics Canada, *The Daily*, Thursday, November 8, 2001; Tudiver, *Universities for Sale.*

23. Statistics Canada data cited in *CAUT Almanac of Post-Secondary Education in Canada*, 24–25.

24. Tom Booth, "Our Universities Facing 'Creeping Privatization,'" *CAUT Bulletin* 48 (February 2001), 1.

25. Statistics Canada, *Educational Quarterly Review* (2000), table 1; Drakich and Stewart, "A Profile of Women Faculty," 3.

26. Statistics Canada, Educational Quarterly Review.

27. Daniel O'Brien, "Average Grant Per Arts Student, 2001–2002," *President's Report, St. Thomas University* (February 24, 2002), 33.

28. The Honourable Andy Scott, "Letter to Brian Tobin, Minister of Industry, on Issues Surrounding Post-Secondary Education," July 1, 2001, 3. In the possession of the author.

29. Nova Scotia Human Rights Commission, *Trends in Creating Quality of Life in Nova Scotia: Human Rights in Community, Workplace and Governance* (Halifax: NSHRC, 2003), 1–33.

30. Ann Oakley, "Introduction: Globalization, Academia and Change," in Ann Brooks and Alison Mackinnon, *Gender and the Restructured University* (Buckingham, UK: The Society for Research into Higher Education and the Open University Press, 2001), xiii.

WORKING IN
CORPORATE U

CHAPTER 1

DESPOILING PROFESSIONAL AUTONOMY: A WOMEN'S PERSPECTIVE

Dorothy E. Smith

MY SOCIOLOGICAL WORK IN the women's movement started as a critique of the conceptual and methodological practices of sociology. These practices constructed a world on paper that represented society and people as objects. The exclusion of women as subjects in sociological discourse was an effect of the suppression of people as subjects in a discourse in which the universal subject was male. In finding an alternative place to begin, I started with the standpoint in the daily life and work of a housewife and mother and designed a sociology that would explore the world outwards from the local actualities of people's lives.

In so doing, I discovered what I have called the "ruling relations."[1] If you start in the everyday world and look within and beyond it to how it is organized and shaped, these relations come into view as the abstracted conceptual and extra-locally organized relations of state, professions, corporations, academic discourses, mass media, and so on. The knower positioned where her body is, in the actualities of her everyday world, discovers a contrasting order of relations or social organization that coordinates people's doings outside and beyond the necessarily local sites of our bodily being. These relations are, of course, to be understood as they are produced by people's local activities. The concept of "ruling relations" doesn't cut the cake up into government, corporation, mass media or even institutions. The ruling relations are a generalized form.

Different functions and forms of social organization as they are today have emerged within a new and textually mediated mode of co-ordinating people's activities across local settings of people's work or other activities. They are to be understood as *an objectification of consciousness and agency*, in specialized social forms, superseding at the level of the organizing and regulation of societies those forms of consciousness that, however formalized, have been identified with individuals and individualized forms of consciousness — "thinking heads," to use Marx's vivid term.[2] In traditional forms of authority, according to Weber, domination is clearly identified with the consciousness and agency of individuals and with particularized relationships among people. Those who exercise authority are "(t)he masters" and "(o)bedience is owed not to enacted rules but to the person who occupies a position of authority."[3] Weber contrasts the notion of rational legal authority with the traditional form. Those in authority are legitimated by the rule of law; their capacities to act are defined by the office they hold; the functions of offices are rationally designed with the goals or general functions of the organization in mind. Weber's concept is limited to one type of objectified mode of ruling — bureaucracy.

What the concept of the ruling relations captures are more general phenomena that are particular characteristics of contemporary society, namely the general forms of objectified social consciousness and agency, independent of particular thinkers and knowers, imposed upon the latter as media of thought, knowledge, agency and imagination, and organizing people's activities in multiple local sites. As well as being systems of communication, knowledge, information, regulation, control, management, and the like, mediated by texts and textual technologies (print, film, radio, television, computers), they are, it must be stressed, media in and through which people act.

People participate in the ruling relations in forms that are separable from them as individuals — they occupy offices or positions, they have roles to play, and so on. How they know is mediated to them by knowledges, information and facts that supersede and displace their personal experience. Or they may be the objects of institutional work as patients, social work clients, students and other categories that create distinctive forms of participation without agency. At work, they are for the most part "employees," that is, those who are "used," and the organizations they work for don't arise out of or seek goals that are theirs as individuals. They do not create art, music, songs, plays and stories in the context of their ongoing relationships with family, friends and neighbours; these are created by paid specialists and delivered to them in the same standardized forms that they are delivered to anyone else watching the same channel, listening to the same band on the radio, picking up the same newspaper or reading the same textbook in class.

The development of the ruling relations accelerated rapidly at the turn of the nineteenth and twentieth centuries in North America and other developed countries. Rapid innovations were made that have permanently transformed the way in which the social is organized at the level of the society at large.[4] Developments in the bureaucratization of the state, familiar in Weber,[5] were accompanied by radical innovations in the management of business enterprises and in the new form of the corporation, which was a move away from the identification of business with individual owner/managers.[6]

The advance of the ruling relations was both created by and a basis for the emergence of a new middle class of people who earn their living in textually mediated forms of work — in business, government, professions, universities, the mass media — and associated forms of enterprise. After the Second World War, this intelligentsia became increasingly important and increasingly powerful. It has played a role in the expansion of the ruling relations and, in particular, in the invention and deployment of the new technologies of information, communication, management and organization that have made possible the current developments. Right after the Second World War, American sociologists were writing about the emergence of a New Class — the intelligentsia — who held a new form of power.[7] The kind of power that was attributed to this group depended on the existence of institutions through which power and initiative could be exercised independently of capital. Universities, government (to some extent), the mass media and the professions were the primary institutional bases of such independence.

This was the intelligentsia that was radically disciplined, particularly in the United States, in the McCarthy era. McCarthyism bore mostly on the radicals in universities and colleges and in government, and particularly heavily on the relatively new forms of mass-media movies and radio. The McCarthy onslaught, together with the revelations of Stalinist tyranny, were immensely successful in breaking the links that had been established between a progressive intelligentsia and working-class struggles. Both sides withdrew: trade unions in both Canada and the United States ejected the Communist Party and built what became traditions that repudiated association with the intelligentsia. For its part, the intelligentsia, particularly in the social sciences, set to work to redefine their disciplines in order to divorce them from their more radical past.[8]

In the 1960s and 1970s, an entirely new radicalism emerged, linked intimately in its origins to the civil rights movement, which was based in a free speech movement that rejected what was seen as the establishment's implicit compact with the oppressor, and opening up an intense public debate about the course of the war in Vietnam, the credibility of government and the deep inequalities of American society. Again, the primary institutional bases for these initiatives were (a) the universities and (b) the mass media — the forms of public communication that mediated demonstrations in Chicago, riots in Watts (Los Angeles) and uprisings in other African-American communities. In both Canada and the U.S., the public debates were based to a very large degree on the established autonomy of the university as an institution as well as a degree of freedom in the media that still, at that time, survived the steadily increasing concentration of ownership.[9]

The women's movement of the 1970s and early 1980s sought to appropriate a share of institutional bases of power for women. Though far from the only struggle in which women were active, the struggle for parity in the professions — particularly in law and medicine — and in universities was a major focus in part, of course, because many women activists were themselves members of the intelligentsia or, as students, were its neophytes. Ironically, as women were gaining ground in these institutions with varying degrees of success, the independence of these institutions from the rule of capital was being progressively undermined.

In the past two or three decades, the ability of an intelligentsia to represent their interests and concerns has been profoundly undercut in two ways: one, by the hegemony of a discourse that has deprived them of a terrain on which they speak and which directly attacks their autonomy from capital, and two (which is perhaps more effective), through changes in the regimes of accountability that govern their work.

Dorothy E. Smith

THE HEGEMONY OF NEO-LIBERAL DISCOURSE

In the 1990s, Ellen Messer-Davidoff explored how right-wing U.S. think tanks and foundations manufactured an attack on liberalized higher education. On the basis of her field research, she describes an ideological campaign waged by an apparatus aimed at securing control of the concepts, ideologies and theories that co-ordinate multiple-sites of power and knowledge that are generated by the ruling relations.[10] In this context, it is misleading to identify these bases of support for a right-wing intelligentsia purely in terms of the metaphor of right and left as a political spectrum. These new institutions were the direct creations of the American business corporations, and their goal was to transform the political and educational culture of the United States, if not beyond. Information- and policy-generating think tanks have been established, including an institute for training journalists as recruits to replace the predominantly liberal professional journalists of today. A multi-headed attack on liberal higher education, and particularly on "multiculturalism" and on the gender and ethnic diversification of the university curriculum, was launched. The major campaign on this front had two objectives: (1) to establish the discourse of neo-liberalism (as contrasted with the discourse of public good of the welfare state) as hegemonic in the public sphere, and (2) to discredit the legitimacy and authority of those speaking in terms of social justice and the public good.

Policy in North America has become increasingly formulated in neo-liberal terms, emphasizing the ascendancy of the private sector, the role of a "free market" and the individual's responsibility for her or his welfare, as contrasted with conceptions of the public good. In the media, new vocabularies discrediting those who raise issues of social justice and the interests of disadvantaged groups were established. The silent majority were differentiated from the newly marginalized social movements now represented as "special interests." The publicly authoritative voice achieved by the social movements of the 1960s and 1970s were discredited. Susan Faludi, for example, describes the media's systematic discrediting of the voices of feminism that started in the early 1980s:

> The media's (pseudo) cheerleading stopped suddenly in the early '80s ...
> "Feminism is dead," the banner headlines announced all over again and
> "The women's movement is over," began a cover story in the *New York
> Times Magazine*.[11]

NEW REGIMES OF ACCOUNTABILITY

From the time of Ronald Reagan's ascendance to the presidency of the United States, right-wing control of public discourse through command of concepts, ideologies and theories has been successful in securing the ideological heights.[12] Ideological command of the field of text-mediated relations is immensely powerful, the more so as it is largely invisible as power, and the right-wing, or perhaps more realistically the U.S. capitalist class, aims at and is increasingly effective in securing it. As Herbert Schiller wrote, "Today, a remarkable edifice of invisible control has been constructed, permitting the most far-reaching measures of social domination to escape significant public attention."[13]

The controls that Schiller describes as "invisible" are new forms of regulation that undermine the autonomy of the professions and increasingly subordinate the practice of the professions, either directly to the organizational forms of capital or, in the public sector, to the demands of capital accumulation for lower taxation, reduced government deficits and extended privatization. Some current thinkers on the changes that are taking place in the organization of contemporary societies have argued that the new social forms of power represent an extension and intensification of the professionalization that emerged at the end of the nineteenth century.[14] John Meyer, for instance, writes:

> In recent decades, the expansions in numbers of scientized professions and professionals have been remarkable. Any given organization is now surrounded by a much denser system of organized people and groups of this sort, and they claim much more extensive cultural content with more intensive authority.[15]

This view of the expansion of the professional character of occupational organization recognizes, of course, the increasing significance of a labour force that is highly trained in relevant skills, for example, in business administration, computer use and computer technology, engineering and the natural sciences. It does not attend, however, to the progressive diminishing of the autonomy of the professions whether collegially or in terms of the independence of individual professional judgement. The increase of density on which Meyer comments is seen here to suggest the increase in forms of regulation that subdue the professional intelligentsia to the project of capital accumulation.

Though journalism is not strictly speaking a profession according to the classic model set by medicine, it has increasingly involved university training and, in the 1960s and 1970s, acquired considerable increments of power, particularly in the area of investigative reporting. Here is a notable instance of a recent and striking loss of autonomy, particularly in the U.S. Traditional practices in newspapers separated the news gathering and publication decisions from the commercial side of newspaper management. Of course, the degree of independence of the newsroom was always limited by the overall policies of the company that owned the paper. Nonetheless, news was at least formally a territory onto which the interests of the commercial side, particularly the interests of advertisers, would not encroach. Beginning in the late 1980s, newspapers in North America were re-organized as a way to subordinate the news functions of newspapers to market-driven interests: the concept of "the total newspaper" was introduced as an ideological coding, subordinating news and the newsroom to the overall interests of the news corporation's profitability. As Doug Underwood expresses it:

> Most journalists are finding it tougher to question authority out in the world when they are being pressured to become loyal corporate soldiers inside their organizations ... reporters are expected to fulfill their role within the system dutifully and without complaint ... No matter how fervent their protests, the lives of newsworkers have become increasingly circumscribed by performance standards and management systems designed to insure greater productivity, by bosses trained in the new techniques of scientific management, by research and surveys, and by editors who have joined the marketing team.[16]

Underwood's use of the term "newsworkers" marks the reduction in journalists' status and autonomy within the newsmaking process. The subordination of news and the work of journalists to the market objectives killed the autonomy of journalism and the exercise of journalists' critical judgement, which had characterized what had come to be called the "adversary journalism" of previous years.

In the public sector, the drive to reduce taxation and to reduce government expenditure has been associated with the introduction of new forms of management into the public service. These have been specifically consequential for professions such as social work and nursing and for various branches of education. Systems for establishing formal criteria of performance and explicit procedures for rendering these accountable within an overall structure of financial management have been set up. In nursing, for example, systems of categorizing patients in order to define the level of care required are complemented by a standardization of the categories of care to be delivered to the relevant type of patient. The new managerial procedures regulate staffing and patterns of care on wards and link them directly to the hospital financial management.[17] The decision-making of nurses in respect to their patients becomes contaminated with administrative criteria.[18]

Formerly, social workers in child-protection services would work closely with families, helping them to solve their economic and relational problems as well as dealing directly with problems of abuse. New forms of management have reduced the role of social workers to one in which they evaluate the risk to children presented by a given case, following strictly scripted risk-assessment procedures and making arrangements for alternative care depending on the level of risk identified.[19] Social workers can thus carry more cases and, at the same time, the risk of scandals based on children dying as a result of parental abuse while under child protection is minimized for the government. There is little room for the social worker to apply trained professional judgement, and certainly insufficient time for the practice of family-oriented casework.

The government-based educational system, including schools and community colleges, has introduced outcomes or performance-based criteria that can be determined independently of the judgement of instructors who are responsible for transmitting skills and knowledge to students. In Ontario, the redesigning of the organization of the public school system has been aimed specifically at reducing the scope of teachers' professional autonomy. Alison Griffith puts it this way: "Standardized tests, standardized report cards, standardized staffing formulas are constructed to exert central office control over most aspects of school life."[20]

At one time, the curriculum set at the provincial level was presented as "guidelines" to be interpreted at the board level and by teachers. The new curriculum, which was introduced in 2000, no longer had the form of guidelines: performance objectives were assigned to every topic and the school principal was made accountable for overseeing the teachers' classroom practices. Determination of what should be taught thus passed from the professional teacher to the centralized administration.

Community colleges, too, are becoming more directly linked to local businesses. At one time oriented almost exclusively to the provision of training programs geared to specific occupations and developed by faculty who represented the skills and knowledge of that occupation, community colleges are now extensively involved in providing courses or programs that fill the specific skill requirements of local industry.[21] The autonomy of instructors to design courses and programs to train students in the areas of their skills has been radically reduced, and the new accounting procedures that followed have increased the subordination of faculty to administration.[22] "What's relatively new in the college sector is that the drive to reduce costs has now moved beyond periodic haggling over the price of our labour to the heart of the labour process — power and control."[23]

Claire Polster has written of how knowledge production in Canadian universities is being reshaped as an instrument of industry.[24] Government research funding promotes research as a service to business. Students are encouraged to view themselves as consumers and to evaluate their courses and grades in terms of how relevant they are to their future prospects on the labour market. The World Bank has made explicit its proposal to promote the "marketizing" of universities by which the corporations would be the clients, the students the consumers, and the faculty the employees available to meet the requirements of clients and consumers.[25] Though such a program meets with considerable resistance among academics, it seems clear that governments are at least interested in such possibilities. Certainly in Canada the promotion of research that is oriented towards business partnerships is indicative and, behind the backs of academics, the Canadian Association of University finance officers have adopted cost-revenue accounting procedures that, as they move into effect in universities, place the onus of meeting cost-revenue standards on departmental units.[26]

*

The instances I have described here are intended to provide examples of the directions of the change taking place today. They are not, on the surface of things, directly gendered but, as collected instances, they can be seen to have specific implications for professional areas in which women have been traditionally dominant, that is, in those sectors of public institutions that focus on reproductive work — education, social work and nursing. In reducing the autonomy and discretionary power of professionals working in these areas, the voice and influence of women professionals is also diminished. In addition, women's gains as faculty members in universities and community colleges (since the initiatives of the women's movement starting in the late 1960s) have been balanced by an increase in the university's use of low-waged, highly qualified sessional lecturers, the majority of whom are women.[27] We have yet to evaluate the gender implications of the shift in university priorities towards science, engineering and business — professions dominated by men — and away from the humanities in which women faculty and students are still disproportionately represented. Recent right-wing government moves in Ontario and British Columbia to reduce the power of teachers' associations to influence educational policy are also moves that significantly reduce the part women can play in society as professionals representing their values and concerns.

Though it is not possible to see with full clarity the kind of society that is emerging in North America, the straws in the wind that I have caught and exhibit here point to capital's increasingly comprehensive capacity to subordinate, either directly or indirectly, the forms of the ruling relations that organize people's everyday lives. If we add to the capture of the professional intelligentsia the extension of a mass media in North America regulating the images, norms and languages of everyday life under the control of a highly and increasingly small number of large corporations, we are beginning to see, I believe, the emergence of what might be called a totalitarianism of capital, in contrast to earlier totalitarianisms of state power.

The progressive undermining of the bases of professional autonomy has had and will have special implications for women who have had and still have a special role in the reproducing of people's everyday lives. Capital as a mode of production has no essential interests in whether and how people live or die, except insofar as they earn a wage and deliver their labour and as they are able to buy the commodities capital produces. This is not new. What is new is the progressive disappearance in society of bases from which voices and influence representing other interests and concerns can be effective. The challenge of our time and of our future is to discover new ways in which we can be effective both in the immediacy of what is happening and in what we are able to transmit to the generations to come.

NOTES

1. Dorothy E. Smith, "The Ruling Relations," in *Writing the Social: Critique, Theory, and Investigations* (Toronto: University of Toronto Press, 1999).

2. Karl Marx, *Capital: A Critique of Political Economy* (London: Penguin Books, 1976), 101.

3. Max Weber, *Economy and Society* (New York: Bedminster Press, 1968), 226–227.

4. J. R. Beniger, *The Control Revolution: Technological and Economic Origins of the Information Society* (Cambridge, MA: Harvard University Press, 1986).

5. Weber, *Economy and Society*, 226–227.

6. W. G. Roy, *Socializing Capital: The Rise of the Large Industrial Corporation in America* (Princeton, NJ: Princeton University Press, 1997); Albert Chandler, Jr., *The Visible Hand: The Managerial Revolution in American Business* (Cambridge, MA: Harvard University Press, 1993); and David F. Noble, *America by Design: Science, Technology, and the Rise of Corporate Capitalism* (New York: Oxford University Press, 1979).

7. Alvin W. Gouldner, *The Future of Intellectuals and the Rise of the New Class: A Frame of Reference, Theses, Conjectures, Arguments, and an Historical Perspective on the Role of Intellectuals and Intelligentsia in the International Class Contest of the Modern Era* (New York: Seabury Press, 1979).

8. P. Diesing, *Science and Ideology in the Policy Sciences* (New York: Aldine Publishing Company, 1982).

9. B. H. Bagdikian, *The Media Monopoly* (Boston: Beacon Press, 1997).

10. Ellen Messer-Davidoff, "Manufacturing the Attack on Liberalized Higher Education," *Social Text* 36 (1993), 40–79.

11. Susan Faludi, *Backlash: The Undeclared War Against American Women* (New York: Doubleday, 1991), 76.

12. S. Blumenthal, *The Rise of the Counterestablishment: From Conservative Ideology to Political Power* (New York: Times Books, 1986).

13. H. I. Schiller, *Information Inequality: The Deepening Social Crisis in America* (New York: Routledge, 1996), 1.

14. J. W. Meyer, J. Boli, et al., "Ontology and Rationalization in the Western Cultural Account," in W. R. Scott and J. W. Meyer, eds., *Institutional Environments and Organizations: Structural Complexity* (Thousand Oaks, CA: Sage Publications, 1994), 9–27.

15. John W. Meyer, "Rationalized Environments," in Scott and Meyer, eds., *Institutional Environments and Organizations,* 28–54.

16. Doug Underwood, *When MBAs Rule the Newsroom: How the Marketers and Managers Are Reshaping Today's Media* (New York: Columbia University Press, 1993), 164.

17. M. L. Campbell, "Information Systems and Management of Hospital Nursing: A Study in Social Organization of Knowledge" (PhD diss., University of Toronto, 1984).

18. J. Rankin, "Texts in Action: How Nurses are Doing the Fiscal Work of Health Care Reform," *Studies in Cultures, Organizations and Societies* 1 (2002), 251–267.

19. H. U. Parada, "The Restructuring of the Child Welfare System in Ontario: A Study in the Social Organization of Knowledge," (PhD diss., University of Toronto, 2002).

20. Alison Griffith, "Texts, Tyranny and Transformation: Restructuring Ontario Education," in J. P. Portelli and R. P. Solomon, eds., *Social Democracy and Educational Restructuring* (Calgary: Detselig Press, 2001), 84.

21. D. E. Smith and S. Dobson, *Storing and Transmitting Skills: The Expropriation of Working-Class Control. New Approaches to Lifelong Learning.* Retrieved from <http://www.oise.utoronto.ca/depts.sese/csew/nall>. February 2002.

22. See N. Jackson, "'These Things Just Happen': Talk, Text, and Curriculum Reform," in M. L. Campbell and A. Manicom, eds., *Knowledge, Experience, and Ruling Relations: Studies in the Social Organization of Knowledge* (Toronto: University of Toronto Press, 1995), 164–180, and L. McCoy, "Accounting Discourse and Textual Practices of Ruling: A Study of Institutional Transformation and Restructuring in Higher Education" (PhD diss., University of Toronto, 1999).

23. Ron Brown, "Taylorism Triumphant?" *Faculty Matters: Views and News of Douglas College Faculty Association Members* 3 (2002), 1.

24. Claire Polster, "From Public Resource to Industry's Instrument: Reshaping the Production of Knowledge in Canada's Universities," *Canadian Journal of Communications* 23 (1998), 91–106.

25. K. Campbell, "When Even Your Accountant Betrays You," *CAUT/ACPPU Bulletin* 45, no. 9 (1998), 28.

26. Ibid.

27. Ron Brown describes a parallel development in community colleges, though he does not refer to its gender ratio. See Brown, "Taylorism Triumphant?"

CHAPTER 2

CORPORATE CHALLENGES TO ACADEMIC FREEDOM AND GENDER EQUITY

Jennie M. Hornosty

ACADEMIC FREEDOM — the freedom to engage in critical teaching and research in an "honest search for knowledge" — is considered by academics as a hallmark of the modern liberal university. Although the idea of academic freedom arguably goes back to the time of Socrates, the struggle to establish academic freedom in Canadian universities is relatively recent, and has been both arduous and long.[1] For feminists in the academy, the appeal to academic freedom brought varied results. Feminists have successfully used academic freedom principles to establish feminist pedagogy as part of university curriculum and to institute Women's Studies programs. At the same time, some academics (usually senior white men) have sought recourse in academic freedom arguments to justify their opposition to curriculum or institutional changes which challenged their privileged position. The shift towards a more gender-balanced university has its roots in the late 1960s and early 1970s, when an increasing number of female students and faculty came to the academy. Shortly thereafter, we saw the creation of courses that endeavoured to reflect women's experiences and realities; universities also began to establish polices and procedures that promoted gender equity. In the current economic and political climate, as universities increasingly embrace commercialization of the academy, the gains that academic women have achieved could be in jeopardy.

In this chapter, I reflect on the ways in which the corporate agenda can both erode academic freedom and threaten the various gains academic women have made since the late 1960s in terms of feminist scholarship and gender inclusivity. The impact of corporatization in universities is far-reaching: it influences governance structures, research priorities, course curriculum, notions of excellence and weakens academic freedom. These changes, some subtle and some more conspicuous, like shifts in language and logos, will change academic life for both women and men. However, my aim is to suggest how the practices and values of corporatization in the academy can undermine a feminist agenda for transforming the university into a more inclusive place.

ACADEMIC FREEDOM

Our modern conception of academic freedom is rooted in the Enlightenment and is generally understood to be of benefit both to academics and society at large. However, it was only in 1940 that the American Association of University Professors (AAUP) articulated its principles of academic freedom, which guaranteed intellectual freedom in teaching, research and publication. In 1958, the Canadian Association of University Teachers (CAUT) became involved with the issue in a serious way when Harry Crowe was dismissed from the United College in Winnipeg in for his remarks that were critical of the principal's policies.[2] This landmark case helped to establish the importance of collegial governance structures and the right to criticize university administrators without fear of reprisal as important components of academic freedom.

The current CAUT *Policy Statement on Academic Freedom* outlines the basic tenets of academic freedom subscribed to by all universities in Canada. It states, in part:

> The common good of society depends upon the search for knowledge and its free exposition. Academic freedom in universities is essential to both these purposes in the teaching function of the university as well as in its scholarship and research ... Academic members of the community are entitled, regardless of prescribed doctrine, to freedom in carrying out research and in publishing the results thereof, freedom of teaching and of discussion, freedom to criticize the university and the faculty association, and freedom from institutional censorship ... Academic freedom carries

with it the duty to use that freedom in a manner consistent with the scholarly obligation to base research and teaching on an honest search for knowledge.[3]

This statement reflects the two aspects of academic freedom as we understand the concept today: university autonomy and individual freedom for free and open inquiry.[4] As history has shown, these two aspects have come under external pressures from the church, state or other powerful interests which in turn has meant that administrators and boards have not adequately protected academic freedom for individuals.[5] Implicit in these principles of academic freedom is the understanding that universities have a civic responsibility to ensure that the creation of knowledge serves the public good.

Academic freedom provides the university community with the necessary safeguards to protect independent research and teaching and protect the right to express ideas that are critical of university administration, governments, media and multinational corporations, or the corporate world generally, without fear of retribution. A critical and "free" spirit, necessary for academic scholarship, can only be guaranteed, however, if tenure and collegial governance remain an intrinsic part of the university's organization. However, the university's increasing reliance on corporate funding and partnerships raises serious questions about university autonomy and academic integrity.[6] The commercialization and privatization of knowledge is in fundamental contradiction with the pursuit of knowledge for the betterment of society and with the cultural environment necessary for the preservation of academic freedom.[7] Women's location in the academy means they may have the most to lose.

The articulation and practice of academic freedom always occurs within a social context that defines the possibilities and limits of academic freedom.[8] As different scholars have argued, the principle of academic freedom has never been absolute.[9] Rather, it is embedded in a historical, social and organizational milieu, which defines its parameters and interpretation. How scholarship, "truth" and knowledge are defined and understood are mediated by those who govern the university at a given point in time. As well, these understandings are shaped by the political milieu outside the academy. For example, historically, various Marxists, radicals and feminist were denied tenure because their research and publications were judged as "not scholarly." Similarly, during the

McCarthy era, American universities did not extend academic freedom to individuals with politically left views.[10]

Today, threats to academic freedom and university autonomy are resurfacing with renewed vigour, reflecting changes in the political landscape and the university's increased reliance on corporate funding. For example, the American Council of Trustees and Alumni published a report entitled *Defending Civilization: How Our Universities Are Failing America and What Can Be Done about It*, which condemns those academics who were critical of the American government's response to terrorism following the attacks of September 11, 2001. Likewise, Campus Watch, an organization dedicated to monitoring scholarship and teaching on the Middle East, has published a list of names of academics who should be disciplined for their views and institutions that should be monitored. Included are Concordia University, University of Toronto, University of Victoria and York University.[11] When Sunera Thobani, a professor of Women's Studies at the University of British Columbia, spoke out against America's war of retaliation, there were numerous calls for her dismissal.[12] The recent high-profile cases in Canada involving Dr. Nancy Olivieri, Dr. David Healey and Dr. David Noble are further testimony to how the practise of academic freedom can easily come into conflict with corporate interests.[13]

In the current context of globalization and transnational capital, there is a shift from upholding the university as a public institution serving the interests of society to an institution more in keeping with a corporate agenda and the needs of global capitalism. This shift, also evident at the international level, threatens both academic autonomy and the principles of academic freedom which depend on it. For example, at the World Conference on Higher Education (October 1998), the World Bank's Reform Agenda entailed an "outright attack on academic freedom, tenure, collegial governance, curricular control by faculty, and faculty organization and unionism." What is more insidious is the fact that a group led by the International Association of Universities (IAU) issued a statement that undermined strong statements adopted by the UNESCO General Assembly in 1997 concerning academic freedom. The IAU position, which garnered majority support, is that "faculty members are too liberal in viewing academic freedom as a right of free expression rather than as a duty 'to uphold the balance' between 'the spiralling demand for higher education on the one hand, and the globalization of economic, financial and technical change on the other.'"[14] Such a position is anathema to the concept of the liberal university embodied in the basic tenets of academic freedom.

The role of a university is to provide an environment where faculty can examine, challenge and criticize existing beliefs, values and assumptions of society, the institutions within it, as well as the university itself. It is a place for independent research, where scholars engage in "the quest for new knowledge, and ... open up new avenues of enlightenment."[15] This role is pivotal for maintaining a democratic and free society — democracy is contingent on its citizens thinking critically and having independent views.

Over the last three decades, academic women have successfully introduced feminist paradigms that have challenged male privilege and the hegemony of the traditional canon in the university. The principal of academic freedom was a crucial vehicle in getting women's voices heard. Similar gains in terms of curriculum were won by other marginalized groups, which saw the creation of new academic fields such as Gay and Lesbian Studies, Native Studies and Black Studies. A university culture that fosters critical thinking and debate is a precondition for new knowledge. However, with increasing corporatization of the university, and its penetration into all aspects of academic life, the social context in which academic women and men operate is changing in significant ways: ways that could undermine university autonomy, academic freedom and the progress made towards establishing a woman-friendly institution.

WHAT IS CORPORATIZATION?

Private and corporate funding in Canadian universities is not entirely new; for example, there were corporate funds provided to universities prior to the First World War. However, the major involvement by corporations in university life, which began to grow significantly in the 1980s, brought with it a corporate agenda and corporate values. These, in turn, affected curriculum offerings, research priorities and the university culture. As many have shown, corporatization has had a major affect on the culture, values, practices and conventions of the university.[16] Before considering some of these changes and their possible implications for academic women and feminist scholarship, I will briefly discuss what corporatization means.

In essence, corporatization refers to the commercialization of all aspects of university life. Current examples include the use of corporate logos, outsourcing and privatizing non-academic labour, appropriating corporate language, circumventing collegial governance structures, modifying course delivery with labour-replacing technologies, redirecting academic research to support corporate partnerships and converting intellectual property into private property. In this new environment, market principles and considerations shape the day-to-day operations of the university. This is well illustrated by the language and discourse in vogue at many universities today. For example, a workshop held last year for faculty and staff at the University of New Brunswick provided hints, tips and checklists for how to best "interact with our clients ... to provide excellent customer service."[17] Implicit here, in what could easily be mistaken for an announcement for Wal-Mart employees, is the idea that the university is just another business, providing mass-produced consumer products to non-discerning clients. In speaking about a recent increase in student enrolment, the Director of Student Recruitment and Integrated Marketing, explained: "We operate like a business, using a targeted strategy ... based on solid market research and performance measurement."[18] These are concrete examples of the appropriation of corporate language and assumptions within the university environment. Students, once viewed as eager minds searching for knowledge and truth, have now been redefined as "customers" and "clients." Professors, once considered scholars and mentors are now viewed as "service providers," "facilitators" or "trainers" whose main responsibility is to satisfy "consumer demand."[19]

However, the primary danger of corporatization is the subtle intrusion of a corporate ideology, which works to redefine the university's priorities. As a result, traditional academic values of scholarship become subordinated to corporate priorities. Research and knowledge once considered ends in themselves are increasingly viewed as marketable commodities for commercial ends; academics are rewarded for becoming entrepreneurs and attracting private capital and corporate partnership for their work.[20] When the university is influenced by corporate values, critical and independent thought and knowledge for its own sake take a back seat to the needs of the global market. Faculty, if they are concerned with maintaining their careers, find themselves adjusting to this new corporate context. In this subtle way, academic freedom is in danger of being weakened.

A culture that advances academic freedom is fundamentally at odds with one that respects market principles. Commercialization of university life entails a shifting away from the values and priorities traditionally at the heart of liberal education. Ideals of "truth," citizenship, humanism and equality become subordinate to concerns for cost-minimization, productivity, marketability and consumer satisfaction. Furthermore, when corporate interests pay for services, they expect a major say in what those services will be and how they will be provided. As a result, collegial governance structures and university autonomy can easily be eroded. Independence from corporate agendas is a prerequisite for autonomy and academic freedom. Arthur Lovejoy summarized it well:

> There are certain professional functions generally recognised to be indispensable in the life of a civilized community which cannot be performed if the specific manner of their performance is dictated by those who pay for them, and ... the profession of the scholar and teacher in higher institutions of learning is one of these.[21]

There are numerous examples of how corporate involvement can affect university autonomy: some clearly evident, others more subtle. At the University of Toronto, the Rotman Foundation was willing to pledge $15 million for the school's Faculty of Management if the university agreed to contribute matching funds to create six endowed chairs. In addition, this agreement would have mandated search committees to consult an advisory committee of external business people in future Faculty of Management appointments.[22] At Dalhousie University, the Institute of Canadian Bankers is directly involved in designing curriculum, and an equally blatant example of corporate control is taking place at the University of Pennsylvania where the terms for the Reliance Corporation Professor (a privately funded chair) state explicitly that the individual must be "a spokesman [sic] for free enterprise."[23] A more subtle example is a case at the University of New Brunswick, where a proposal for a modified MBA program was sent to the executive committee of the School of Graduate Studies for consideration without any mention of its academic merit but with substantial comment about the new employable skills students would receive and the large support it received from local business.[24] More subtle, yet pernicious, implications are seen when, directly or indirectly, administrative decisions about which departments receive additional research funding and new faculty are influenced by corporate agendas. For example, when a university needs to find matching funds for a corporately endowed chair in an engineering or computer science program, fewer funds are available for programs in liberal arts such as Women's Studies.

To consider more specifically how corporatization can negatively effect academic women, women's research and feminist praxis, I consider the three broad areas of curriculum and teaching, research priorities and university culture. In each of these areas, I endeavour to show how protections of academic freedom could be eroded. My purpose is to outline possible scenarios and not make any claims to inevitability.

CURRICULUM AND TEACHING

Teaching and research are the two most important missions of the university. With corporatization, emphasis in the curriculum is placed on teaching "marketable skills" rather than critical thinking. The new buzz words include "strategic investment," "innovation agenda," "the new economy," "accountability" and "performance indicators," all of which speak powerfully to an ideological shift taking place. As a result, notions of what constitute "good courses" and "good teachers" begin to change. The focus of teaching is shifted to "skill acquisition" and "competitive advantage." Curriculum decisions are framed in terms of promoting entrepreneurship rather than increasing social awareness or challenging traditional beliefs and practices. It is hard to imagine in such an environment much support for areas like feminist theory and Women's Studies.[25] Equally at risk are courses with radical or critical agendas, which can quickly become marginalized as irrelevant and the professors teaching them penalized through poor course evaluations. The example of a part-time sociology professor in Wisconsin who felt compelled to eliminate inequality topics, such as poverty, gender and race, from her course content after students punished her on evaluations for teaching such material provides a chilling example.[26] Although this violates her academic freedom to teach material central to her discipline, she has little recourse if she wants to have her contract renewed. Presumably from the students point of view these topics are seen as irrelevant for future employment. In this situation, there is little room for appeal. The corporate university is more concerned with pleasing its financial partners than protecting academic freedom.

Women's Studies and feminist scholarship grew at a time when universities became more open and democratic. At the heart of feminist pedagogy is a mandate to question the status quo, to take action against sexual, racial and class inequality and to make links between the personal and the political. The material taught does not impart specific employment skills, nor does it lead to specific products for the market place. The current trend in some universities towards "digitization" and "on-line courses" is also at odds with the dialectical teaching methods at the heart of feminist pedagogy. A question that needs to be asked is, Will there be administrative pressure put on faculty to adopt the latest informational technologies for course delivery as a means of saving money?[27] There is no academic freedom if, for example, faculty must change their method of teaching and communicating with their students because that is the direction in which the university is going. The parameters of academic freedom become constrained when the curriculum is driven by market priorities.

New marketing strategies for student recruitment stress the training and utilitarian function of higher education.[28] Recruitment fairs and promotional literature often explicitly promote entrepreneurial fields like business, engineering, computer science and information technology. Both of these approaches to university education have an affect on students' expectations and demands and, indirectly, on course selection and curriculum development. The fields that could be most affected are the social sciences and humanities, including Women's Studies. If students enter university with a corporate mindset, they will choose only courses and programs that they believe have an "exchange value" in the market place. Those holding an instrumental view of university education will see little need to take "interest courses," which could open new horizons or broaden their thinking. Students who are concerned only with getting practical, skill-related courses to enhance their job opportunities will have little or no interest in Women's Studies or feminist scholarship. As one student frankly told me when I suggested she consider taking some Women's Studies courses for interest's sake: "Why bother? They won't get me a job. They're a waste of time."[29]

The long-term impact of this instrumental approach to education will be a dramatic shift in curriculum development and staffing priorities. These effects can be readily seen in Australia, Britain and the United States where certain departments, like classics, have been eliminated. At other places, even traditional science disciplines such as chemistry, physics and math are fearful of their demise, as funds are re-allocated to areas that generate revenues and mesh with immediate business needs.[30]

Pressures already exist in many Canadian universities to drop low-enrolment courses and to add courses that are more skill-related. These decisions are based not on pedagogical grounds but on concerns for cost-efficiency and marketability. However, if the primary criterion for allocating program funds is based solely on market principles, arguments can easily be made, as we have seen above, to divert the university's limited resources (both financial and staff) into programs that are more profitable. This could have a disastrous effect on Women's Studies if, as happened at the University of New Brunswick, there is a further decline in student enrolment — without adequate resources, Women's Studies programs will be unable to offer a diversity of courses. With limited course selection, even fewer students will enrol due to timetable conflicts or lack of interest. If academic values are subsumed by corporate values, pedagogical arguments based on assumptions about the intrinsic value of a liberal education will have little legitimacy. Similarly, arguments about academic freedom or the importance of women's scholarship will carry no weight.

When universities are viewed as just another "business," market principles generally dictate what is valued and what is promoted. As Gerber argues, many supporters of corporatization "see liberal education as a waste of time and resources, because they fail to see the immediate 'payoff' of the liberal and fine arts, and because they are willing to allow the market to determine what should and should not be taught."[31] Under these circumstances, institutional autonomy and academic freedom are compromised. Similarly, critical epistemologies based on the transformative potential of knowledge are eclipsed in favour of utilitarian approaches that value education for its "use value," which is more appropriate for commercial and industrial interests.[32] Disciplines that further corporate interests — engineering, computer science and business — are granted more faculty positions and given larger amounts of a university's operating budget. And disciplines that don't facilitate the new corporate agenda are at risk of becoming underfunded or ultimately eliminated. Many of these disciplines are in the social sciences and humanities where, it must be remembered, women make up a larger proportion of the faculty.

When Women's Studies programs were introduced, they encountered significant resistance and hostility, particularly within male-dominated disciplines such as engineering and computer science.

Feminist scholarship was dismissed as biased, methodologically inferior, intellectually bereft or simply as male-bashing. Academic freedom was a vehicle that feminists successfully used to promote research on women's issues and to incorporate women's knowledge into the curriculum. However, the socio-historical context in which this occurred corresponded to a period of radical transformation in the academy, when the ideals of liberal education were at the forefront and intellectual debate was widespread and highly valued. It was a time when principles of collegiality and university autonomy were paramount, although I do not mean to suggest that everything always worked as it should. (I am not trying to paint some utopian image here of the university prior to the onslaught of commericalization. In the past, collegiality was violated, academic freedom was ignored and feminists were harassed.)

With the emergence of corporatization, these liberal principles shift and become invalid. The changes that result can be slow and subtle and will manifest themselves differently in each institution. Nevertheless, I am suggesting that when corporate ideology gains hegemony in a university, certain fundamental things change. For example, when knowledge is commodified, certain courses appear irrelevant, are devalued or, from the perspective of the political right, are targeted as subversive. From a corporate mindset, it is difficult to see much value in courses that examine the intersection of race and class in the exploitation of women, or those that address the unpaid work of women and how this furthers the interests of capitalism. A drug company is unlikely to sponsor research to determine whether commonly prescribed medications could have a long-term negative impact on women's health. Yet many academic women are engaged in this kind of critical scholarship which challenges the status quo. If there is little or no support for their work, academic women will have a more difficult time remaining in the academy and the space for feminist scholarship will diminish. In this new context, the question of academic freedom becomes increasingly irrelevant. As Ursula Franklin bluntly states: "What we are to teach and how to teach it appears no longer a subject of academic and social discourse, but has become a 'market decision.'"[33]

RESEARCH PRIORITIES

The influence of corporate ideology on the research mission of the university is equally troubling. Previously, it was generally understood that the purpose of academic research was "to advance the frontiers of knowledge,"[34] to engage in a spirit of free inquiry in the pursuit of "truth." What is meant by "truth" can differ, as intellectual debates between feminists and positivists testify. Nevertheless, there was general agreement that university research, even if "applied" as opposed to "pure" research, was driven by intellectual curiosity not monetary gain. Academic freedom was important in protecting this right. However, as many have demonstrated, with the growing commercialization of universities, we see a major shift that is giving priority to entrepreneurial-type research.[35]

The shift in research priorities is evidenced by the growing number of corporate–university partnerships and the recommendations made by the federal government's Expert Panel on the Commercialization of University Research.[36] This new context can alter the research priorities of individual faculty and university departments. For example, the recommendations of the Expert Panel would radically change the reward systems in universities and privilege research that led to the production of marketable products. One of its recommendations is that universities make commercialization a core function, by adding it as a fourth component to faculty responsibilities, along with the traditional duties of teaching, research and community service. The Panel went even further to recommend that a professor's track record at commercialization be considered part of the promotion and tenure process. These recommendations have clear gender implications. For example, if implemented, those who do research in the humanities and social sciences, where a majority of female academics are located, would be penalized for not doing research that has commercial benefits. Also, a need to engage in proprietary-type research that adds to the academic workload would disproportionately disadvantage female faculty, who are the ones generally responsible for family and childcare. These recommendations have been vigorously opposed by faculty associations as a threat to intellectual integrity and academic freedom.

The right to define one's research priorities and interests, to engage in scholarship and research in one's pursuit of truth, is rendered meaningless if assessment decisions are influenced by a professor's track record of attracting corporate sponsorship or producing marketable products. Commercial priorities would devalue more traditional academic research that sees knowledge creation as a social and public good. In essence, the commercialization of research would undermine feminist

research on issues such as sexual harassment, the feminization of poverty, mothering, domestic labour, woman abuse and gender socialization,
which would carry little weight in tenure and promotion considerations.
As a result, those who work in these areas would be faced with either
changing their research interests, foregoing promotions and other benefits like research funding or leaving the university altogether. The
long-term effect would be that new knowledge in certain areas would
diminish; programs, like Women's Studies, which depend on this
research would shrink or disappear. In other words, the commercialization of research can easily skew the types of research programs that are
developed and hence the type of knowledge-creation that is generated.
Although academic freedom would still protect one's "right" to research
any area, this becomes a nebulous right if the real choice is between having a successful academic career or pursuing one's research passion. I am
not arguing that such dramatic changes are inevitable, but rather am
pointing to some real dangers inherent in the current directions and
underlying ideology. The commercialization of university research could
alter what we consider to be "useful" or "productive" research as well as
what we mean by "useful knowledge."

Similar unintended consequences are evident in the granting councils' (NSERC and SSHRC) requirement that researchers secure external
partnerships as a condition of receiving research grants.[37] This requirement too has gender implications. Directly or indirectly, it is likely to
have a significant impact on the kind of research academics do, for certain research areas are more conducive to finding partnerships, especially
corporate ones, than others. This suggests that certain kinds of research
done by Women's Studies scholars could have greater difficulty being
competitive since research priorities of the granting councils are influenced by the priorities of the corporate sector. Topics such as equity
issues, women's history, female sexuality, feminist theory, lesbian identity, women in politics, to mention only a few are not likely to receive
much support or interest from industry. Academics with interest in these
areas, especially younger non-tenured faculty, an increasing number of
whom are women, may feel substantial pressure to shift their research
agendas to areas with the greatest likelihood of funding success.

The introduction of Industrial Research Chairs is a further example
of how corporate agendas can alter research priorities and departmental
needs.[38] The university ends up committing its financial resources and

support to those academic areas and research foci that can command industry partnerships. Many have also argued that the Canada Research Chairs program may provide significant funds for individual stars but it diverts funds and resources away from hiring new junior faculty, a large portion of whom would be women.

Experience to date suggests that the infiltration of corporate values and structures poses a serious danger to academic freedom. It is clear that independent inquiry and objective analysis directed by societal issues is in major conflict with the growing tendency to promote proprietary technology, and that the decisions about what constitutes knowledge and the research that is supported begin to represent outside vested influences.[39] As I have suggested above, research critical of industry and corporate ideologies is unlikely to attract major corporate funding. Academic freedom is also eroded when faculty feel pressure, because of external influences, to change their research area, teaching styles, methods of evaluation or course content for fear of losing their jobs or being denied tenure. The case of Dr. Nancy Olivieri provides a dramatic example of how the health of patients and the public's interest can be put in jeopardy when universities and individuals rely on corporate sponsorship for research funding.[40] The refocusing on the needs of industry and the redirection of research funding are reshaping academic life and with it academic freedom.

Institutional autonomy *is* "inextricably linked" to academic freedom. The 1988 "Statement on Academic Freedom and Institutional Autonomy" supports this viewpoint: "Historically there has been a struggle for university autonomy, arising from the conviction that a university can best serve the needs of society when it is free to do so according to the dictates of the intellectual enterprise itself." This autonomy is threatened when corporations or governments exert pressures that "unduly influence the intellectual work of the university."[41] Such is the situation that many fear is occurring today.

UNIVERSITY CULTURE

Culture, as the shared beliefs and values of a group of people, shapes the group's perception of the world and the structural arrangements that are deemed "natural." It provides a reference point for determining which things are important and how things are done. The culture's ideology provides a worldview to which most members subscribe. For example, the liberal university culture, shaped by the struggles beginning in the 1960s, includes shared beliefs about collegiality, academic freedom, university autonomy and, more recently, principles of equity and diversity.[42] Within institutions, the idea of culture refers to an organization's "way of being" in the world and the values, meanings and perceptions that the organization's participants bring with them to work.[43] The infusion of corporate ideology and corporate practices poses a serious threat to the academic environment: it alters the organizational culture and hence the everyday working environment for academics.

In the last few decades, women academics in Canada have made important gains in gender representation, program development and policies. When the problem of systemic discrimination was recognized in the early 1980s, the universities put in place employment equity policies and positive action goals designed to increase the number of women academics across all ranks and departments. One can debate how successful these policies have actually been, given that women academics still make up only 25.1 percent of tenured faculty and 39.1 percent of tenure-track faculty positions. Nonetheless, these numbers are better than the 1960 figure of just over 11 percent.[44] Besides policies against sexual harassment, most universities now have maternity, parental and adoptive leave policies in their collective agreements or faculty manuals. Some agreements recognize that the "tenure track" and the "baby track" often occur at much the same time, and some universities have on-site childcare facilities. Together these have created a more "woman-friendly" environment.

However, the experience elsewhere suggests that these gains could be at risk with the growing influence of corporate ideology. The introduction of corporate managerialism in Australian universities, for example, indicates that principles of employment and educational equity become secondary when a business mentality determines a university's values and priorities. A focus on cost-minimization and increased productivity shifts the emphasis in official university policy, from concerns about access and equity to efficiency and accountability. Both substantially disadvantage women and undermine formal equity initiatives.[45] Two recent incidences at UNB suggest how at-risk women's gains actually are.

Two years ago, the associate vice-president of human resources decided, without consulting the Joint AUNBT–UNB Employment Equity Committee, not to fill the vacated full-time employment equity position for financial reasons. We were told that the monies saved from that position were needed to hire someone to assist with professional training and development.[46] Shortly after, there were announcements for workshops on "developing customer relations" and meeting "consumer needs." During the last round of collective bargaining, the management team opened Collective Agreement articles relating to maternity, parental and adoptive leave in an attempt to clawback our excellent provisions in these areas by restricting eligibility and limiting future entitlements if government legislation changes. They were, again, looking for ways to save money[47] and the gender implications of their actions did not appear important. Both of these attacks suggest that there has been some shift in university values and priorities when it comes to gender equity.

The use of "performance indicators" is another corporate tool used to evaluate academic work, and it has a particularly negative effect on the university culture.[48] Increased standardization, rigid accountability practices and decreased autonomy and control over one's work are used to increase productivity. Not only are such practices inimical to academic freedom, they are bound to be especially difficult for women with family responsibilities. Margot Prior paints a vivid picture of such practices in Australia:

> Every day brings a request for an account of something: Work completed over the past 12 months, work projected over the next 12 months, how many grants applied for, how many publications, expected number and cost of projected graduate student projects over the next two years, accounts of student selection processes, reports on visitors, seminars, research group activity, course outlines, books of readings for courses for the next two years, library lists, self-appraisal statements, etc., and all required by next week (or yesterday).[49]

The gendered division of labour in our society means that women still continue to find ways to balance their desire to nurture with their desire to achieve professionally. Stress and fatigue are the price many academic women pay when they juggle their private and public roles to take care of children and family responsibilities. Given the current difficulties in balancing academic work with home life, it is not surprising that family conflict is identified as one of the key reasons for gender imbalance in the academy.[50] For this reason, academic women have fought hard to institute policies guaranteeing maternity, parental and adoptive leave, along with sick leave and provisions for childcare. An increase in the already high academic workload will hurt junior faculty embarking on their career the most. It will be especially stressful on young academic women in the prime of their childbearing years who face increased demands to compete for research grants, supervise more students and publish more frequently while beginning a family. While maternity and parental leaves are available, a change in the university's culture could exert pressure on women to reduce the time they take or forego these leaves altogether in order to stay competitive.[51]

Decreased autonomy, more demands for accountability and a heavier workload will make the struggle for equity for women academics even more difficult. An "'adequate' family life in today's society and 'tenure worth' research activities are difficult to balance … [W]omen pay a price by not being promoted … by resigning, or by failing even to consider an academic life as a career choice."[52] The use of corporate managerial practices in higher education may mean that even more women find themselves "choosing" between an academic career and having a family. If fewer women become academics, especially in the traditionally male-dominated fields, employment equity polices to promote hiring of women will be rendered meaningless.

To increase managerial flexibility and lower costs, universities today rely more and more on contractually limited and part-time appointments.[53] Again, due to the gendered division of labour, casualization of academic labour will put women at a greater disadvantage than men in competing for full-time positions. Since women generally are the ones who juggle work and family responsibilities, they have less time and energy to devote to being super high achievers, especially during their early childbearing years. This coincides with the period when many academic women are just beginning their careers. As a result, if fewer tenure-track jobs are available, the increased competition will work to the disadvantage of women. In the United States, Nigel Wilshire argues that part-time instructors are being employed deliberately to undermine tenure, with the consequence that a "permanent class of gypsy scholars" is being created.[54] This class of gypsy scholars, concentrated in contractually limited job ghettos with few benefits and protections, will have a female face. The implications of corporate managerialism in Australian universities has meant that "women remain concentrated in the lowest [and least secure] positions, [at the same time] the shift from collegial to managerial decision-making [further] entrench[es] the gendered character of university power relations."[55] In short, the transformation of academic work along economic rationalist principles and corporate ideology can easily undermine the equity agenda women academics have fought hard to establish.

*

Although gender equity has not been fully achieved in Canadian universities, women academics have made significant gains during the last thirty years. Feminist scholarship and research have been integrated into the mainstream in many disciplines. Women's Studies programs exist on most campuses. Policies aimed at creating a more inclusive and gender-sensitive environment have been well established. Positive action strategies and employment-equity goals to increase the number of female academics in male-dominated disciplines have been institutionalized in most universities. Principles of academic freedom have been at the heart of the debate over the nature of knowledge and the mission of the university. These principles are necessary, although not sufficient, to ensure an inclusive and diverse institution. Academic freedom, despite some troubling cases, has successfully protected faculty rights for the most part.

However, as I argued in this chapter, the fundamental academic values on which all these principles are rooted are being undermined by the commercialization of university life. A culture based on business managerial practices and a corporate ideology are transforming the core mission of the university. As Bertelsen writes:

> [When] higher learning is recast as a service industry for capitalist enterprise, the impact on academics in considerable. Knowledge becomes "information," a commodity to be manufactured, packaged, bought and sold, and intellectual work a matter of goods being cost-effectively manufactured on a production line.[56]

In this new environment, academics become merely "human resources" whose work can be outsourced when the costs become too high. Curriculum matters and hiring priorities are driven by business needs rather than academic ones. Corporate funding, rather than intellectual curiosity or societal needs, determines the issues university researchers study or whether findings can be published. Such funding promotes proprietary research and courses are expected to produce marketable job skills. As a result, the independence of university researchers and teachers is greatly reduced.

The university culture is in a process of change. While different universities will respond to corporatization in different ways, depending on whether a critical mass exists to oppose the intrusion of market values, I would suggest that over time, if this trend is not abated, the academy as we know it will be radically different. The impact of corporatization is likely to occur faster at research-intensive universities where disciplines such as engineering, business and computer science are especially strong. How this will affect areas like Women's Studies will depend on a variety of institutional factors, including how well established such programs are, the number of supportive faculty, university revenues, student demands and so on. I am not suggesting that the results will be identical in all institutions. Rather, my argument is that the move towards corporation in the academy will bring structural and ideological changes that will reduce our independence as scholars and teachers.

The extent to which principles of academic freedom can defend individual faculty rights in a corporate university environment will also be eroded. Academic freedom is always mediated by the social context, shaped by the dominant values and beliefs within the university. But as we have seen, the underlying philosophy operating in a corporate university are antithetical to the traditional liberal values of free inquiry and scholarly discourse. Academic freedom requires that universities be independent from external economic or political pressures. Without this independence, academic freedom loses its hegemonic position. Consequently, our integrity as scholars can easily be compromised, often in subtle ways. This can occur, for example, through pressures to select certain types of course material, engage in particular types of research or compromise family responsibilities to meet new standards and expectations. Those who are least powerful in the academy, usually women, will be most affected.

For academic freedom to thrive, we need universities which are open, transparent, free from external forces, democratic and pluralistic. A university shaped by corporate values and practices endangers these very precepts and undermines academic freedom that sustains intellectual inquiry. This will have serious implications for the academic work of men and women alike. My purpose in this chapter, however, has been to highlight some of the ways in which the potential consequences of corporatization are gendered. We have reasons to be concerned that feminist scholarship, Women's Studies programs and equity gains, as well as academic freedom, for which many of us have fought so hard, could become no more than a memory from the past.

NOTES

1. Michiel Horn, *Academic Freedom in Canada: A History* (Toronto: University of Toronto Press, 1999).

2. See Horn, *Academic Freedom in Canada* for a detailed history of the case.

3. CAUT, "Model Clause on Academic Freedom," *Policy Statement on Academic Freedom.* Approved by CAUT Council May 1977, Ottawa.

4. Jon Thompson, Patricia Baird and Jocelyn Downie, *The Olivieri Report* (Toronto: James Lorimer, 2001).

5. Horn, *Academic Freedom in Canada.*

6. Larry Gerber, "'Inextricably Linked': Shared Governance and Academic Freedom." Retrieved from <http://www.aaup.org/publications/Academi/01mj/mj01gerb.htm>. July 2002.

7. Claire Polster, "Intellectual Property, Higher Education, and Women's Inequality: Exploring Connections/Proposing Solutions" (paper presented at CRIAW Conference, Sudbury, Ontario, 1999).

8. Jennie Hornosty, "Academic Freedom in Social Context," in Sharon Kahn and Dennis Pavlich, ed., *Academic Freedom and the Inclusive University* (Vancouver: University of British Columbia Press, 2000).

9. See, for example, Marlene Dixon, *Things Which Are Done in Secret* (Montreal: Black Rose Books, 1976); Horn, *Academic Freedom in Canada*; Ellen Schrecker, *No Ivory Tower: McCarthyism and the Universities* (New York: Oxford University Press, 1986).

10. Schrecker, *No Ivory Tower.*

11. The American Council of Trustees and Alumni, *Defending Civilization: How Our Universities Are Failing America and What Can Be Done about It* (2002) is available on-line at <http://www.goacta.org/ publications/Reports/defciv.pdf>. To see the activities of Campus Watch, see their Web site at <http:// www.campus-watch.org>.

12. In the case of Dr. Thobani, the UBC administration acted quickly to defend her academic freedom to put forth unpopular ideas. Both the AAUP and the CAUT have spoken out against ACTA and Campus Watch, as have numerous individual academics.

13. See Thompson, Baird and Downie, *The Olivieri Report* for an excellent detailed description of what happened to Dr. Nancy Olivieri. Partly in response to these cases, the CAUT established a special Academic Freedom Fund at its November

2001 Council Meeting.

14. See "UNESCO Declaration Puts Academic Freedom at Risk," *CAUT Bulletin* (January 1999).

15. E. Ann Clark, "Academia in the Service of Industry: The Ag Biotech Model," in James Turk ed., *The Corporate Campus: Commercialization and the Dangers to Canada's Colleges and Universities* (Toronto: James Lorimer, 2000), 85.

16. See, for example, Neil Tudiver, *Universities for Sale* (Toronto: James Lorimer, 1999); Howard Buchbinder and Janice Newson, *The University Means Business: Universities, Corporations and Academic Work* (Toronto: Garamond Press, 1998); Clark, "Academia in the Service of Industry"; William Graham, "Academic Freedom or Commercial Licence?" in Turk ed., *The Corporate Campus;* Turk, "What Commercialization Means for Education" in Turk ed., *The Corporate Campus.*

17. Stroplegram sent on May 27, 2002. Two other e-mails to this effect were sent out to the university community within a few weeks of each other. One specifically about "customer service to international students" (July 8) and the other on "providing excellent customer service" (May 29).

18. "Recruitment Performance: A Good News Story," *UNB Perspectives,* 10 March 2003, 2.

19. On the same topic see Turk, "What Commercialization Means for Education"; Tudiver, *Universities for Sale;* and Colin Symes, "Selling Futures: A New Image for Australian Universities?" *Studies in Higher Education* 21, no. 2 (1996).

20. J. Fry, "College as Business" (paper presented at the 29th Annual Conference, The Academy in the New Economy: Transitions and Change, New York, Baruch College, April 1-3, 2001).

21. Quoted in Horn, *Academic Freedom in Canada,* 258.

22. Graham, "Academic Freedom or Commercial Licence?" Fortunately, this agreement failed after the conditions were made public to the University of Toronto faculty and there was significant faculty opposition to the proposal.

23. David McNally, "Welcome to the Corporate University." Retrieved from <http://www. fortunecity.com/victorian/byron/895.mcnally.html>. August 2000.

24. Personal information. I was a member of the executive committee of the School of Graduate Studies at the time this proposal came forward. What surprised me most was how few people on the committee saw this as a problem.

25. I expect that lip service will be paid to notions of diversity and equal opportunity for women. After all, these enhance business opportunities and make one more competitive. However, this is radically different from the critical thinking and social action that are at the core of Women's Studies and feminism.

26. Tom Brennan, "More Thoughts on the Future of Higher Education," *The Harbinger* (2000). Retrieved from <http://www.the harbinger.org >. April 2001.

27. I am not suggesting that the new informational technologies save the university money. In fact a great deal of evidence is there to suggest it does not. However, the administration often uses the money argument in its support.

28. Symes, "Selling Futures."

29. I don't remember the exact words spoken, but they were to this effect. This happened during an advising session for sociology students. Faculty members at other institutions have told me of similar experiences. This attitude seems to be growing.

30. See, for example, William Bostock, "The Global Corporatisation of Universities: Causes and Consequences," *AntePodium* (1999). On-line journal of the School of Political Science and International Relations at Victoria University of Wellington. Retrieved from < http://www.vuw. ac.nz/atp/articles/ bostock.html >. August 2000; B.A. Sethuraman, "Corporatizing the University" (1999). Retrieved from <http://music1.csudh.edu/cfa/htm/Corporatizing. html >. August 2000; and Nigel Williams, "Declining Enrollments, Funds Threaten Small Departments," *Science* 275 (1997), 747.

31. Gerber, "'Inextricably Linked.'"

32. Symes, "Selling Futures."

33. Ursula Franklin, "What Is At Stake? Universities in Context," in Turk, ed., *The Corporate Campus,* 21.

34. This phrase is taken from an UNESCO document on academic freedom quoted in Wayne Renke, "Academic Freedom, Teaching, and Administrators" (paper distributed at the CAUT Grievance/Arbitration Conference, Ottawa, Ontario, February 2002).

35. See, for example, Clark, "Academia in the Service of Industry"; Franklin, "What is at Stake?"; Graham, "Academic Freedom or Commercial Licence?"; and Polster, "Intellectual Property, Higher Education, and Women's Inequality."

36. CAUT, "Commentary on the Final Report of the Expert Panel on the Commercialization of University Research" (September 30, 1999). Retrieved from <http://www.caut/english/issues/commercialization/commentary.asp>. April 2001. Although the recommendations of the Expert Panel have not, at this stage, been implemented, the tone they have set indicates government priorities and their expectations of university research. While some administrators have been critical, others have embraced the recommendations.

37. Turk, "What Commercialization Means for Education." Not all SSHRC grants have this requirement, although it appears that there is a move in SSHRC to give low priority to pure curiosity-driven research. The emphasis is on research that has specific policy implications. Increasing monies are allocated to strategic research that requires partnerships. In some cases, the partners are community-based and not from the corporate sector, for example women's organizations and government departments. However, the size of the grants tend to be somewhat less than those given to research with corporate partnership — especially in cases which require matching grants. In NSERC corporate partners are the norm and the monies available to researchers are significantly greater.

38. Clark, "Academia in the Service of Industry."

39. Ibid.; Franklin, "What is at Stake?"

40. Thompson, Baird and Downie, *The Olivieri Report.*

41. Association of Universities and Colleges in Canada, "Statement on Academic Freedom and Institutional Autonomy" (Ottawa: AUCC, 1988), 1.

42. This is not to suggest that all these values operate without problems. Equity and diversity, for example, continue to be an ongoing struggle, and certainly not all academics embrace them wholeheartedly. However, there is at least lip service that the values are important ones.

43. See, for example, Elaine Butler and Lucy Schultz, "Women and the Politics of University Work: An Agenda for the Organization," in Anne Maree Payne and Lyn Shoemark eds., *Women, Culture and Universities: A Chilly Climate?* (Sydney, AUS: University of Technology, 1995).

44. Data from "CAUT Almanac of Post-Secondary Education in Canada" (Ottawa: CAUT, 2003), 13. Women are still, however, significantly underrepresented in engineering, computer science, physics and mathematics.

45. George Lafferty and Jenny Fleming, "The Restructuring of Academic Work in Australia: Power, Management and Gender," *British Journal of Sociology of Education* 21 (June 2000), 257–268.

46. In April 2002, the University hired an employment equity officer on a contractual basis, primarily to complete the Compliance Review required under the Federal Contractor's Program and to assist with the goal-setting exercise mandated under the Collective Agreement. After protest to senior management, the contract was extended "indefinitely," yet no final decision exists on whether this will revert back to a permanent full-time position.

47. Such leaves do not cost the university money. Faculty members who take maternity, adoptive or parental leave are not replaced while they are gone. Occasionally, a department may receive a stipend for someone but often not. In fact, based on the data the union's negotiating team had, such leaves actually save the university money.

48. See William Bruneau and Donald Savage, *Counting Out the Scholars: How Performance Indicators Undermine Universities and Colleges* (Toronto: James Lorimer, 2002) for an excellent discussion of the topic.

49. Quoted in Karen Coleman, "Women and Corporate Management in Universities," in Payne and Shoemark, eds., *Women, Culture and Universities*, 114.

50. Jennifer Rindfleisch, "Change from Within: The Attitudes of Senior Management Women towards Methods of Collecting Gender Imbalance in Australian Organizations," in Payne and Shoemark eds., *Women, Culture and Universities*.

51. Anecdotal evidence at the University of New Brunswick suggests that this is already the case in some faculties (engineering and computer science, for example). I have heard examples from faculty at other Canadian universities as well.

52. Report prepared by the Queen's University Faculty Association Subcommittee on Women and Tenure quoted in Jennie Hornosty, "Balancing Child Care and Work: The Need for a 'Woman-Friendly' University," in Jacqueline Stalker and Susan Prentice eds., *The Illusion of Inclusion: Women in Post-Secondary Education* (Halifax: Fernwood Publishing, 1998), 190.

53. J. Schuster, "Who Will Be the Academic Employees of the Future?" (presentation at the 29th Annual Conference, The Academy in the New Economy: Transitions and Change, New York, Baruch College, April 1–3, 2001). In the United States, for example, there has been a decline in the number of tenure-track/probationary appointments whereas part-time appointments have increased. Over 43 percent of all faculty are on part-time appointments; of those on full-time appointments, only 39 percent have tenure-track/probationary appointments.

54. Bruce Wilshire, *The Moral Collapse of the University: Professionalism, Purity and Alienation*, cited in Bostock, "The Global Corporatisation of Universities."

55. Lafferty and Fleming, "The Restructuring of Academic Work in Australia," 264.

56. Eve Bertelsen, "Degrees R Us" (2001). UCT Academics' Association. Retrieved from <http://www.uct.ac.za/org/aa/chomsk.html>. April 2001.

CHAPTER 3

TEACHER EDUCATION OR MARKET LOTTERY?
A LOOK AT RECENT SHIFTS IN KNOWLEDGE, CURRICULUM AND PEDAGOGY IN A FACULTY OF EDUCATION

Linda Eyre

PROCESSES OF MARKETIZATION are rapidly transforming universities[1] and public education[2] in Western nations by restructuring management, controlling curriculum and research, and by threatening professional autonomy, collegial relations, equity and social justice. Nowhere are these combined forces more likely to be felt than in teacher education. As well as having obligations to university policies and structures, faculties of education have concomitant historical relations with provincial departments and ministries of education. Faculties of education thus provide a site where the hegemonic discourses of university and state are co-ordinated, forming the "ruling relations"[3] of capital that regulate public institutions and threaten to undermine feminist research and pedagogy in the academy and in the schools.

My purpose in writing this essay is to contribute to feminist scholarship on marketization of education[4] by analyzing how women are positioned in market discourses[5] and analyzing the effects this cultural positioning has on the construction of knowledge in a particular site — a faculty of education. Education is an important place to look at the gendered effects of market-driven processes and practices as it is generally a discipline with a strong representation of women faculty, a high ratio of women students and a history of practices that both support and undermine critical feminist work. My analysis reflects Miriam Henry's argument that the relationship between university and state is "simultaneously tighter and more anarchic," reflecting processes of "political globalisation." She writes:

> Political globalisation does not mean the surrendering of national sovereignty. But in relation to education it does mean that bodies with an interest in education operating at supranational (e.g., the European Union), regional (e.g., the forum for Asia Pacific Economic Cooperation), international (e.g., the OECD or the World Bank), multinational (e.g., McDonald's) and local levels may now be seen analytically as more strongly implicated in the educational machinery of contemporary nation states.[6]

Henry argues that more work is needed to track what is happening and to track its gendered effects.

My point is not to hark back to a bygone era where all was supposedly well for women; a huge amount of feminist research over the centuries has revealed deeply entrenched oppressive practices in education. Nor do I wish to suggest that making education policy is straightforward and uncontested. As Jenny Ozga says, education policy is "struggled over, not delivered in tablets of stone, to a grateful or quiescent population."[7] Moreover, I try to be open to the possibility that globalization may have some positive as well as negative effects in education and may offer promise as well as danger for feminist theory and practice.[8] My analysis reflects a feminist reading of the relation between gender and power in corporate education practices — practices that continue to unfold.

The essay is grounded in my own experience as a feminist academic in a faculty of education in New Brunswick. Turning my gaze reflexively on my own situation is indicative of contemporary approaches in critical theory and understanding personal experience as a source of knowledge is in keeping with feminist case study research.[9] In narrating my own experience, I am located in a particular context and tell a particular story, as Barbara Kamler explains:

Stories do not tell single truths, but rather represent a truth, a perspective, a particular way of seeing experience and naming it. Stories are partial, they are located rather than universal, they are a representation of experience rather than the same thing as experience itself.[10]

In writing this critique, I recognize that while government representatives are not neutral bodies[11] they are required to implement decisions made in the premier's office, and that administrators in faculties of education are expected to be sympathetic to government interests. I acknowledge too that we are all implicated in marketization processes, myself included. My point is to show how market discourses are being taken up in teacher education, and the effects this cultural positioning is having on critical feminist scholarship and research. I begin by providing some context about recent developments in public education in New Brunswick.

New Brunswick In/corporate/ed

In the last decade, the province has forged ahead with a neo-liberal economic agenda for education, health and social services. In 1996, the province dissolved school boards and replaced them with parental advisory boards, groups without legislative power. The province intensified its control over the curriculum through attempts at outcomes-based education and an expansion of standardized testing. At the same time, it downsized its curriculum development branch, downloaded management responsibilities onto individual schools and formed public–private partnerships for school construction and curriculum-resource development. Furthermore, it attempted to deregulate the teaching profession through cutbacks and contract hiring and placed gag orders on teachers to prevent them from participating in a critique of government policies and practices.[12] Many of these changes were implemented despite public concern and without the consent of the province's teacher organizations. While the present Conservative government has implemented some changes (e.g., in 2001 the province created district education councils with elected members and power to influence education decisions), a neo-liberal economic agenda prevails.

Recently, the province faced a challenge to the assumed effectiveness of its public education system. The Organisation for Economic Co-operation and Development (OECD) ranked New Brunswick students' performance in literacy, science and mathematics as the lowest in

Canada.[13] This ranking created a crisis that required the government to respond. Prior to his recent election call, Premier Bernard Lord announced the release of *A Quality Learning Agenda*, a blueprint of education reform for the province. The *Agenda* is directed at "raising academic achievement and excellence, improving quality teaching, and ensuring greater accountability of the school system to students and parents."[14]

The first policy statement of the *Agenda*, entitled *Policy Statement on K–12: Quality Schools, High Results*, states that the province will implement targets for grades K–12 and closely monitor student, teacher and school performance; the province even claims that it will track the "prevalence of parents reading to pre-school children." The province's stated goal is to place New Brunswick "in the top three provinces in Canada for academic achievement, high school graduation rates, and participation in post-secondary learning." *Quality Schools* also promises more effort to "ensure quality teacher training ... and on-line professional development opportunities." It says post-secondary institutions must "adapt their programs to meet the ever-changing needs of society and its economy" and that the province will monitor teacher education programs to ensure that teachers "have the skills, training, and resources to be able to teach what needs to be taught."[15] As Valerie Hey says, "Performance and assessment indicators are the new instruments of managerialism — a key element of the repositioned logic of state surveillance that flourishes despite the rhetoric of devolution and local autonomy."[16]

Ostensibly, *Quality Schools* is about improving public education in New Brunswick. Few would question the need for more government support of public education in the province. When looked at through a market lens, however, the document also has to do with bolstering global neo-liberal economic policies. Such policies work, internationally, to further corporate involvement in public education and, provincially, to decrease government expenditures and increase employment by attracting the business sector to the provinces.[17] A privatized education system has the potential to reap huge profits for the corporate sector. Indeed, Wayne Ellwood describes OECD as a "rich nations club where most of the 'Global Fortune 500' — the biggest and wealthiest corporations — are based."[18] New Brunswick, on the other hand, is among the economically poorest provinces in Canada: it suffers dearly from high unemployment and severe cuts to its federal transfer payments, yet has one of the lowest corporate tax rates in the country.

Rather than questioning OECD research methodologies or situating the data in the socio-economic context of the province, the government promulgates individualistic discourses about what parents, students, schools and teachers must do to improve literacy levels in the province. National and provincial media also proclaim notions of good families that care about education and bad families that don't, proliferating in their texts language that demonizes single mothers, dead-beat dads and ineffective teachers. OECD researchers also take up individualistic discourses blaming students, teachers and parents, especially single mothers, for low literacy and math scores.[19] Add to this mix the work of bodies such as the Atlantic Institute for Market Studies, which used OECD research findings to create a comparative grid on schools in the region and raised the ire of school administrators in the province.[20] Also influential is the Vancouver-based Fraser Institute, which, as Patricia McAdie illustrates, distorts OECD research findings in an attempt to persuade government and the public that public education is failing and privatization is the answer.[21]

New Brunswick's health-care reform agenda bears some similarity to the marketization of its education system. The province is moving ahead with cutbacks to health services, contracting out of services formerly in the public domain, supporting public–private partnerships and adopting management techniques of the corporate sector. The government's agenda is shored up by federally and provincially funded studies that report high rates of obesity, inadequate nutrition and substance use in the province — data that, effectively, construct a crisis in the province's health-care system.[22] OECD researchers, AMI, the Fraser Institute, governments and the media proliferate individualistic discourses that blame individuals for their health status, that is, for making so called inappropriate *lifestyle* choices.[23] Decontextualized statistical data and individualistic blame-the-victim discourses deflect attention away from the irrefutable connection between poverty and health, thereby absolving the government of responsibility and opening a space for the privatization of health care in the province.[24] It is no coincidence that there is growing government interest in Western nations in "lifestyle regulation," "medical contracts" and "fat food taxes," as well as suggestions that "Canadian Medicare start charging different contributions according to the lifestyles of payees."[25] In the UK, for example, a "pills for promises" government document suggests that people who are overweight could be asked by their GP to sign a contract pledging to go on a diet in return for treatment under the public health system.[26]

Not surprisingly, *Quality Schools* also includes targets related to child and youth health. The province says that it is interested in "developing the whole child" and "there will be a renewed emphasis on art, music, health, and physical education."[27] Attention to health education is sorely needed: the elementary/middle-school health curriculum is limited and a high-school health curriculum does not exist; a few years ago the province reduced the number of qualified physical education specialists in the elementary schools. The irony of the province's belated attention to health education, however, is that teachers will have little time for teaching about health given the current panic over provincial literacy scores. This situation creates a space for corporate bodies that want access to youth and schools, a point to which I return later.

What is the impact of these neo-liberal ideologies and market discourses on individuals and programs in faculties of education? What are the effects of the changes upon the individual subjectivities and professional identities of people who work in these places? What counts as knowledge in this restructured place? What are its gendered, raced and classed effects? How are faculty resisting the demands of conformity to an instrumental approach to education? Are they? What happens when they do? As Valerie Hey asks, "Who in short are the winners and losers in the market lottery?"[28]

TEACHER EDUCATION

In higher education, cuts in transfer payments to the provinces have forced universities to create more wealth by increasing enrolment, offering a more flexible delivery of courses (on-line and off-line) and seeking corporate sponsorship for programs, facilities and research endeavours. New Brunswick is no exception. Indeed, the province is especially disadvantaged because of its smaller resource base and the inequitable distribution of research funds across the country.[29] The faculty of education where I work has increased class sizes as well as undergraduate and graduate enrolment, and has cut low-enrolment courses. A reduction in the number of faculty due to early retirement incentives and only a few new appointments has stretched remaining faculty to the limit. At the same time, there has been an increase in the number of courses taught by stipend and part-time faculty and by graduate students, contributing to what Jill Blackmore names a "casualized academic labour market."[30]

Program changes are also underway. The Bachelor of Education (BEd) program, which in the 1990s was a collaborative faculty effort to reflect progressive approaches to teacher education, is now being restructured under the direction of the administration with the consent of the faculty council.[31] Paradoxically, at a time when the university is supposedly attending to equity and social justice issues, education courses that raise these very questions are under threat. For example, in an effort to attract and retain prospective math and science specialist teachers, the faculty has agreed to pilot a shortened BEd program for a select group of math and science students — a program that is not only discriminatory but also excludes the foundation courses in "Social, Cultural and Political Contexts of Education" (an area of study that includes courses in critical and feminist studies, Aboriginal studies, equity and social justice issues). Indeed, as I write this essay, current administrative interest in equity and social justice issues in education lies in a proposed Multicultural Research Centre, but even that is framed by an economic discourse of attracting newcomers to the province.

Processes of marketization are becoming part of the cultural hegemony of the faculty. As I write this piece, the faculty administration is requesting feedback on a series of initiatives that reflect taken-for-granted marketization processes, including a further increase in undergraduate enrolment with the additional sections of courses to be covered by more stipend appointments; the hiring of a project officer who will seek out gratis teacher professional development and contract work for the faculty; proposals for the establishment of research and teaching centres that will appeal to philanthropists, including a centre for literacy upgrading; and proposals to market the BEd program globally. The idea that the BEd program be shortened from four terms to perhaps three, or even two, also hangs over the faculty.

While many aspects of these market discourses require a gender, race and class analysis, a concern I wish to address here has to do with what Catherine Casey describes as "the hidden curriculum of the discursive practices of the new work order."[32] Through an analysis of three critical episodes in the faculty where I work, I wish to show how shifts in government education policies towards a for-profit market model affect curriculum and pedagogy in the faculty and how these shifts affect the individual subjectivities and professional identities of the critical and feminist scholars who work there. The episodes are merely indicative of what is happening and illustrate why academics interested in equity and social justice issues should be concerned.

Critical Episode 1: Literacy Skills or Situated Practice?

[Within ten years] all New Brunswick students will leave grade 2 with an ability to read — 90% will read at grade-level, and 20% of these students will read at a superior level ... Within four years, all New Brunswick teacher training institutions, in cooperation with the Atlantic Provinces Education Foundation (APEF), will provide new teachers with the strategies needed to bring their students to the provincial literacy standards.[33]

Following the release of *Quality Schools*, the faculty administration announced that a newly established ad-hoc faculty committee (made up of two faculty administrators and two faculty members) would be reviewing all programs in the faculty, beginning with literacy. Faculty who instruct literacy courses were requested to meet with the committee to address a list of predetermined questions that had to do with how they were responding to the provincial literacy targets in their respective courses. In essence, faculty members were involved in an unexpected process of accountability framed around the province's skills-based, assessment-driven approach to literacy.

While increased attention to this area of the curriculum is welcome, the list of questions put forward by the committee appeared to reflect an uncritical acceptance of the province's assessment-driven approach. The Department of Education's directive and the committee's response did not reflect contemporary approaches to literacy, especially the range of literacies explored in the critical/feminist literacy courses offered in the faculty. However, acquiescing to the Department's literacy agenda could have far-reaching consequences. If children are not successful in meeting the province's literacy standards, a situation that is highly likely given the Department's unrealistic expectations, the faculty could be blamed for not providing teachers with the right strategies and ultimately be held accountable for larger structural problems in the province. Furthermore, compliance with *Quality Schools* could implicate the faculty in the province's highly questionable plans to extend its testing program to second-grade students; and the province's stated desire to focus on "developing strategies to improve the literacy achievement level of boys"[34] has been criticized by feminist scholars as typical of a masculinist anti-feminist agenda.[35]

The Department's assessment-driven literacy discourses also surfaced in a proposal put forward by the faculty administration which recommended that the Faculty of Education seek philanthropic funding for the establishment of a centre for literacy upgrading in the province, to be led by practitioners from outside the faculty. Critical and feminist scholars in the faculty with internationally recognized expertise in literacy were not consulted during the development of the proposal or even prior to its release. Feminist scholars are now writing an alternative proposal for a research and teaching centre that would be devoted to situated literacies, to be led by faculty along with practitioners. When looked at from a critical/feminist perspective, *Quality Schools* could have potentially negative effects on literacy development in the province. Although it has stimulated feminist praxis and opened up conversations about approaches to literacy in the faculty, whether the province is open to such discussions remains to be seen.

Critical Episode 2: Teacher Education or Training?

> We will continue to support student health and well-being by providing students with an understanding of the principles of healthy living including physical, emotional, psychological and social health and ... [ensure] that physical safety and disease prevention are addressed within the curriculum and modelled in our schools.[36]

Following its stated commitment to health education, the province changed its requirements for teacher certification: a course in health education is now required for elementary teacher certification in the province.

Although I would have preferred a broader understanding of health than the government advocates, as a health educator, I welcome more attention to this area of the school curriculum. The province's decision to change teacher certification requirements, however, created a problem for the faculty — how could a health education requirement be incorporated into the Bachelor of Education (BEd) program, especially one with limited faculty resources? The faculty curriculum committee addressed the problem and brought a motion to faculty council. The committee recommended that the core/foundation courses in the area of "Social, Cultural and Political Contexts of Education" no longer be required for students in the elementary program. Instead, students would be required to take a course in health education.

Faculty members who teach in this core area (including myself) expressed concerns with the proposal. We questioned why courses related to equity and social justice issues had, effectively, been singled out for deletion from the elementary BEd program. My suggestion was to integrate health education with other school subjects, a suggestion that would be more in keeping with the province's support of an integrated elementary curriculum. But the committee insisted that a course in health education replace one in the core area. As a compromise, the committee added a second core area as an option ("History, Philosophy and Practice") and said that students could use an elective credit for the health education requirement in the (unlikely) event one was available to them. The committee brought its revised motion to a subsequent faculty council meeting when, unfortunately, most faculty who teach courses in "Social, Cultural and Political Contexts" were unable to be present. The motion passed.

Although the faculty's attention to health education is long overdue, there are overriding concerns. First, the lack of prior consultation with faculty directly affected by a proposed curriculum change is an indication of the abandonment of established university collegial processes. In effect, a small group of people recommended a program change that could have long-term consequences for faculty and for prospective teachers and students in the public-school system. Second, prospective teachers can now earn a BEd degree without ever having addressed issues of gender, race, class and sexuality, or questions of diversity, equity and social justice (or problems to do with the history and philosophy of education and professional practice). Yet, in the early 1990s, when the program was revised, the faculty regarded these areas of study as an essential foundation for all BEd students. Ironically, *Quality Schools* also speaks to the importance of a curriculum that

> provides [students with] the core knowledge and skills required for becoming ... socially responsible members of society ... ensuring every person ... has the opportunity to learn and work in an environment where he or she is safe, respected and valued.[37]

Although these targets suggest the province's support for equity and social justice in education, the statements prove hollow when it does not deem this knowledge essential for teacher certification.

Critical Episode 3: Community Involvement or Corporate Control?

> Parent and community involvement in public education will never reach the level needed to ensure successful schools and successful students until New Brunswickers become fully convinced of the value of education and committed to becoming partners in supporting learning.[38]

Quality Schools confirms the province's interest in public–private partnerships, a position endorsed by OECD and other corporate driven bodies.[39] For me, such partnerships raise many concerns for the future of public education. Let me explain.

In 1997, the Department of Education invited me to participate in the development of a Web-based educational resource on alcohol for twelve to fourteen year olds, funded by the Brewers Association of Canada (hereafter referred to as the Industry) at a cost of $1 million.[40] The resource was to be developed in a partnership involving the Industry, two provincial universities (one anglophone and one francophone), the Department of Education, Health and Community Services, NBTel and a local technology company. I was to be a writer for the anglophone project and the then dean of my faculty was the project manager. The Industry said it would take a no-strings-attached position, leaving the content of the resource up to the team. It soon became apparent, however, that the Industry, in keeping with its other educational programs favoured a *responsible drinking* approach; an approach that provides technical information about the effects of alcohol, which, it is assumed, will enable people to make wise choices about alcohol use.[41]

The Industry also stipulated issues that could be addressed (drinking and driving) and those that could not — namely, alcoholism, fetal alcohol syndrome, alcohol use in combination with other drugs, issues for specific groups and corporate advertising. I expressed my concerns about the limitations of this approach at numerous meetings and in the monthly reports I submitted to the Industry. I argued that alcohol is not simply a matter of drinking responsibly because individuals are not equally positioned in terms of choice. I also argued that a responsible drinking approach could normalize drinking for young people and implicate them in illegal practices. I suggested a more critical approach, one more in keeping with contemporary approaches to health education.

But the Industry's interests prevailed. Four months into the partnership, the Industry decided that I would no longer be a writer for the project. I resigned. The project went ahead and the Industry hired two private male consultants to write the text. The final version of the resource is now on the Internet hosted by SchoolNet, a federally funded initiative that connects schools to the Web. The Industry still maintains that it "had no involvement in developing the website's content."[42]

What is particularly relevant here is how the Industry controlled what counted as knowledge in the preparation of the resource. Students were denied access to information about how alcohol works socially, economically, politically and globally. I was merely a commodity producer, and students were positioned as the consumers. This case fits so well into Jane Kenway and Elizabeth Bullen's analysis of "promiscuous corporations desiring school children" where companies, especially those engaged in risky health practices, seduce schools by developing "expensively produced learning materials ... usually overlaid by some apparent educational purpose."[43] The global marketing via the Internet of the idea of responsible drinking and the ideologies it sustains, of course, has unlimited economic potential for industry and government; according to the Industry, in 1998, "governments in Canada ... received almost $4.6 billion generated by beer in taxes and other revenues."[44]

The way I was treated is also extremely relevant, and for me not to speak about the violence I experienced working within this corporate sector would be a betrayal of feminism. As I have written elsewhere:

> Not being introduced to newcomers on the team, being excluded from the morning handshake ritual, side comments just loud enough for me to hear, continuing sidebars while I was speaking, and secret meetings about me during breaks were some of the ongoing practices to intimidate me and undermine my status as a writer for the project. The other team members, all men, read themselves into the script. They knew not to come near me. They knew not to publicly show interest in my concerns; they knew not to engage in discussions about research ethics or about the politics of texts. In this masculinized environment I behaved badly. The Industry wanted to buy my labour, my body not my ideas, surely, the most degrading form of commodification.[45]

Some Common Threads

These three episodes illustrate how the discursive practices of corporate bodies, government and university came together in mutually sustaining ways. As Wayne Ellwood says, "Their sheer size, wealth and power means that multinationals and the business sector in general have been able to structure the public debate on social issues and the role of government in a way which benefits their own interests."[46] In each episode, corporate-driven neo-liberal individualistic discourses shaped provincial education policy which, in turn, framed the social construction of knowledge in the faculty. The faculty administration was either unwilling or unable to challenge the dominant discourses of the state; its views on matters related to what counts as useful knowledge appeared to coincide with those of the provincial government, producing a powerful hegemonic effect. Together, these episodes are symbolic of a larger shift towards a neo-liberal economic agenda for education, health and social services in the province, what Valerie Hey describes as the "imposition/amplification of the imperatives of individualism and consumption."[47]

Each of the episodes also illustrates how the processes of marketization influence feminist teaching, research and scholarship in education. Assessment-driven, skills-based literacy programs and individualistic approaches to health education shore up market agendas and deny students an opportunity to engage in critical analyses of the world around them. The elimination of courses that address questions of equity and social justice reduces teacher education to what Ann Brookes describes as a "more technocratic, instrumental emphasis in terms of knowledge, language and goals."[48] Indeed, I would argue that the faculty is now in a situation similar to that described by Jenny Ozga in which "economy and efficiency are justified *as if they were values*, and other values are deprecated as ideological."[49] Moreover, what happens in early levels of teacher education has a spiral effect on graduate programs and research. When critical feminist thought is undermined, graduate enrolment, course offerings and, ultimately, the future of critical and feminist scholarship in education is threatened.

Corporate discourses not only have an impact on the construction of knowledge in the faculty, they also affect the individual subjectivities and professional identities of faculty and students who work there, the majority of whom are women. As Jill Blackmore and Judith Sachs argue, the "privileging of management discourses over academic discourses"[50] has a damaging effect on professional autonomy, academic freedom and established processes of academic collegiality. While feminist scholars have historically been situated on the margins in the academy, processes of marketization further legitimize exclusionary practices.

Nevertheless, the episodes do show that resistance is possible. In each case, critical and feminist scholars, either individually or collaboratively, worked at different levels (publicly and subversively) to challenge the dominant relations of power. We pointed out contradictions and paradoxes and offered alternative solutions. While perhaps none of us succeeded to the extent that we wished, we were able to at least question some taken-for-granted marketization processes and practices.

How Do We Proceed?

This essay reflects my interpretation of how marketization has affected critical and feminist scholars in a faculty of education and the implications for research and pedagogy in the academy and the schools. While the essay is located in a particular context, it provides a glimpse at the ruling relations that are rapidly changing teacher education. The essay illustrates how and why the fragile gains made by feminist scholars in the academy, especially the establishment of courses and programs that engage with critical and feminist inquiry in education, are under renewed threat, requiring increased vigilance and a concerted response.

How, then, do we proceed? Naive suggestions for change do not fit into an increasingly corporatized environment, especially when, as Ozga points out, "the market itself has been marketed to those caught up in it."[51] Moreover, anti-feminist discourses are symptomatic of the gendered relations of power that are still part of the taken-for-grantedness of daily life in university communities. It is as if the neo-liberal economic discourses and neo-conservative ideologies that work together in the current market-driven climate have given new life to "old" sexist, racist, classist and heterosexist practices, reinscribing what counts as knowledge, framing teaching and research practices and legitimating structures of inequality.

However, feminist scholars in the academy must continue to critique the institutional discourses that undermine critical feminist scholarship and construct women as Other. At the same time, it is important to remember that the power to confront is not equally available to all women. Knowing some strategies may help, as Alison Taylor writes:

> Hegemonic discourses are not necessarily consistent and unified, but rather contain elements that may be contradictory. Counter-hegemonic work involves highlighting these contradictions and attempting to decouple/rearticulate discursive elements in the process of developing alternative visions.[52]

Certainly there were many contradictions in the vision of teacher education evident in the episodes presented here, and those of us involved attempted to articulate them and offer alternative suggestions. Whether our individual and collective efforts have opened up opportunities for future dialogue in the faculty and with the department remains to be seen. Taylor points out how important it is to explore why hegemonic discourses appeal to particular groups of people. She writes that it may be because the discourses "correspond to the lived realities of students, parents and teachers."[53] She also comments that academics may have to acknowledge "a little bit of truth" in hegemonic discourses.[54] The province's literacy scores and health statistics *are* cause for concern, and as Kari Dehli says, "Critics of marketisation cannot ignore the depth of rage and frustration about public schools that many people feel."[55] However, this does not mean that students, parents and educators should be held completely responsible for educational outcomes, especially when testing, and test results may be more indicative of systems of privilege and oppression than literacy development. Nor should BEd programs and school curricula automatically be restructured to fit an assessment-driven agenda. As with all research, OECD research methodologies and findings require a critical in-depth analysis, not a knee-jerk compliant response.

Taylor further suggests bringing teacher organizations on side "to challenge the top-down policy approach of government" and "developing alliances across social divisions ... with mainstream and marginalized groups of parents and students as well as with organized labour groups."[56] Working with unions on issues dealing with equity, however, may be difficult: the province's teacher organization, for example, has been historically reluctant to take up equity issues. Building relations with parents and students, especially from marginalized groups, would be strategically difficult but may be more fruitful. Parental concerns helped stifle the province's commitment to outcomes-based education and, recently, *Quality Schools* was overshadowed by voters' concerns about automobile insurance rates, an issue that almost brought the government down.

Further research that explores what is happening in faculties of education across the country and beyond might help us better understand how marketization works in different contexts and may provide useful examples of different forms of counter-hegemonic practice. Identifying tactics of resistance not only helps to fill gaps in theories of power but it also has the potential to foster change at the local level. The response of faculty administrators, especially women, to market-driven policies and practices also requires further investigation. Their willingness, as well as their reluctance or inability, to challenge hegemonic practices might help us better understand how women academics negotiate corporate rule. An understanding of how feminism works at different levels will contribute to understanding the role of resistance and could lead to greater collaboration in feminist efforts for social change.

At the same time, it is incumbent upon us not to forget the advocacy work that is still needed. Prospective teachers deserve more than a regressive skills-based *training*. If universities are to fulfill their promise of a quality liberal education and if faculties of education are to live up to their title they must, at the very least, provide the conditions that enable prospective teachers to explore a range of contemporary pedagogical approaches. They must offer programs that engage prospective teachers in critical questions about the social, economic and political contexts of their lives and the gendered, raced and classed effects on teaching and learning. Faculty members must continue to question the neo-liberal economic values and practices that are being taken up by corporate bodies, government and university — values and practices which, if left unchallenged, will have harmful long-term effects on public education.

NOTES

1. See, for example, Ann Brooks and Alison MacKinnon, eds., *Gender and the Restructured University* (Buckingham, UK: The Society for Research into Higher Education and Open University Press, 2001); Neil Tudiver, *Universities for Sale:*

Resisting Corporate Control over Canadian Higher Education (Toronto: Lorimer, 1999); James L. Turk, ed., *The Corporate Campus: Commercialization and the Dangers to Canada's Colleges and Universities* (Toronto: Lorimer, 2000).

2. See, for example, Trevor Harrison and Jerrold Kachur, eds., *Contested Classrooms: Education, Globalization, and Democracy in Alberta* (Edmonton: University of Alberta Press, 1999); Jane Kenway, ed., *Marketing Education: Some Critical Issues* (Victoria, AU: Deakin University Press, 1995); Simon Marginson, *Markets in Education* (St. Leonards, NSW, AU: Allen and Unwin, 1997); Heather-jane Robertson, *No More Teachers, No More Books: The Commercialization of Canada's Schools* (Toronto: McLelland and Stewart, 1998); Alison Taylor, *The Politics of Educational Reform in Alberta* (Toronto: University of Toronto Press, 2001); Geoff Whitty, "Creating Quasi-markets in Education: A Review of Recent Research on Parental Choice and School Autonomy in Three Countries," in Michael Apple, ed., *Review of Research in Education* (Washington, DC: AERA, 1997).

3. See Dorothy Smith, chapter 1 in this volume.

4. See, for example, Brooks and MacKinnon, eds., *Gender and the Restructured University;* Miriam David, "Choice and Markets in Education: A Critique of Some Key Texts," *Discourse* 17 (1996), 417–421; Valerie Hey, "'A Game of Two Halves'—A Critique of Some Complicities: Between Hegemonic and Counter-hegemonic Discourses Concerning Marketisation and Education," *Discourse* 17 (1996), 351–362; Jane Kenway and Debbie Epstein, "Introduction: The Marketisation of School Education: Feminist Studies and Perspectives," *Discourse* 17 (1996), 301–315; Mary Beth Krouse, "Women and the University as Corporation," in Sommer Brodribb, ed., *Reclaiming the Future: Women's Strategies for the Twenty-first Century* (Charlottetown, PEI: Gynergy Books, 1999).

5. Kehri Dehli, "Between 'Market' and 'State'? Engendering Education Change in the 1990s," *Discourse* 17 (1996), 371.

6. Miriam Henry, "Globalisation and the Politics of Accountability: Issues and Dilemmas for Gender Equity in Education," *Gender and Education* 13 (2001), 95.

7. Jenny Ozga, *Policy Research in Educational Settings: Contested Terrain* (Buckingham, UK: Open University Press, 2000), 1.

8. See Fazal Rizvi and Bob Lingard, "Globalization and Education: Complexities and Contingencies," *Educational Theory* 50, no. 4 (Fall 2000), 2, and Jill Blackmore, "Warning Signals or Dangerous Opportunities? Globalization, Gender, and Educational Policy Shifts," *Educational Theory* 50, no. 4 (Fall 2000), 3. Retrieved from <http://www.ed.uiuc.edu/EPS/Educational-Theory/Contents/2000_4.asp.> July 25, 2003.

9. Jeff Hearn, "Academia, Management and Men: Making the Connections, Exploring the Implications," in Brooks and MacKinnon, eds., *Gender and the Restructured University;* Shulamit Reinharz, *Feminist Methods in Social Research* (New York: Oxford University Press, 1992).

10. Barbara Kamler, *Relocating the Personal: A Critical Writing Pedagogy* (Albany: State University of New York Press, 2001), 45.

11. Sandra Taylor, Fazal Rizvi, Bob Lingard and Miriam Henry, *Educational Policy and*

the Politics of Change (New York: Routledge, 1997), 31.

12. Elana Scraba, *Schools Teach, Parents and Communities Support, Children Learn, Everyone Benefits: Review of the New Brunswick Education System* (Edmonton, AB: Education Consulting International, 2002).

13. Organization for Economic Co-operation and Development, *The OECD Program for International Student Assessment Knowledge and Skills for Life — First Results from PISA 2000*. Retrieved from <http://www.pisa.oecd.org/>. July 20, 2003.

14. Office of the Premier, New Brunswick, News Release, "Quality Learning Agenda: Ten-year Vision to Strengthen N.B.'s Education System" (2003). Retrieved from <http://www.gnb.ca/cnb/news/edu/2003e0414ed.htm>. July 3, 2003.

15. New Brunswick, *A Quality Learning Agenda. Policy Statement on K–12: Quality Schools, High Results* (Fredericton: Province of New Brunswick, 2003), 15, 16, 18, 20, 25, 31. Also available online at <http://www.gnb.ca/0000/publications/comm/1894-Publication-E.pdf>.

16. Hey, "'A Game of Two Halves,'" 354.

17. Harrison and Kachur, eds., *Contested Classrooms*.

18. Wayne Ellwood, *The No-Nonsense Guide to Globalization* (Toronto: New Internationalist Publications, 2002), 100.

19. Elizabeth Sloat and J. Douglas Willms, "The International Adult Literacy Survey: Implications for Canadian Social Policy," *Canadian Journal of Education* 25, no. 3 (2000), 218–233; J. Douglas Willms, *Vulnerable Children: Findings from Canada's National Longitudinal Survey of Children and Youth* (Edmonton: University of Alberta Press and Human Resources Development Canada, 2002); Elizabeth Blaney, "Continuing the Conversation: The International Adult Literacy Survey," *Canadian Journal of Education* (in press); Nayda Veeman, "A Response to Elizabeth Sloat and Douglas Willms' 'The International Adult Literacy Survey,'" *Canadian Journal of Education* 25, no. 4 (2000), 353–357.

20. See *Grading Our Future: Atlantic Canada's High Schools' Accountability and Performance in Context* and *Interactive High School Report Card: You Decide What Counts*. Available on-line from the Atlantic Institute for Marketing Studies <www.aims.ca>.

21. Patricia McAdie, "The Fraser Institute and the War Against Public Education," *Our Schools/Our Selves* 12, no. 3 (2003), 20–24.

22. See Colleen Fuller, *Caring for Profit: How Corporations Are Taking Over Canada's Health Care System* (Ottawa: Canadian Centre for Policy Alternatives and New Star Books, 1998); Health Canada, *Towards a Healthy Future: Second Report on the Health of Canadians* (Ottawa: Health Canada, 1999); and Health and Community Services, *Provincial Student Drug Use Survey* (Fredericton: HCS, 1996).

23. Select Committee on Health Care, *A Wellness Strategy for New Brunswick. Second Report of the Select Committee on Health Care* (Fredericton: SCHC, 2001); Willms, *Vulnerable Children*.

24. Pat Armstrong, Carol Amaratunga, Jocelyne Bernier, Karen Grant, Ann Pederson and Kay Willson, *Exposing Privatization: Women and Health Care Reform in*

Canada (Aurora, ON: Garamond Press, 2002).

25. Barbara Amiel, "I Recommend Weeding Out Biomedical Ethicists at Birth," *The Daily Telegraph*, 23 June 2003, 18.

26. Mary Riddell, "The Fat Fatwa Won't Work: The Rich Get Thinner and the Poor Get Larger. That's Why Obesity is a Pressing Political Issue," *The Observer*, 8 June 2003, 26.

27. New Brunswick, *Quality Schools*, 32.

28. Hey, "'A Game of Two Halves,'" 354.

29. See Tudiver, *Universities for Sale;* Turk, *The Corporate Campus.* For New Brunswick, see John McLaughlin, "The Future of Canada's Universities and Colleges," CAUT Hearing, University of New Brunswick, Fredericton, 9 February 2002.

30. Jill Blackmore, "Disciplining Feminism: A Look at Gender-Equity Struggles in Australian Higher Education," in Leslie G. Roman and Linda Eyre, eds., *Dangerous Territories: Struggles for Difference and Equality in Education* (New York: Routledge, 1997), 78.

31. The faculty council is being restructured to include faculty associates (former administrators and teachers on short-term appointments, seconded from the public school system) and has abandoned quorums for meetings.

32. Catherine Casey cited in Jill Blackmore and Judyth Sacks, "Women Leaders in the Restructured University," in Brooks and MacKinnon, eds., *Gender and the Restructured University*, 56.

33. New Brunswick, *Quality Schools*, 22, 27.

34. Ibid., 34.

35. Pierrette Bouchard, Isabelle Boily and Marie-Claude Proulx, *School Success by Gender: A Catalyst for Masculinist Discourse* (Ottawa: Status of Women Canada, 2003).

36. New Brunswick, *Quality Schools*, 32.

37. Ibid., 32, 46.

38. Ibid., 38.

39. Taylor, *The Politics of Educational Reform in Alberta*, 13.

40. Brewers Association of Canada, "'Tiens-toi' French Alcohol Education Site Launched," *On Tap* 14, no. 3 (2000), 1. For a detailed analysis of the partnership, see Linda Eyre, "'No Strings Attached? Corporate Involvement in Curriculum," *Canadian Journal of Education* (in press).

41. Brewers Association of Canada, *Quiet Victories: Community Partnerships and Responsible Drinking Initiatives* (Ottawa: BAC, 2001).

42. Brewers Association of Canada, "Youth Alcohol Education Program Launched in Alberta," *On Tap* 14, no. 5 (2000), 2.

43. Jane Kenway and Elizabeth Bullen, *Consuming Children: Education-Entertainment-Advertising* (Philadelphia: Open University Press, 2001), 90, 97.

44. Brewers Association of Canada, *BAC Annual Report: Partnerships* (Ottawa: BAC, 1998), 3.

45. Eyre, "'No Strings Attached?"

46. Ellwood, *The No-Nonsense Guide to Globalization*, 63.

47. Hey, "'A Game of Two Halves,'" 360.

48. Ann Brooks, "Restructuring Bodies of Knowledge," in Brooks and MacKinnon, eds., *Gender and the Restructured University*, 15.

49. Ozga, *Policy Research in Educational Settings*, 7.

50. Jill Blackmore and Judyth Sachs, "Women Leaders in the Restructured University," in Brooks and McKinnon, eds., *Gender and the Restructured University*, 47.

51. Ozga, *Policy Research in Educational Settings*, 20.

52. Taylor, *The Politics of Educational Reform in Alberta*, 307.

53. Ibid., 309.

54. Ibid., 302.

55. Dehli, "Between 'Markets' and 'State,'" 372.

56. Taylor, *The Politics of Educational Reform in Alberta*, 308, 309.

CHAPTER 4

"THE CAPTIVE SCIENTIST": CORPORATE INFLUENCE OVER SCIENTIFIC RESEARCH

Ella Haley

There is no science uninfluenced by politics. This is a plea to get the
politics out of hiding.
— Sylvia Tesh, *Hidden Arguments*[1]

THERE IS GROWING PUBLIC CONCERN about undue corporate influence
on scientific research in universities and in government. The more
recent visible cases involved Dr. Nancy Olivieri who was disciplined by
a pharmaceutical company for disclosing the side effects of a trial drug
that she was using on her patients; Professor David Healy who was fired
after he went public about the dangerous side effects of Prozac; and
researchers within Health Canada who were pressured by corporations
to authorize their products. I'll touch on each of these briefly. Corporate
funding and influence over research is not a new phenomenon. For
comparative purposes, I'll review two more historic cases: one involving
the delayed recognition of an occupational disease because of the
funder's "gag clause" and the other involving corporate influence on
fluoride research and related inquiries.

Toronto's Hospital for Sick Children (HSC) is a fully affiliated teaching hospital with the University of Toronto. In 1996, Dr. Olivieri, a specialist at HSC, "identified an unexpected risk with a drug that she was testing to treat a rare blood disorder. When she began to inform patients of this risk as was required by medical ethics, the drug manufacturer, Apotex, terminated the research trial and threatened to take legal action."[2] Dr. Olivieri faced allegations, which were later proven to be false, had her scientific integrity questioned and was temporarily removed from her position.

Simultaneously, the University of Toronto was in the midst of negotiations to receive a multimillion-dollar donation from Apotex.[3] One catch was that Apotex requested the University of Toronto president to lobby the Canadian government against proposed changes to drug patent regulations that would hurt the company's revenues. President Prichard wrote to the Prime Minister noting "the proposed government action could jeopardize the building of the University's proposed new medical sciences centre."[4] These actions by Apotex raise serious questions about research ethics and academic freedom. The features of Dr. Olivieri's story are not unique —

> It could occur at many institutions across Canada … it is essential to put in place measures to ensure that, in the conduct of clinical research trials, the public interest is protected from inappropriate action by trial sponsors.[5]

In 2000, David Healy, a world-renowned research psychopharmacologist from Wales, was hired by the University of Toronto-affiliated Centre for Addiction and Mental Health (CAMH).[6] He had been warned by a key advisor to the pharmaceutical industry that his career "would be destroyed" if he kept going public about the hazards of antidepressant medications known as SSRIs.[7] Healy was dumped by the University of Toronto just after he gave a lecture in which he linked Prozac, Paxil and the other SSRIs to suicide. In the same lecture, Healy also spoke about "conflict of interest with drug companies and the increase(d) challenge doctors face in avoiding it"[8]:

> [Researchers like myself] get money from the pharmaceutical industry. We speak for pharmaceutical companies, run trials for them, and it does bias you. We probably all hope that the bias is going to be a small little bias and it's a risk we just have to take.[9]

A CAMH official explained that Healy was fired because of his "unscientific lecture," in which he exhibited extreme views, based on inadequate science.

At issue is the role of pharmaceutical companies in shaping medical research. More than half of the research funds in the CAMH came from drug companies. As in the Olivieri case, the University of Toronto was expecting a large donation ($1.5 million) from a pharmaceutical company — in this case, Eli Lilly, the manufacturer of Prozac.[10] Healy had given expert testimony in court cases against the company. In defending Healy, James Turk of the Canadian Association of University Teachers argued,

> Here we have one of the top, if not the top psychiatric research facility and teaching hospital in the country saying we don't want someone who raises a certain set of fundamental questions about one of the most pre-scribed, widely prescribed classes of medicine in Canada.[11]

Healy has filed a multi-million dollar breach of contract lawsuit against the CAMH and the University of Toronto and will donate any settlement that he wins to the Academic Freedom Trust Fund.[12]

In 1998, Health Canada scientists went public about the pressure put on them by corporations seeking approval for their products. At issue was Health Canada's "willingness to accept data and money from companies seeking approval to market drugs in Canada."[13] Dr. Shiv Chopra testified before the Senate Standing Committee on Agriculture and Forestry, saying, "We have been "pressured and coerced to pass drugs of questionable safety, including rBST."[14] Recombinant Bovine Somatotrophin (rBST or bovine growth hormone) increases milk production in cows. Dr. Chopra and Dr. Margaret Hayden recommended that rBST not be approved because of demonstrated research concerns about the side effects in cows, and concerns about a possible link to cancer in humans from a byproduct of rBST.

Doctors Hayden and Chopra testified that they were pressured by their supervisors to approve the drug anyway. These researchers felt that the regulatory intent of the *Food and Drugs Act* was being compromised. "Our members are being pressed by management to ignore rigorous professional standards of practice, thereby creating unacceptable and unnecessary risks in the drug assessment process."[15] When neither their department nor the Prime Minister responded, they went public with their concerns. Following this they were officially reprimanded and given gag orders, both of which they appealed and won. In her decision, the judge ruled,

> Where a matter is of legitimate public concern requiring a public debate, the duty of loyalty cannot be absolute to the extent of preventing public disclosure by a government official. The common law duty of loyalty does not impose unquestioning silence.[16]

Behind these disciplinary actions is a shift by the Health Protection Branch in its role and in the standards that it applies to determine food safety. Department scientists are instructed that their clients are the food and drug manufacturers that are seeking approval of their products. There has also been a shift from the precautionary principle (preventing harm from happening) to risk management where regulators manage any negative environmental or human health impacts. In April 1999, in an audit of Canada's meat supply, the European Union found

> widespread use of cancer causing hormones, antibiotics, endocrine disrupters and other hormonally active substances, all of which are banned in Europe ... there were the same substances that department scientists had recommended against approving.[17]

Professor Ann Clark, a plant researcher at the University of Guelph, is particularly concerned about how the biotechnology industry is influencing academic research and teaching:

> The chilling effect of industrial encroachment on academic freedom is increasingly viewed as a threat to academia as we know it. The withdrawal of "public good" funding and the requirement for matching funds to access what is left effectively control the research questions that we can ask, and hence, the lessons our students can learn.[18]

Clark is also greatly concerned about how professors act in a third-party role, appearing as independent scientists:

> The impact of such professors is prolonged and indeed exacerbated when they enact their third-party role — replacing factual discourse with value-laden diatribes to camouflage and further the goals of external vested interests — through the very graduate students they are entrusted to teach.[19]

Take for instance, a graduate student paper discrediting Percy Schmeiser, the canola grower who was sued by Monsanto for having Monsanto's patented Roundup Ready gene in canola on his land and for not notifying Monsanto to come and remove it. Clark analyzed how a Monsanto-linked professor "shielded himself" through a graduate student's paper that emulated "the distinctive writing style" of the student's faculty adviser."[20] She illustrates how the paper uses tactics that she calls "double-speak" to discredit Mr. Schmeiser's case. These include

- replacing factual discourse with emotion-laden symbolism,
- deliberate fabrication to encourage conformity to a vested interest, and
- hiding vested interests.

Clark worries that when academics teach students how to discredit detractors through strategies such as these, and when academics commit themselves to proprietary research of "no apparent redeeming social value," that we are "perilously close to the values of Orwell's *1984.*"[21]

Sometimes it seems as if the federal government is learning from the above cases. In January 2004, after a campaign by the Council of Canadians that focused on the influence of the biotechnology industry on the federal government, Agriculture Canada announced that it would end its work "with biotech Monsanto to develop wheat that is genetically modified to make it resistant to the herbicide Roundup."[22] Yet even as we struggle with the reoccurrence of the mad cow crisis, Dr. Shiv Chopra has again been suspended for criticizing the government publicly. "Chopra was cited as saying the suspension relates in part to comments he made that department officials ignored internal calls for a ban on animal feeds suspected of causing bovine spongiform encephalopathy, or mad-cow disease."[23]

Some of the authors who have contributed to *Inside Corporate U* are concerned about increasing corporate influence over academic research. While university autonomy did begin to falter as governments began withdrawing funding in the 1980s, universities in Canada have long served business interests.[24] Neil Tudiver argues that usually this relationship has been at arm's-length, the universities "supplying trained graduates, independent studies, expert advisers, and contract research."[25] What's new is that the government now acts as a matchmaker to marry business and research interests.

Historically, since 1919, the government has supported business-related research in mining, fishing, agriculture and forestry. Government-industry linked research in mining stems back to 1842 at McGill University. Since 1900, the Canadian Manufacturers Association has lobbied for closer relations between industry and universities. By 1916, most graduate fellowships at the University of Toronto were subsidized by corporations.[26] In the same year, the

Honourary Advisory Council on Scientific and Industrial Research, later known as the National Research Council (NRC), was set up. During the Second World War, the federal government invested heavily in munitions manufacturing, spending $7 million to support twenty-one new laboratories conducting wartime scientific research. After the Second World War, the NRC played a key role in encouraging government-industry-university research in science and engineering. Gradually it trimmed its size, dividing its research divisions into three separate divisions: the Defense Research Board, Atomic Energy of Canada and the Medical Research Council. In 1966, the Science Council of Canada was set up to promote university research to serve industry.[27]

Industry-funded scientists both inside and outside the university can be co-opted and can have the direction of their research and the analysis and circulation of their findings monopolized and controlled by the industry that hires them.[28] It is not unusual for scientists to be used by the party hiring them to legitimate industrial pollution. Take for example the case of the radium dialworkers. As early as 1915, Dr. David Edsall, a founder of Harvard's Department of Industrial Hygiene and later dean of both the Harvard Medical School and the School of Public Health, cautioned researchers against investigating individual cases of occupational illness and reporting them to government agencies. "Employers are afraid of what the State [Compensation] Board may do and it might injure the hospital to be identified as being in close cooperation with them."[29] Between 1918 and 1922, the Department of Industrial Hygiene relied completely upon business contributions. Even the editor of the *Journal of Industrial Hygiene*, based out of Harvard, found that she had to "exercise discretion in choosing articles for publication, so as not to lose financial support for the program."[30]

During the First World War, about 2,000 teenage girls and young women worked in factories where they applied luminous numbers on watch and instrument dials with paint that contained radium.[31] When some of the young women began to get sick and die, the National Consumers League, an organization devoted to the problems of working women, prompted Dr. Alice Hamilton to investigate; Hamilton was a renowned toxicologist and Harvard professor in industrial hygiene. She learned that three colleagues in her department had conducted research for the United States Radium Corporation on the industrial hygiene of dialpainting, in its factory in Orange, New Jersey. These researchers included "Cecil Drinker, a founder of Harvard's industrial hygiene program and Assistant Dean of Public Health at Harvard."[32] When Drinker and his colleagues found that the radium in the paint was causing the necrosis ("jaw rot") in the dialpainters, they abided by the radium dial company's stipulation that they not publish their findings.

In the radium dialworkers' case, Claudia Clarke argues that the recognition of an occupational disease was delayed because of "governmental-industrial-academic collusion" that is largely based on industrial funding of research and experts.[33] At issue is how corporate-funded university researchers and experts failed to help the dialpainters, posing instead as "neutral" experts.

Clark argues that in keeping his silence, Dr. Drinker "was acquiescing in further exposures and preventing dialpainters from seeking compensation."[34] Only when Dr. Drinker found that the radium company had issued a "forged report" in his name to the Department of Labor that exonerated the company of any responsibility in the illnesses of the girls, did he finally set out to publish his data. But, as the radium company's lawyer reminded him:

> It is my understanding that you were retained by and at the expense of the Radium Corporation to make the investigation in question ... While, of course, the Radium Corporation did not desire this fact to in any way affect your investigation and conclusions, it certainly assumed that in case your conclusions were adverse to its claims you would not publish ... This is the first occasion in my experience covering many years with doctors and other expert witnesses of high character when any expert has ever threatened, during the pendency of litigation, to publish a report adverse to the party to such litigation who had retained him.[35]

Once New Jersey's Labor Department received Dr. Drinker's full report, it acted to enforce all recommended safety procedures. The radium company left town and reopened in New York City. In 1925, a few years later, the radium company referred several employees to Dr. Frederick Flinn, "an expert" on radium poisoning, who reassured them that their health concerns were not related to radium. Although Dr. Flinn published the results of his studies ruling out any cases of jaw necrosis (radium poisoning) in the Orange factory, he knew from his earlier research how to recognize radium poisoning, and he confided privately to Dr. Drinker that he felt the radium was to blame for the dialpainters' symptoms.[36]

Dr. Flinn was, in fact, employed by the radium company and, although he was examining and diagnosing radium exposed workers, he was not a physician. Instead, he was a physiologist from Columbia University's Department of Industrial Hygiene and later became chair of the department. After being challenged by Dr. Hamilton about his connection with the radium company, Dr. Flinn finally published another article acknowledging that the radioactive material lay at the heart of the women's health problems.[37]

These case studies illustrate some of the unacceptable costs of close links between university academics and private industry. There is growing concern about the continued push towards this relationship, which David Suzuki refers to as the "industrialization of the university." He writes:

> My most serious concern is with the vital role of the academic as both critic and source of knowledge for society. Without an ax to grind, the scholar is in a unique position to provide a balanced point of view ... They are sufficiently detached from the priorities of various interest groups like business, government and the military to point out flaws in our current social truths.[38]

In my doctoral dissertation, I examined the influential network of academics and corporate and government officials who were involved in research on industrial fluoride emissions and the strategies that they used to control and co-ordinate how the issue was defined and dealt with.[39] Like the example of the research on the dialworkers, the literature on industrial-funded fluoride research reflects how some academics have enhanced the role of what Dorothy Smith refers to as "ruling relations," which is an internally co-ordinated complex of administrative, managerial, professional and discursive organization that regulates, organizes, governs and otherwise controls our societies.[40]

Beginning in the 1930s, fluoride-emitting industries, especially aluminum and phosphate processing factories faced extensive litigation fines against aluminum and phosphate processing factories, in particular, for their toxic fluoride emissions.

> In the early thirties, Alcoa and other manufacturers of aluminum were in trouble, serious trouble. They had a waste product, sodium fluoride, which represented a serious disposal problem. It could not be dumped on the ground because it poisoned vegetation, animals and humans. Alcoa's Vancouver, Washington, plant was fined in 1950 for

dumping fluoride into the Columbia River and poisoning domestic animals.

Fluoride was the culprit in other extensive litigation throughout the country. Fluoride gases and solids escape from smokestacks and settle on vegetation in the immediate surroundings and many miles distant. They poison vegetation, livestock and humans ... Many of the lawsuits were settled out of court ... In the *Martin vs. Reynolds Metals* suit it was proven, for the first time, that fumes from an aluminum reduction plant had damaged human health.[41]

A great deal of fluoride research was funded by the Mellon and Kettering Institutes. The Mellon Institute was founded by the Mellon family, owners of Alcoa as a research institute for the U.S. "businessman." The intent was that

when a manufacturer is in trouble ... he goes to the Institute. For $6,000 or more he gets a fellowship entitling him to employ a scientist for a year and use laboratory facilities ... The scientists' job is either to improve the product or to find a new use for it ... When the research is satisfactorily completed, all discoveries are turned over to the manufacturer exclusively. Thus, findings incriminating to the companies need not be reported to the medical and veterinary professions.[42]

The Kettering Laboratory, in the Department of Preventive Medicine at the University of Cincinnati, was founded by the Ethyl Gas Company, Frigidaire and DuPont deNemours to study health hazards in industry. As at the Mellon Institute,

findings are made available to the professions and to the public only upon approval by the donor of the grant. Article 8 of the contract agreements between the corporations and the Laboratory provides that the University "disseminate for the public good any information obtained." However, before the issuance of public reports or scientific publications, the manuscripts thereof will be submitted to the Donor for criticism and suggestions. Confidential information obtained from the Donor shall be not be published without permission of said Donor.[43]

Corporate-funded researchers basically operated as "captive scientists," enabling industries that had toxic fluoride emission to reconceptualize fluoride as necessary for healthy teeth. This scientific research was used by fluoride emitters to defend themselves in lawsuits and in official inquiries related to industrial fluoride emissions. The documents from these inquiries perpetuated an ideological control through their texts. My research illustrates not only how scientists were "captives" of industry but were also very influential "captains" of industry.

In the Hall Inquiry,[44] which investigated industrial emissions from a phosphate processing factory in Port Maitland, Ontario, key academics with close ties to government and industry determined the terms of reference of the public inquiry. Key testimony and data were blocked from being entered into the public record. Key witnesses were instructed not to discuss the factory involved nor its emissions. Although the Commission had two esteemed academics on the Commission, it failed to demonstrate proper scientific methodology in collecting, analyzing and sharing its data. A search at the Ontario archives for the background records of the Hall Inquiry (Reference Code: RG 18-155) yielded very little information — only the final reports and the transcript of the proceedings.[45] While commissions from the 1960s onwards have tended to deposit more records with the provincial archives, they are under no obligation to do so. Royal Commissions are not included under the *Archives Act,* or the *Freedom of Information and Privacy Act.*[46] The head of a Royal Commission does not have to deliver any background documents if she or he so chooses. These special privileges of the Hall Commission make it very difficult to investigate the accuracy of its report, and work against the standards expected of any peer-reviewed scientific research report.

David Suzuki has reflected on the "industrialization" of academia and worries that in entering into a "Faustian bargain" with private industry, we risk losing sight of the broader context of that activity:

> Academics who accept grants or investments from the military or the pharmaceutical, forest, and computer industries ... will be reluctant to jeopardize that support by criticizing those industries when necessary.[47]

He is particularly concerned about biotechnology — the "genetic engineering of organisms for commercial purposes." While biotech companies are "sprouting up on campuses like mushrooms," few academic meetings are discussing the potential "misuse or hazards" of this technology:

> Surely an academic community of scholars who maintain an arm's-length relationship with vested interests of society should be expected to raise those questions. Who else will do it?[48]

In the fall of 2002, academics gathered together with journalists to share these concerns at the "Disciplining Dissent Conference." They drew up resolutions, which this book also reflects, to reinforce

academics' commitment of working together:
- "to promote public service values,
- to strength and advance the cause of teaching and research in the public interest,
- to encourage a diversity of voices, and
- to ensure that the independence and integrity of academic research through adequate public funding."[49]

We will need this commitment in this era of funding cuts as we try to ensure that pure research in Canadian universities is fostered — research that is freely shared and independent from market demands, and that allows academics to "collaborate in collegial rather than entrepreneurial competition."[50]

NOTES

1. Sylvia Tesh, *Hidden Arguments: Political Ideology and Disease Prevention Policy* (New Brunswick, NJ: Rutgers University Press, 1988), 177.

2. Jon Thompson, Patricia Baird and Jocelyn Downie, *The Olivieri Report* (Toronto: James Lorimer, 2001), back cover.

3. Ibid., 6.

4. Ibid., 11.

5. Ibid., 15.

6. Rick Giombetti, "Prozac, Suicide and Dr. Healy." Retrieved from <http://www.counterpunch.com/prozacsuicide.html>. January 9, 2004.

7. Canadian Broadcasting Corporation, "CBC News and Current Affairs: The David Healy Affair" (June 12, 2001), 3. Retrieved from <http://www.pharmapolitics. com/cbcnational.html>. January 9, 2004. SSRIs are Selective Seratonin Re-uptake Inhibitors which are prescribed as anti-depressants.

8. Ibid., 8–9.

9. Ibid., 9.

10. Ibid., 6.

11. Ibid., 10.

12. Giombetti, "Prozac, Suicide and Dr. Healy."

13. James Baxter, "Scientists 'Pressured' to Approve Cattle Drug: Health Canada Researchers Accuse Firm of Bribery in Bid to OK 'Questionable' Product," *Ottawa Citizen*, 23 October 1998, A1.

14. Ibid. At present rBST is approved in the U.S., but not in Europe or Canada.

15. Nova Scotia Allergy and Environmental Health Association, "Whistleblowers at Health Canada Protect Food Safety: Update" (Summer 2000), 1. Retrieved from <http://www.environmentalhealth.ca/summer01blow.html>. January 9, 2004.

16. Ibid., 2.

17. Ibid.

18. E. Ann Clark, "Industry and Academic Biotechnology: Teaching Students the Art of Doublespeak" (paper presented at the Canadian Association of University Teachers Conference, Discipling Dissent: The Curbing of Free Expression in Academia and the Media, Ottawa, November 1–3, 2002), 7. Clark is citing G. Toomey, "Letting the Gene Out of the Bottle," *University Affairs* (October 2002), 20–25.

19. Ibid., 9.

20. Ibid.

21. Ibid.

22. "Ottawa Abandons Monsanto Project," *CBC News* (Saturday, 10 January 2004). Retrieved from <http://www.cbc.ca/stories/2004/10/monsanto040110>. January 11, 2004.

23. Paul Waldie, "Health Canada Suspends Scientist: Microbiologist Criticized Ottawa for Failing to Enact Animal Feed Ban," *The Globe and Mail*, 20 December 2003, A13.

24. Neil Tudiver, "Capitalist Research: A Marriage of Convenience," *Universities for Sale: Resisting Corporate Control over Canadian Higher Education* (Toronto: James Lorimer, 1999).

25. Ibid., 139.

26. Ibid., 140.

27. Ibid., 141, 143.

28. Murphy Raymond, *Rationality and Nature: A Sociological Inquiry into a Changing Relationship* (Boulder, CO: Westview Press, 1994), 207.

29. Ibid., 9.

30. Ibid.

31. Ibid.

32. Ibid., 151.

33. Claudia Clark, "Physicians, Reformers and Occupational Disease: The Discovery of Radium Poisoning," *Women and Health* 12, no. 2 (1987), 156.

34. Ibid., 154.

35. Ibid., 147.

36. Ibid., 161.

37. Ibid., 160–162.

38. David Suzuki, "The Prostitution of the Academic," *The David Suzuki Reader* (Vancouver: Greystone Books, 2003), 192–193.

39. Ella Haley, "Methodology to Deconstruct Environmental Inquiries Using the Hall Commission as a Case Study" (PhD diss., York University, 2000).

40. Dorothy E. Smith, *Writing the Social: Critique, Theory and Investigations* (Toronto: University of Toronto Press, 1999), 49.

41. George Waldbott, *A Struggle With Titans: Forces Behind Fluoridation. A Scientist's Look at Fluoridation* (New York: Carlton Press, 1965), 130.

42. Ibid., 115, 119. Dr. Waldbott is citing from the article on the Mellon Institute in *Life Magazine* (May 9, 1938), 48.

43. Waldbott, *A Struggle With Titans*, 123.

44. Ontario, *Committee of Inquiry on Allegations Concerning Pollution in the Townships of Dunn, Moulton, and Sherbrooke* (Toronto: Queen's Printer, 1968). Reference Code: RG 18-155.

45. In a note in the file, M. Weissengruber of the Hall Commission says that he turned over the records of the Commission to the Minister of Health, Matthew B. Dymond (Michele Dale, Senior Archivist, Education Portfolio, Archives of Ontario, personal discussion with author, January 12, 2004). My search through the archives of the Department of Health produced a few piecemeal documents.

46. Michele Dale, Senior Archivist, Education Portfolio, Archives of Ontario, personal discussion with author, January 12, 2004.

47. Suzuki, "The Prostitution of the Academic," 193.

48. Ibid., 194.

49. "Conference Statement" from Disciplining Dissent: The Curbing of Free Expression in Academia and the Media Conference, Ottawa, November 1–3, 2002.

50. Jim Marino, "Clearcutting in the Groves of Academe," Gordon Laxer and Trevor Harrison, eds., in *The Trojan Horse: Alberta and the Future of Canada* (Montreal: Black Rose Press, 1995), 213.

WOMEN'S
CAREERS
IN THE
GENDERED
STREAM

CHAPTER 5

SHIFTING PROGRAMS OR UNDERCUTTING EQUITY?
A PRELIMINARY STUDY USING THREE UNIVERSITY ACADEMIC CALENDARS

Jane Gordon & Ilya Blum

CANADIAN UNIVERSITIES EXPERIENCED a phenomenal growth during the 1960s. New universities were founded, existing ones grew in size and expanded the number and level of their programs. An academic infrastructure began to emerge, along with the expansion of granting councils, university presses, scholarly societies and discipline-based journals. This growth was driven by the increased number of students (the baby boomers) who were seeking higher education and by government policy-makers who wanted higher participation rates in post-secondary education. Universities protected their autonomy by refusing to accept corporate funds and by relying on government money, at a time when it was available in abundance. However, when the availability of government money began to decline in the 1970s and 1980s, universities began to focus on how to replace it. As Janice Newsom and Howard Buchbinder describe it, the financial constraints of the time led to greater linkages with the corporate world.[1] This resulted in the universities reorienting their research aims from a scholarly based approach to a more practical application, which led to the subsequent devaluing of teaching and undergraduate education.

These trends continue today. While often couched in the name of sound economic practice, there has been a change in the nature of university governance, with an expansion and reliance on administrative rather than collegial structures, an emphasis on cost recovery and contracting out of work previously done by university employees, such as the running of bookstores and the provision of food services, housekeeping and grounds maintenance. This is most evident in those aspects that touch the education process directly, especially around issues of faculty appointments — there has been a dramatic growth in part-time or limited-term faculty who are frequently governed by collective agreements with set salary scales. The growing literature on the corporatization of the campus documents the many different effects that this shift is having on the university environment.[2]

During this period — the 1970s to the present — there has also been increased advocacy around issues of gender equality on campus. Feminist academics and others involved in the equity movement — including groups within faculty associations at the local, regional and national level and administrative groups — sought change in multiple ways. Some of these changes were women's admissions to undergraduate, graduate and professional programs, campus-based child care, sexual harassment policies and access to the high-status job of professor. These efforts led to the development and implementation of the Federal Contractor's Program, which required employees doing business with the federal government to do a census of employees and report on the hiring of four under-represented groups: visible minorities, individuals of Native ancestry, people with disabilities and women.

Paralleling these efforts were women's efforts to revise curriculum and institutional policies and practices. Among the policies that were problematic were time limits for students to complete academic programs, the absence of financial support for part-time students and the physical layout of campuses and campus buildings. All of these policies affected students with disabilities, mature students, part-time students and students with work or family obligations, and some affected faculty and other university employees.

As a consequence of greater access to graduate programs and open-hiring processes, the number and percentage of women faculty increased during this thirty-year period. Today, women represent 25 percent of the tenured faculty and 40 percent of those faculty in tenure-stream positions. However, the effect of recent corporate-oriented practices on women and other equity groups suggests that there are problems.[3] In our attempt to more fully understand how corporatization is influencing women in the changing academic environment, we decided to focus on the academic calendars that universities publish on an annual basis. These calendars, though widely used, are often taken for granted. They are used by students to make choices about which institution they will attend and to select programs and courses once they have made their choice. Universities use them for promotional purposes and for informing prospective students, faculty and other employees about their academic offerings. However, calendars are often more than that. They can provide us with a glimpse of a university's culture, and give us information about the university's structure and composition as well as the number, distribution and scholarly qualifications of its faculty. They also provide insight into a university's character and its values, which can be used to glean information above and beyond the particular educational programs offered. These calendars are public documents and are available to interested individuals outside the academy and around the globe.

As documents that have been created for other purposes, these university calendars allow us to examine change in a relatively objective way. As social science researchers know, unobtrusive or non-reactive measures commonly provide insight into social phenomena.[4] The collection of a university's calendars over an extended period of time provides perspectives into that institution's history and allows researchers to develop original ways to examine change within it.

In this essay, we report on how we used university calendars to examine some of the transformations that have occurred over the past twenty-five years, changes that are concomitant with the emergence of academic corporatization.[5] The calendars provided us with pre-existing data for analysis — data as neutral and objective as one can get in what is otherwise a very political debate. While we focus here on the faculty information contained in these calendars, we also note that they contain other useful information: the programs available, the courses required in each program and the extent and variety of the university's administration. The calendars we examined are from three small undergraduate universities situated in the Maritimes and span the period from the mid-1970s to the mid-1990s. Our data consisted of the faculty listings in these calendars — their names, department affiliations, ranks and credentials. In some of the institutions, we also found information about the faculty's full-time or part-time status, their sabbaticals and other leaves. From these data, we were able to obtain more information. Through first names, for example, we could usually infer gender. The year in which an individual's name first appears allowed us to infer the initial hiring date. We could also infer attachment to an institution, by looking at the total number of years during which an individual was listed as a faculty member.

In discussions about corporatization in the academy there is often a discussion about the casualization of academic labour. Although Statistics Canada may provide data on the numbers and percentages of part-time faculty, that information is sketchy — it often focuses on institutions, not on individuals. Calendars can thus provide information beyond that which Statistics Canada makes available. We could, for example, learn what proportion of faculty were in a given rank each year, but not how many of the existing faculty were rising stars soon to be promoted. We could look at numbers and percentages in each rank or other employment category, but we didn't know whether it was the same individual or a different individual year after year. We could also glean the duration of a faculty member's working arrangements and terminal rank — two measures that cannot be obtained from Statistics Canada data. These variables are useful in assessing the impact of corporatization and other changes because they measure a degree of stability and academic growth in a particular university's faculty.

The three universities we examined are located in a peripheral region of the country and are probably less touched by corporatization than those located in Canada's cental core. All are located in the same province to minimize change caused by interprovincial funding differences. We also chose three institutions roughly similar in size, at least at the starting point of our data collection. However, these institutions differ significantly in several ways and each has its own distinctive culture. One of the universities is located in a major urban centre, while the other two are located in rural areas, within one and two hours commuting distance of the urban centre. All three fall under the small, primarily undergraduate universities as categorized annually in *Maclean's*[6] and two of the three have, over the years of the survey, been among the highest ranked in that category. One of the three currently has a high proportion of professional programs, while the other two are predominantly focused on Arts and Science.

We chose these institutions for a number of reasons. There was a convenience factor. We had the co-operation of the archivists and librarians as well as the staff in the registrar's office in locating calendars for our use. We are familiar with these institutions from our own educational and professional lives and we also had informants at each institution who helped us with questions on names and genders when necessary. We felt that because of their size, the calendars from small universities were likely to provide more complete faculty lists. While smaller universities offer a more limited number of programs than larger institutions, they face the same financial pressures from government funding and change within the institution might be easier to see. We believe that because of their connections to particular geographic regions and an orientation towards their local and alumnae communities, these institutions are likely to be more cumbersome in dealing with change or slower to change than the larger ones.

THE FOUR ISSUES UNDER REVIEW

In our examination of corporatization we focused on four specific issues: (1) the changes in the distribution of faculty in the disciplines over time; (2) the length of the attachment of faculty members to their university; (3) gender composition of the faculty; and (4) the highest rank achieved by faculty. We chose these four issues because we believe they reflect the growth of corporate influence in the academy.

The first issue, for example, helps us see what has happened to the core disciplines of a liberal education, whether the number and variety of professional programs have changed and how distribution of faculty has been affected. In the second issue, we wanted to look at the length of the faculties' relationship with their university. The 1950s model described by Theodore Caplow and Reece McGee in *The Academic Marketplace* was of a faculty member at a university for a life-time career.[7] The mobility options of faculty hired during the expansion of higher education in Canada in the 1960s, however, did not survive the cutbacks of the 1970s. Newson and Buchbinder suggest that the economic pressures on government caused by rising unemployment, plant closures and an ideological shift towards conservatism was reflected in the cuts to the higher-education budget and a decline in per-capita spending on higher education in that decade.[8] Stability for those faculty already in place and new career patterns for those faculty seeking positions was the prevalent pattern. Our examination of the length of faculty involvement at their current institutions allowed us to examine faculty growth, issues around full- and part-time appointment status and the question of community allegiance, including whether the types of contracts offered to faculty were tenure stream or short term.

Looking at the third issue, we wanted to establish the gender composition of the faculty. From the 1970s on there has been increasing pressure on universities to be more inclusive of women and other groups that have historically faced discrimination. This has resulted in changes in curriculum (discipline based and interdisciplinary courses on women, incorporation of gender and gender issues into other courses), policies (sexual harassment, availability of campus childcare, parental leave for employees) and staffing at all levels. In 1980, the starting point of our investigation, women made up a very small percentage of the university faculty in Canada. During the 1980s, universities experienced growth in both student and faculty numbers, but it was growth often driven or influenced by the need to secure funding from corporate rather than governmental sources. We were interested in finding out what an increasingly market-driven university meant for women faculty. An examination of the role of women in the corporate academy also tells us something about its adaptation to one particular kind of change.

A second reason we wanted to look at gender composition was to see how program changes affected gender equity. Recent statistics document that women and men still tend to earn advanced degrees in different disciplines, although the extent of the differences have diminished. What does the discipline distribution in the academy mean for women faculty? Are efforts at achieving greater equity likely to be nullified by the new directions in which universities are moving?

The fourth issue helped us to determine the highest rank attained by faculty. Promotion to the rank of professor is earned through significant scholarly or professional achievements and the maintenance of solid teaching and service over periods of ten years or more. The fewer number of faculty who attain the professor rank may indicate a greater reliance on a more marginal or contingent labour force.

Our Methodology

At this point it seems appropriate for us to provide a little more detail on our methodology. We examined copies of university calendars for each year during the period 1975 to 1995 and recorded the information contained in the faculty listings. At each site, each listing included the faculties' last and first names, rank, department affiliation, credentials and institutions where these credentials were earned. One of the sites included part-time academic faculty and identified their status. A second site did not list any part-time faculty members. A third site listed part-time faculty in a separate section. We also included faculty who were on sabbaticals or taking other leaves and those with appointments shorter than twelve months. However, for the purposes of this study, we excluded administrative personnel as well as retired or emeriti faculty.

Since the names of faculty members were not always spelled consistently from year to year, and sometimes changed due to marriage, divorce or membership status in a religious order, the first step of the analysis was used to identify individuals uniquely. We also inferred the gender of each individual from the name, and in cases of doubt we consulted current or retired faculty members from the respective universities. In approximately 7 percent of the listings, we were unable to identify the gender, and we excluded those individuals from the analysis.

We categorized academic departments into three broad categories, namely Arts and Science (A&S), Human Services Oriented Professions (HP) and Market Oriented Professions (MP). A&S consisted of the traditional Arts and Science disciplines; HP consisted of professions such as Education, Human Kinetics, Recreation Management, Family Studies, Nutrition and Food Science; and MP consisted of departments such as Commerce, Business Administration, Engineering, Public Relations, and Information Technology. It is important to point out that department names sometimes change over time. For example, in one university, the Department of Typing and Shorthand became Secretarial Arts, then Office Management and is now Information Technology.

We then computed two variables for each individual faculty member. The first of these, called "attachment," counts the number of years during our period for which that person is listed in the institution's calendar. Those listed between one and six times and not listed in the final year of our research period were classified as "low attachment." (We reasoned that many of those with six or fewer years of experience who were on staff in the final year of our period of study may well have stayed on a few more years.) In the second variable, we computed each individual's highest rank attained during the same period. We labelled those who achieved the rank of professor in any year for which we had calendar data as "eventual professors" or EPs. Admittedly, some faculty members may have been promoted in the late 1990s, after the cut-off point for our data, but would not be so recognized by our variable. We believe these two variables capture the degree of affiliation and the recognized achievement of faculty at their respective institutions. We then examined changes occurring in the 1980s in the distribution of faculty among the three areas by gender and changes in the proportions of faculty with low attachment and of faculty who eventually attained promotion to the rank of professor within each area at each site.

We realize that as a methodology, our use of calendar data is not perfect. If anything, it underestimates the number of faculty in any particular year, since the printing date for the calendar may not coincide with the end of hiring — a time-lag issue that may also affect rank and credentials.

AN OVERVIEW OF THE RESULTS

We emphasize at the outset that the numbers below reflect individuals who taught at the three universities but not necessarily with full-time positions. Table 1 summarizes some essential demographics about the three institutions we examined. We can see that the overall faculty numbers were comparable at the three sites, and that University A was predominantly female (64 percent) in its faculty composition, while the others were predominantly male.

These institutions also differed substantially in the distribution of their faculties among the three areas of study. During the 1980s, University A typically had 30 percent in Human Services Oriented Professions (HP), 20 percent in Market Oriented Professions (MP) and 50 percent in Arts and Science (A&S), while University B had approximately 17 percent in HP, 12 percent in MP, and 70 percent in A&S. University C was similar to University B, in that it had just under 70 percent of its faculty in A&S, 20 percent in HP and 10 percent in MP.

Table 1: Demographics of the Institutions

INSTITUTION	LOCATION	FULL AND PART FACULTY		PERCENT FEMALE	
		1980	1990	1980	1990
University A	Urban	134	247	58%	64%
University B	Rural/Urban	223	284	15%	23%
University C	Rural	166	225	24%	28%

We next examined the faculty composition in each of the three areas at the three sites. In 1980, the HP faculty at two of the sites, University A and University C, were predominantly female (80 percent and 60 percent respectively) and these proportions increased slightly throughout the 1980s. The HP faculty at University B was predominantly male, with only 20 percent female in 1980, but rising to 50 percent female by 1990.

The MP faculty at University A was 60 percent female in 1980, but dropped to about 50 percent by 1990. In MP, both University B and University C were 20 percent female in 1980. At University B this percentage declined somewhat during the 1980s, while at University C, it increased to 24 percent by 1990.

A&S faculty at University A was 60 percent female in 1980 and increased slightly by the end of the decade, while at the other two sites, the percentage of female faculty was well below 20 percent in 1980, and increased significantly by 1990, to 25 percent at University B and to 20 percent at University C.

We also wanted to determine what proportion of the 1990 faculty at each institution consisted of members who first appeared in the calendar after 1980 and what the gender distribution of the more recent hirings were. These findings are summarized in table 2.

Table 2: 1990 Full-time and Part-time Faculty by Institution and Date of First Listing

INSTITUTION	ALL FACULTY N	ALL FACULTY STARTING AFTER 1980 (% of all faculty)	FEMALE FACULTY STARTING AFTER 1980 (% of all faculty hired after 1980)
University A	247	70%	63%
University B	284	44%	32%
University C	225	45%	41%

Even though the percentage of female faculty members rose substantially at Universities B and C, where the faculty in 1980 was predominantly male, we observed that their success in attracting women during the 1980s was still below 50 percent. The experience of University A may indicate that women were available to be hired during that period.

We also examined rates of "low attachment." If you recall, we defined faculty listed in six or fewer calendars and not in the final calendar included in our data as having "low attachment." How did the attachment of faculty members vary across the three sites and areas and how did it change during the period? The overall results are summarized in table 3.

Table 3: **Faculty with Low Attachment by Institution**

INSTITUTION	ALL FACULTY N		ALL FULL- AND PART-TIME FACULTY WITH LOW ATTACHMENT (% of all faculty)		FEMALE FACULTY WITH LOW ATTACHMENT (% of faculty with low attachment)	
	1980	1990	1980	1990	1980	1990
University A	146	247	36%	32%	50%	60%
University B	223	284	18%	19%	25%	38%
University C	123	225	11%	16%	38%	36%

These results seem to indicate little change in the universities' reliance on faculty members who only remain on staff for a few years, and suggest that the presence of women in this group is increasing. A more detailed look at the subject areas in each university reveals quite a different pattern.

During the 1980s, University A relied heavily on faculty members with low attachment. In HP, at University A, almost 40 percent of the faculty had low attachment in 1980, and this percentage increased to about 45 percent by 1985 before dropping to 30 percent by 1990. The cohort of low-attachment faculty was two-thirds female in the early 1980s and almost 100 percent female by 1990. In MP, at University A, the proportion of low-attachment faculty was similar, but its gender composition was less than 50 percent female throughout the period. In A&S, the percentage of low-attachment faculty was much lower in 1980, at 10 percent, but it rose significantly and steadily to over 20 percent by 1990. Within the A&S, females were in the majority of the low-attachment faculty, but this declined from almost 100 percent to about 60 percent during the 1980s.

At University B during this period, the highest reliance on low-attachment faculty was in MP, where it held steady at 20 percent. In A&S, the percentage of low-attachment faculty increased from 10 percent to 15 percent, while in HP it decreased from 15 percent to under 10 percent by 1985 and held steady. In all three areas, females were in the minority in the low-attachment cohort in 1980, but increased to almost 50 percent by the end of the decade.

At University C, the HP had no low-attachment faculty at all in 1980, but 20 percent by 1990, the majority of whom were female. MP, however, included 20 percent low-attachment faculty in 1980, but this dropped to almost 0 percent in 1990. MP low-attachment faculty were predominantly male. In A&S, less than 10 percent of the faculty had low attachment throughout the period, and almost all were male.

What about faculty achievement during the 1980s? We identified those who succeeded in achieving the rank of "eventual professor" during the period for which we had calendar data (the cut-offs were 1995 for one of the institutions and 1997 for the other two). At University A, in HP and MP, the proportion of EPs was under 10 percent and entirely male throughout the period. In A&S, the proportion of EPs was 35 percent in 1980 and dropped to 25 percent by 1990. The majority of the EPs in A&S were female.

At University B, in A&S, the average proportion of EPs over the period was 60 percent, declining from 65 percent in 1980 to 50 percent in 1990. Almost all the EPs in A&S were male. In HP, the proportion of EPs held steady at around 40 percent, but the proportion of females among the EPs increased from 5 percent to 40 percent over the decade. In MP, the proportion of EPs declined from 30 percent to 20 percent by the middle of the decade, and then leveled off. Here, as in A&S, the presence of females was virtually nil.

At University C, in the HP area, the only 20 percent of the faculty employed in 1980 eventually achieved the rank of professor. Of those employed in 1985, 30 percent eventually became professors. In HP, about two-thirds of the EPs were female. In MP, the proportion of EPs held steady at about 20 percent, while in the A&S, the proportion dropped dramatically from 60 percent in 1980 to 40 percent in 1990. Almost none of the EPs in these areas were female.

DOCUMENTING THE SHIFTS IN EQUITY

It is clear that overall faculty numbers have increased during the 1980s, and it is encouraging to see that the proportion of females has increased, though they still are far below the 50 percent level at two of the institutions. Unfortunately, these numbers do not necessarily reflect full-time academic appointments. Furthermore, the observed increase of women among the faculty with low attachment raises the concern that women faculty are considered contract labour who are hired either on a per-course basis or on limited-term contracts. We note that such an increase in female faculty with low attachment was not observed at the site located in a rural area and far from an urban centre. The overall presence of faculty with low attachment has not changed greatly at the institutions we studied. The noted increase in the number of women reflects a reduction in the number of men. This might mean that male faculty with low attachment may have found other employment opportunities.

University C, located in a rural area, has most of its female faculty members in the Human Services area, which includes many of the traditionally female professions. In HP, both the proportion of female faculty and the proportion of low-attachment faculty increased during the 1980s. In the Arts and Science area, the initially low proportion of females has shown some growth but only reached 20 percent by the end of the period. Similarly, in the Market Oriented area, the proportion of women increased but only to 24 percent by 1990. There has been little change in the presence of women in the faculty at University C.

In the traditional Arts and Science Professions at Universities A and B, the gender ratios followed the same progression as the A&S at University C, with little growth in the overall proportion of women and low reliance on female faculty with low attachment. However, the professional areas at these universities underwent significant change and moved in opposite directions. The Human Services Profession saw large growth at University B and moderate growth at University A in the proportion of female faculty, and increases in the proportion of females with low attachment. In Marketing Oriented Professions, though, the overall participation of women declined somewhat over the period, as did the overall reliance on low-attachment faculty. At each of these two sites, the proportion of females in the low-attachment group increased significantly. Again, this may reflect the undesirability of the available low-attachment positions for male faculty.

Overall, little change was observed over the period in the proportion of EPs. The eventual attainment of professorial rank for female faculty is very low at Universities B and C, except in the area of Human Services. In A&S, female EPs were present in significant proportions at only one site, University A, with its predominantly female faculty. However, at this university only 30 percent of faculty members were EPs compared with 60 percent at the other two sites. This may mean that significant barriers to female promotions still exist, or it may mean that high-achievement female faculty are choosing employment opportunities elsewhere.

*

In conclusion, the impact of corporatization appears to depend on the university and its culture. The types of changes we documented as happening during the 1980s are not the same at all three of the institutions and reflect the internal choices regarding program shifts. These choices are made in the context of the leadership of each institution and according to the directions of key individuals, including their ability to mobilize faculty and alumni and to raise potential donor support for planned change. Each university in our study has a unique history and contemporary interpretation, and the "spin" given to this history plays a significant role in the rationale for change. For example, one of these institutions uses its historical commitment to the education of women to justify the maintenance of programs that may not be sustainable economically, arguing that it is safeguarding access for women to these areas.

The traditional core of the university, consisting of the Arts and Science disciplines, is at best holding its own within the academy at a time when overall university enrolments are increasing. All three institutions have a common core of Arts and Science disciplines. There are differences in the proportions of faculty in these disciplines at each institution, but in each case, this category did not grow over the time period we studied. We recognize that our findings may be limited by the fact that we concentrated on the 1980s in our analysis. While we used both earlier and later information in our examination of attachment, we have not yet used the data to follow those additoinal changes that have occurred since 1990. We plan to continue this work and hope to communicate further findings from this research.

Our data also document that women have made and are making inroads into the academy, but they have not always achieved equal access to the best positions. The professor rank is still elusive, low-attachment female faculty are increasing in the traditionally strong female disciplines of the Human Services Oriented Professions, and the percentage of women among the low-attachment positions in Market Oriented Professions is also increasing. This raises the concern that the equity movement of the last two decades may be undercut by these program shifts in the academy.

NOTES

1. Janice Newson and Howard Buchbinder, *The University Means Business* (Toronto: Garamond Press, 1988), 9.

2. See the special issue of the *Canadian Review of Sociology and Anthropology* (2002), and the series published by the Canadian Association of University Teachers, including Neil Tudiver, *Universities for Sale* (Toronto: Lorimer, 2000). More recent examples include Henry A. Giroux, "Neoliberalism, Corporate Culture and the Promise of Higher Education: The University as a Democratic Public Sphere," *Harvard Educational Review* 72, no. 4 (2002), 425-439; Shannon Hodges, "Authentic Values and Ersatz Standards," *Academe* 88, no. 6 (2002), 33–36; Katharyne Mitchell, "The Value of Academic Labour: What the Market has Wrought?" *Environment and Planning* 32, no. 10 (2002), 1713–1718; Rachel Silvey, "Sweatshops and the Corporatization of the University," *Gender, Place and Culture* 9, no. 2 (2002), 201–207; and Jeffrey R. Young, "David Noble's Battle to Defend the 'Sacred Space' of the Classroom," *Chronicle of Higher Education* 46, no. 3 (2000), 47–50.

3. Marjorie Griffin Cohen, "Cronyism Thrives in CRC Hiring Process," *CAUT Bulletin* 50 (2003), 5; Claire Polster, "A Break from the Past: Impacts and Implications of the Canada Foundation for Innovation and the Canada Research Chairs Initiatives," *Canadian Review of Sociology and Anthropology* 39 (2002), 275–299.

4. See, for example, Earl Babbie, *The Basics of Social Research* (Belmont, CA: Wadsworth, 1999); Ted Palys, *Research Decisions* (Toronto: Harcourt Brace, 1997); and Eugene J. Webb, Donald T. Campbell, Richard D. Schwartz and Lee Sechrest, *Unobtrusive Measures* (Chicago: Rand McNally, 1972).

5. See, for example, Janice Drakich, Karen R. Grant and Penni Stewart, "The Academy in the Twenty-first Century," *Canadian Review of Sociology and Anthropology* 39 (2002), 249–260; Newson and Buchbinder, *The University Means Business;* Tudiver, *Universities for Sale;* and James L. Turk, ed., *The Corporate*

Campus (Toronto: Lorimer, 2000).

6. See, for example, *Maclean's*, November 18, 2002.

7. Theodore Caplow and Reece McGee, *The Academic Marketplace* (New York: Basic Books, 1958).

8. Newson and Buchbinder, *The University Means Business*, 20.

CHAPTER 6

WILL WOMEN'S STUDIES PROGRAMS SURVIVE THE CORPORATE UNIVERSITY?

Marilee Reimer

THIS CHAPTER DRAWS UPON a research project I undertook of Women's Studies programs in two provinces in which I observed how the processes of commercialization are affecting these programs and the feminist scholarship of the faculty engaged in running them. My interest in these matters comes from observing how Women's Studies programs in my own university and in small universities in Atlantic Canada are being dwarfed by new professional programs, while Women's Studies programs elsewhere in Canada are thriving despite commercialization.

Given that Women's Studies as a field has only appeared in the last thirty to forty years, the survival and burgeoning of new programs might cause one to celebrate, but it is time to give more systematic attention to the conditions under which many of them exist. For instance, I recently encountered a telling example of the university administration's expectations that Women's Studies faculty will continue to carry additional workloads at their own personal expense. I was a part of a group of Women's Studies faculty from the University of New Brunswick and St. Thomas University who met with the Dean of Graduate Studies of UNB to discuss the Dean's proposal to start a master's program in the department. While well intentioned, the Dean had been unable to generate any resources for this initiative — neither a course release for a director nor a course stipend for a graduate seminar. As faculty who were already providing volunteer labour to run the undergraduate Women's Studies and Gender Studies programs at the two campuses, we declined the offer to take on the project because we were reluctant to increase the workloads of our "double day" any further.[1]

My interviews with Women's Studies faculty in some of these programs indicate that all of these academics are struggling with market-oriented campuses where outside commercial interests are hurting their programs. While there is widespread knowledge of the many demands involved in establishing a Women's Studies program, what we are now experiencing is more than just the same old "difficulties" of running a program. What appears to be operating here is a more virulent set of challenges to the continued health of these programs, and particularly at the graduate level. For when it is no longer possible for Women's Studies faculty to sustain graduate education, then we will no longer be able to replace — or refresh — ourselves. In order to continue, Women's Studies requires that we have the time and energy to teach a new generation of graduate students.

According to Jane Rinehart, a "quality" education in a commercialized or "McDonaldized" university is defined in terms of cost efficiency, predictability, calculability and control within the context of faculty workload and access to funds for infrastructure and research.[2] The trends in university financing that are becoming familiar to faculty in postsecondary education are having a dramatic impact on university programming by intensifying labour, increasing expectations that faculty receive greater amounts of grant money and publish more and that their research have more of a commercial orientation. Jan Newson has identified the inception of corporatization as having taken place with the proposals of the Corporate Higher Education Forum and the former Science Council of Canada in the 1980s.[3] It was these bodies that articulated the framework for shifting university resources to meet commercial ends and moving government funding from general research councils into targeted and matched-funding research programs. Women's Studies as a field is positioned in such a way as to be uniquely affected by the new emphasis in funding as it is primarily females who teach it. However, one university recruiter described the new funding programs as having an emphasis on science, engineering and computer science, which included only a few new female hires.[4] The traditional humanities and social science disciplines have had to cope with increasing enrolments without a parallel increase in the number of faculty. Due to the emphasis on commercialization, expansion of Women's Studies programs has often occurred without the proper structures to support it. Working to obtain interdepartmental support can entail enormous amounts of ongoing effort and politicking.[5]

In addition to work intensification, commercialization has a particular way of affecting the specific liberal arts character of Women's Studies and its methodologies. Indeed, Rinehart would go further to suggest that feminism, which began with questioning institutions' gender practices, has now begun to question the prevailing business practices in the university and the accompanying belief in "objective" and neutral science that characterize the corporate university.[6]

Many people wonder why it is necessary to organize feminist studies outside the existing departments, and indeed, given that my own degree was defined as focusing on feminist studies within an existing department (Sociology in Education at OISE/UT), I once wondered the same thing. The difficulties Women's Studies programs encounter in attempting this autonomous existence have revealed the barriers that prevent feminist scholarship from being widely accepted in the corporate university. This discovery is relevant to the success of feminist scholarship and programs that rely upon traditional methods of faculty assessment within the university and within funding bodies. Given the significant role that research productivity plays in faculty advancement and therefore program advancement, the question arises whether universities are suppressing feminist inquiry by allowing the implementation of evaluation methods that have arisen in an era where commercialized research protocols dominate?

In order to assess if a research regime exists in which feminist inquiry is deemed outside the commercial mould, we need to ask what is distinctive about Women's Studies and feminist inquiry. Linda Christiansen-Ruffman and Marilyn Porter have recently identified three distinct characteristics that contribute to feminist scholarship: (1) a broad range of disciplines of knowledge, yielding contributions to the disciplines themselves as well as to an interdisciplinary scholarship on women and gender; (2) the theory, methodology and praxis of the emerging field of feminist scholarship; and (3) the questions that the powerless are asking, with the answers "helping to inform both women's organizations and policy-makers at all levels of their work to bring about equality and social justice."[7]

Feminist researchers have challenged the objectivity of the masculinist model of research, where the predominant form involves the autonomous, independent researcher who is the "principal investigator" or a small team of like-minded researchers who accept the hierarchy involved in the research effort.[8] Feminist methodologies commonly allow for collaborative and interdisciplinary research groups and often build-in the input of community and advocacy groups at all stages of a research project. However, Jane Gordon and Sandra Bell found that for a number of feminists the participatory action, community-based model of research was not recognized as scholarship for the purposes of tenure and promotion, nor was it recognized as scholarly unless it was published in a narrow range of "prestigious" academic journals. These scholars experienced a lack of faculty acceptance of feminist scholarship due to the narrow and rigid standards applied in promotional processes that define scholarship according to a hierarchical model of the research process and the academic audience.[9]

With the recent reorganization of university funding, as Claire Polster argues, the research performance of individuals is linked with the success of the university at gaining such resources as grants and chairs, and the reverse is true as well.[10] Given the new funding initiatives, faculty members' success at research has a significant impact on the willingness of the university to provide infrastructure and funding for programs they initiate. Given the centrality and necessity of research productivity and its recognition, an evaluation of the effects of commercialization must raise the issue of how feminist scholarship is recognized because Women's Studies academics must also advance their own scholarship if their programs are to advance.

With the advance of commercialization on university campuses, we need to know if feminist scholarship, pedagogy and methodology are given full legitimacy in the academy and if programs are supported in practical terms. These are among the questions I raised in the research project (an institutional ethnography) that I carried out in the spring of 2001 in Ontario and Atlantic Canada.[11] In the study, I focused on the Women's Studies faculty at three universities collaborating in a Joint Master's Program in Women's Studies, and at a fourth university offering both a master's and a doctorate in its Doctoral Program.

In these programs there were many feminist faculty who have been required to reapply for promotion or to rewrite grant applications so as to satisfy their assessors, who are critical of feminist research. This additional work not only delays program development but serves to discourage others from participating in Women's Studies research. Many professors who are quite successful researchers find that the commercialization of education at their institutions leads to greatly inflated workloads that impinge on their ability to contribute to Women's Studies programs. My findings reveal that given the particular structure of Women's Studies programs, which entails large amounts of volunteer labour and the long-term commitment to community-based research, commercialization is having a devastating effect on development and research productivity and contributing to faculty burn out.

JOINT MASTER'S PROGRAM

The Joint Master's Program was operating in its fifth year when I began examining how commercialization was affecting it and the three participating Women's Studies programs that comprise it. Set up in 1996, the Program now accepts up to nine full-time master's students annually. It was the faculty's involvement in the broader feminist community that made the collaboration across the three universities possible. Their community activism also allowed them to overcome their respective institutional boundaries in order to create such a collaborative arrangement — a first at these universities. This was fortunate given that not one of the universities could afford to support a master's program in Women's Studies.

The work for the students was in some ways greater than the usual interdisciplinary program if only because they were required to meet the course requirements and the time limits of all three universities. Although the cultures of the three campuses varied greatly — from an undergraduate teaching campus to a research-based university — faculty worked collectively towards the Program's common objectives and goals.

The Joint Master's Program is distinct in its offering of a graduate seminar that involves field-based learning through the women's movement and community-based activity, thereby creating a space where activists and academics can work productively together. In each of the first five years, there have been students from all three universities enrolled in the Program and many have now graduated. However, a year after I conducted these interviews, the largest of the universities announced its intention to pull out and has recently made this official. It remains to be seen if the remaining two universities will be required to change the organization of the Program in order for it to continue.

Given the overall lack of resources available for the support of Women's Studies programming at the three universities, this withdrawal should not be a surprise. That the administration would consider something like the University of New Brunswick model (in which the administration expects Women's Studies faculty to mount a master's program without any resources to support it) as its financial commitment to Women's Studies at the graduate level is indicative of the emphasis being placed on the commercial value of courses. To better understand this, I will discuss how the university's withdrawing from the Program relates to commercialization and what this means for the three Women's Studies programs referred to here under the pseudonyms "Education Is An Art," "Expanding Feminist Faculty" and "Many Sick Faculty."[12]

"Education Is An Art"

The Women's Studies program "Education Is An Art" is housed at a small university (which has fewer than 5,000 students). At first glance this program appears quite fortunate to have received two rare appointments on a campus that has shrunk from 175 to 140 faculty in the last eight years. Within the corporate university, the new pattern seems to be that as the established humanities and social science departments are shrinking overall, more corporate-oriented departments and professional programs are taking the lion's share of new appointments.[13] However, the administration has stated that the Women's Studies program complements several aspects of the university's mission statement. Of the three universities in the Joint Master's Program, this is the only one with appointed staff, made up of two full-time positions joining up to four cross-listed faculty, a cross-listed co-ordinator and a shared chair in Women's Studies. In addition to the graduate program, there is a vibrant undergraduate program that offers a major and an honours degree in Women's Studies and that includes up to a dozen Women's Studies courses as well as a speakers' series.

Upon examining the situation of this apparently strong program more closely, we can see that the priorities of the province and the university administration illuminate the typical orientation of a commercialized campus. The provincial government has cut back considerably on educational spending in the previous five years. Professional programs are developed that rely heavily on corporate sponsorship for such things as co-op jobs and awards to students and that are seen to have vocational outcomes in health, nursing and areas related to the service industry and information technology. Major graduate programs in these professions have been established and more are in the offing.

The co-ordinator of "Education Is An Art" was certain that the program will not be getting further resources, given that the administration is not responsive to such requests in the Arts and Sciences unless the program has large enrolments. The administration, it appears, isn't particularly supportive of the Arts and Sciences in general, with which Women's Studies is affiliated. Although it claims that Women's Studies is an essential part of the university, on the ground, its commitment appears thin. As unusual as two full-time faculty hires may be, they are hardly sufficient to run a program.

On closer examination, it becomes clear that the "double day" of women's work sustains this program, and this is particularly noticeable when anyone takes a sabbatical, as two faculty did in 2000–2001. As well, no one has been willing to be the rotating chair for the graduate admissions and policy committee for the Joint Master's Program — faculty feel tremendous pressure to apply for grants and to complete publications and need to put their energy into pursuing these goals. The Women's Studies master's is the only one in the Arts and Sciences, and to take on additional work of advising is to increase the workload, especially given that faculty already have one of the largest annual teaching loads in the province at six half-courses per year. The fact that workloads have dropped from six to five half-courses almost everywhere else in the region suggests that the union has not taken up an issue that is rather central to the exploitation of the women faculty in this program who continue to be subjected to the "double day."[14]

Unlike faculty in other departments, faculty in Women's Studies are asked to make a lot of appearances, and are regularly invited to speak to the media, at conferences and so on. Not incidentally, faculty are involved with community-based organizations as board members and as volunteers. As with the other two universities involved in the Joint

Master's Program, I found a good number of examples where distinctly feminist, collaborative or community-based research was not given recognition in the department's promotion assessment: four Women's Studies faculty were turned down for promotion and one for a permanent position. The co-ordinator stated that as far as research is concerned, the faculty do a competent job given their workload and that most have received a grant in the past. Nevertheless, the commitment to mount a Women's Studies program has cut significantly into their research time, possibly affecting the likelihood for some to qualify as a principle investigator in a SSHRC grant or for a Canada Research Chair. The co-ordinator also mentioned that the male faculty of this institution recently received inter-university release-time grants at levels that are close to twice the proportion of releases that would be appropriate for their representation in the overall faculty population.

Another difficulty in a commercialized university is that the implementation of an employment-equity policy is not considered a priority. If it was a priority, perhaps more faculty support would be generated for Women's Studies in a range of departments. It is clear that in this university the emphasis is on programs whose courses have a strong commercial value. The student body and the faculty appear to be quite conservative and those programs that attract corporate funding are the ones that grow. Women's Studies is not one of the those and the enrolments, not surprisingly, remain relatively low.

In addition, the program has no money for outreach, and the history of fundraising has not been promising. Faculty have been "stretched" to a point of exhaustion and hardly anyone is willing to be a cross-listed faculty when the workload is not recognized. It is also very difficult to talk someone into being co-ordinator of the program, and the junior staff need to publish and receive tenure before taking on politically risky committee work. The small group of faculty who have sustained Women's Studies from the outset continue to keep the program afloat while fulfilling the requirements of their home departments. As one faculty commented, "The University doesn't want to see Women's Studies go under, but they are perfectly prepared [to maintain the program] on the backs of the women who already work in the program."[15]

The following effects of commercialization are clearly visible in the "Education Is An Art" program: the program is underfunded and the Women's Studies faculty are regularly overworked; an effective employment-equity policy does not exist and feminist research is de-valued; there is a lack of funding for outreach and for publicizing the program; the union is oblivious to the basic concerns of women who are overworked; and the administration showcases "Education Is An Art" to gain support for the university and for its new professional programs. While the administration pays lip service to the importance of the pro-gram, it keeps the finances of the program very, very tight. Just maintaining this program is an art in itself! What kind of a model is this Women's Studies program for the young women of today? Regardless of the challenges it faces, it has had some successes, as one faculty com-mented:

> We graduate some very good students, sound academic students, but we also graduate some students who have a real commitment to working with women. So those to me are criteria for success. I think we also enor-mously enrich the lives of many of the women who go through the program. Not so much the traditional students, but some of the mature students.[16]

"Expanding Feminist Faculty"

Housed at a medium-sized university (5,000 to 24,000 students), this Women's Studies program has achieved status as a separate program encompassing both undergraduate and graduate studies. This university has the familiar emphasis on commercialization and development of professional programs, but faculty have managed a more successful strat-egy that involves the union and that makes sure feminists are hired in such fields as criminology as well as in the Arts and Science disciplines. The Women's Studies program itself, however, has no full-time positions for either the graduate or undergraduate sections, and it relies on course releases to fill the positions of program co-ordinator and chair of the graduate admissions and policy committee. Twenty-eight faculty are cross-listed from the established disciplines. In addition to a speakers' series and a joint chair in Women's Studies, the faculty are involved in a range of international projects that raise the program's visibility.

The strategies the faculty use are interesting, given that the initial group who set up the program was relatively small. The main approach has been to mobilize a core group of women in a sustained effort to improve visibility and attain support throughout the university, as well as maintain gender balance on every university committee. They work closely with the union and receive backing to have a woman on every hiring committee, thus keeping the equity strategy at the forefront. Not only has the union managed to lower their workload to five half-courses annually but it has also added eleven new names in the last year to the Women's Studies faculty list as more feminists are hired in other departments. The program's representatives pressured the administration for better Women's Studies visibility in the Strategic Research Plan and were given it. They have also created a graduate faculty which ensures that the graduate programs have greater visibility with the granting bodies.

It is evident that a very small group and a strong co-ordinator have contributed a great deal of volunteer time in establishing the program and in holding it together. Given processes of commercialization, however, it remains to be seen if the feminists hired across the university will stay, how long it will be before the junior faculty can participate fully in the Women's Studies program, and if their feminist research will disadvantage them in the tenure-promotion and grants process. As well, whether or not the new faculty will be able to participate in advising graduate students may depend on how pressured these faculty are to obtain grants in the new context where individual performance becomes part of the overall university's assessment for chairs and grants.[17]

Although faculty in this program have successfully reduced their overall workload, it would be a mistake not to acknowledge that this program has depended and continues to depend very heavily on faculty who are willing to put in the "double day" of department and program meetings, advising and public appearances. However, maintaining women's representation on committees is more problematic given that faculty are overloaded with the responsibilities for the Joint Master's Program and a school of graduate studies. Nonetheless, the "old guard" will have to maintain the program until the junior hires are ready to step into their shoes. It may be that success will depend on how well the women can live up to a "male" work ethic, that is, producing at a level that assumes one has no family responsibilities and that one has a support system at home.[18]

"Many Sick Faculty"

This third program is located at another medium-sized campus and offers both an undergraduate minor and major in Women's Studies. This campus is perhaps a foreboding example of what a commercialized university does with programs that do not have obvious commercial value. In this example, we see how bringing research grant money into the university can be valued so singularly that even a Women's Studies master's program that has a complementary value to professional programs in health, education and social work ended up being dropped.

Despite the strategies used to create visibility for the Women's Studies program — the usual speakers' series, a chair in Women's Studies and a few scholarships — this program is flagging. A number of feminists who were interviewed made it clear that the overarching commercial emphasis of bringing in research grant money has squashed most of the faculty's active involvement in the program for the simple reason of faculty exhaustion. This is true to the extent that at the time the interviews were conducted the program did not have a co-ordinator for the upcoming year and there were few (if any) graduate students enrolled.

The primary impetus for the erosion of the "Many Sick Faculty" program appears to come from a reward structure based on performance indicators that overwhelmingly reward bringing in research grant money to the university. Due to the expansion of professional programs in the health sciences, there are as many Women's Studies professors in these departments as there used to be in Arts and Sciences. The younger feminists in the health sciences know that large research grants are necessary to fulfill the requirements for tenure and promotion. In the last five years there has been a dramatic push for research money. One faculty member estimated that unless you have "thousands upon thousands" of dollars in grants, it is no longer possible to become a full professor.

The co-ordinator also identified overwork as contributing to the erosion of the program. She mentioned that never before have there been so many sick faculty in Women's Studies. Faculty who have retired or left over the past five or six years have not been replaced, so whoever tries to co-ordinate Women's Studies will simply be overworked. Given that the professors have so many responsibilities to graduate students in their own departments and schools, it is not reasonable to take on more graduate students who are not considered part of their workload. Furthermore, contributions to advising graduate students net faculty little if any workload recognition, and for the many Women's Studies faculty in health sciences, advising graduate students has no influence on the reward structure beyond the first two student advisees in their home discipline. One faculty had fourteen graduate students, including students in the Women's Studies master's program, and still did not receive workload recognition.

Faculty who advise a large number of graduate students find that one of the problems contributing to their overwork is the extremely time-consuming Tri-Council Ethics Review process that they and their students now must follow. A major point of contention is that this review process assesses faculty, especially qualitative researchers, according to normative standards that their disciplines have taught them to avoid.[19] At the same time, the process delays the academic progress of financially strapped graduate students — some of whom have taken off of work to finish a thesis — who waited over six months for approval and still did not receive it, which means they wasted a lot of time and money. Such delays would make sense if these standards were necessary to competently review projects on ethical grounds. But faculty from this university commented that ethical review boards impose the biomedical model of research on applicants in the social sciences, often valuing reductionist strings of variables that focus on the individual out of context of her or his social and economic circumstances. According to this observation, funding bodies favour reductionist, individualistic and non-critical issues such as "How the individual copes with AIDS" or "How they cope with caregiving" or "How people could cope better if they had social supports." Social scientists, and feminist scholars particularly, are more inclined to focus on such issues as "What are the lived circumstances that are leading to the development of a given condition?" — issues that are less likely to be treated seriously than those that are more suited to the biomedical model.

This criticism has been made as a more generic argument by feminist researchers who find the Tri-Council Guidelines on Ethical Research inappropriate for qualitative research.[20] Faculty raised concerns that feminist research topics are not "safe" topics to present to the major funding bodies, suggesting that it is not only qualitative researchers who have run afoul of the standards of assessors for grant money and ethics review. Fewer feminist faculty are applying for funding given the perceived biases of major funding bodies against feminist issues. Not surprisingly, at the last two Congresses of the Social Sciences and Humanities representatives from the Social Sciences and Humanities Research Council have spoken about the insufficient number of faculty applying under the grant category of "Health, Social Work and Women's Studies." It appears that, historically at least, some faculty on university ethical review boards and funding bodies are unfamiliar with feminist methodology and qualitative research and are therefore demanding that researchers meet the requirements of the biomedical model of the health and physical sciences.[21]

The net result of overwork — whether generated by the underfunding of university disciplines, the demand for research money or the requirements of ethical review boards and funding appraisers — is that in the "Many Sick Faculty" program, with people always busy or out sick, the faculty don't have time to contribute to the program. Many professors find that if they support Women's Studies, their own research suffers. If they do take on additional responsibilities in order to keep the program running, they risk overwork and illness. As one professor commented, "I have never seen so many people in Women's Studies become ill — and I mean really ill. People are overworked."[22]

THE DOCTORAL PROGRAM

One of the more successful Women's Studies programs is the Doctoral Program situated within a large liberal arts university as an independent administrative unit. It offers both a master's and a doctoral degree, and its autonomous graduate faculty can appoint faculty and cross-list courses drawing on twenty undergraduate units and twenty-four graduate units. The Program has a research centre, a journal, a library, a speakers' series, a bridging program, two hundred cross-listed faculty who are involved in teaching and 2,000 students enrolled in undergraduate classes. As well, it is funded for five full-time academics (a director and four professors), one contract position and four support staff. It has approximately forty-four students in each of the master's and doctoral programs, and graduated seven PhDs in the previous seven years. Most impressive is the $3 million dollars the Program has raised for scholarships and the library along with the millions in research the faculty has brought in. Such a world-class program attracts students from all over the globe.

Given its funding from the administration and the age of the faculty, the Program should enjoy stability for the next ten years. The strategies used to build this Program include mobilizing a healthy presence of feminist faculty who already work in diverse fields, a high student demand from a fairly politicized constituency and a university administration that includes women in senior administrative positions. They also have a unique fundraising strategy:

> The success in our fundraising was based on a new fundraising strategy for women whose charitable objectives differ from those of men and corporations. We focused on women graduates and faculty. Personal contact was most important. We established scholarships and bursaries … We discovered that women are less concerned about personal recognition and many wish to remain anonymous. Some women give in honour of their mothers and grandmothers. All have some kind of personal commitment to Women's Studies and feminism. We have also had some male donors and their link is often a daughter or wife who is taking Women's Studies courses. When corporations have given to Women's Studies … it is often because one of their female employees (often a Women's Studies graduate) has prompted the company to do so.[23]

Another successful strategy has been the establishment of an alumni association for graduates, which, it is hoped, will play an important role in future fundraising. The strong commitment from the faculty must also be mentioned, as over 90 percent of the Women's Studies faculty contribute financially to the Program. The success of the Program is also an outgrowth of the faculty's outstanding research and publication record, which was so impressive that the administration cited the Program as being one of the university's "gems" in its Strategic Research Plan and allowed it to apply for a Canada Research Chair, which it received.

This example of a Women's Studies program where the "chilly climate" has thawed considerably, and where non-Women's Studies students expect feminist content in their courses, is worth examining to see just how vulnerable such a program might be to corporate priorities. Given the tremendous sacrifice Women's Studies faculty made in the 1980s and 1990s to establishing this Program, and continue to make in terms of workload, it is very hard to entertain the possibility that it would be eroded in the near future.[24] However, this is exactly what is happening. With first-year classes ranging from 150 to 200 students, professors in some units are finding that their third-year classes have doubled from thirty to sixty students and that their senior seminars have increased from twenty-five to thirty-five. Since this university has the largest proportion of arts students in the country and may be a trend-setter, it is worth pondering why the faculty workload is shifting into "voluntary overtime" once again, despite the secure funding and the fundraising accomplishments.

To begin with, an Arts university is not favoured in the government funding game because it lacks the rich alumni of some other universities and it doesn't have two of the top-earning departments — medicine and engineering. The workload is five half-courses (due to union action) and all graduate advising is done on voluntary overtime. In addition, affirmative action isn't "emphasized" by the administration and the union, so fewer women are available for committee work. Those who do take on committee responsibilities are faced with work overload.

Given that the federal and provincial governments are not supportive of the Arts and Humanities, funding difficulties may become exacerbated because of corporatization priorities. For example, the federal government just doubled the level of graduate assistance, but this was conditional upon the university providing half of the money. With provincial cutbacks in operating grants, this money wasn't in the budget and the departments had no say over how many graduate scholarships they would receive. What has changed in the funding process under corporatization is that resources are increasingly controlled by external funders whose resources go to those areas that win corporate donations and Canada Research Chairs. This approach favours business, engineering, natural sciences and information technology. The provincial government has made this situation worse by using performance indicators that include students' speed of completion and post-graduation job attainment. The university experienced funding cutbacks to every department after rating the lowest on these performance indicators for the province. This manner of setting funding levels would appear to penalize institutions that have non-traditional learners from low-income and immigrant backgrounds and a high proportion of women who study the Arts and who have traditionally faced barriers to employment that men haven't faced.[25]

Needless to say, faculty morale has been greatly affected by these cuts and by anticipated future reductions. It has also been affected by the open political stance of the provincial premier, who devalues Arts and plays up his commitment to university training that directly creates "marketable" graduates. In a program that for many years had no corporate sponsors, even maintaining a research centre was dependent on a Women's Studies faculty member having a grant she could use to employ graduate students to run it. The Social Sciences and Humanities Research Council is the one Women's Studies faculty have depended on, however, for the past ten years the Council has not given out infrastructure grants, making it difficult to sustain the research centre. Also, faculty who were interviewed felt strongly that the federal government's allocation of money through the Canada Research Chairs program is an absolute disaster. Faculty who become chairs cannot teach or do any administration work, which requires the other faculty in Women's Studies and home departments to cover this individual's work responsibilities.

When we consider the processes of financial reorganization and the commercial priorities of the government and funding bodies, the basis for the erosion of the current abilities of faculty to contribute to the Program become evident. The Program may be stable for the next ten years, but this may be achieved at some cost to faculty who are shouldering heavier and heavier workloads as cutbacks are fed through the system. The most alarming increase in workload can be seen in the increased class size that has been imposed on many departments and administrative units within Women's Studies faculty. These increased workloads are very important to consider because they are reaching the levels of other universities where workloads are so high that faculty have not received adequate research grants that would qualify them for funding for a single Canada Research Chair.

It is also worth noting that high workloads might affect Women's Studies faculty's ability to qualify for funding from organizations like the Canada Institute of Health Research. At a CIHR presentation I attended, eligibility was defined in a way that favours researchers in the physical sciences who have large corporate grants. To meet the eligibility requirement, it was explained, a faculty member would have to have 50 to 75 percent of her work time protected, and if she didn't have such protection, it might be necessary for her to apply with another faculty member who did have such protection.[26] Obviously, such federal and provincial funding policies may destroy the basis for research-generating academic programs if minimum protected work time is set at a level that disqualifies faculty in the Arts and Humanities.

*

From the interviews with faculty in the Joint Master's Program and the Doctoral Program, it appears quite likely, given the trends in commercialization, that academic support for feminist scholarship and programming will continue to suffer. This will not be remedied unless support is provided to Women's Studies faculty to both deliver graduate programs and produce scholarship that is valued by the university.

One of the immediate effects of corporatization that we are seeing is the systematic disadvantaging of Women's Studies programming. This happens as feminist standards are devalued and as individuals are less able to contribute to their programs through grants and research funding. The biomedical model and quantitative approaches to research are antithetical to the collaborative and labour-intensive community-based work in which so many feminists engage. The dominant commercial criteria are based in the physical sciences and the biomedical model.[27] This disadvantages feminists in the evaluation of their scholarly research and teaching. In addition to using qualitative research methods, which are at odds with the corporate criteria of ethics and research, the overt political orientation of feminism conflicts with more conservative, pseudo-objective approaches that many social scientists have embraced in a conservative era. Women's Studies programs are significantly impacted by the increased time required for feminists to reapply for jobs, promotion, grants and ethical review approvals to meet the standards of the corporate university.

The second form of systematic disadvantaging is related to the fact that the priorities of a corporately driven university are external to academia itself. Women's Studies is an excellent example in that whatever internal merits and justifications the university may have for such programming, and whatever the students' demands, when educational funding is left to the whim of the corporate sector women are disadvantaged. Women's Studies programs are much less likely to obtain corporate sponsors or grants for infrastructure from government and universities given the increasingly commercial objectives of these granting bodies. Equality oriented and feminist work — research on violence against women and children or on equity measures in the workforce that address race, class and gender inequality, for example — isn't necessarily commercially attractive in the short run.

As university priorities are reorganized through government cutbacks and targeted funding, Women's Studies programs are vulnerable to an intensified "double day" given their structural location as interdisciplinary programs. Already situated in a time when volunteer labour has sustained programs, research, advising and so on, the lowering of the boom on the Arts and Humanities in terms of workload may be the factor that increasingly eliminates Women's Studies programs. Women's Studies faculty require financial support so they can produce graduate programs that will educate the next generation of women and men with a feminist vision.

Clearly an alternative needs to be found to the externally driven priority setting in the academy before this wave of feminism is completely drowned out by corporations that are gaining control of the university community's direction and infrastructure. Unless academic policy is held to a higher standard than the vested interests of the private sector, the gains of the women's movement and women's scholarship will be lost.

NOTES

1. This reference to the "double day" that academic feminists perform is taken from Catherine Side, "Rethinking the Women's Studies Ph.D. in Canadian Universities," *Journal of International Women's Studies* 2 (2001), 67–88.

2. Jane Rinehart, "Feminist Education: Rebellion within McUniversity," in Dennis Hayes and Robyn Wynward, eds., *The McDonaldisation of Higher Education* (Westport, CT: Bergen and Garvey, 2001), 3.

3. Janice Newson, "Conclusion: Repositioning the Local through Alternative Responses to Globalisation," in Jan Curry and Janice Newson, *Universities and Globalisation: Critical Perspectives* (Thousand Oaks, CA: Sage Publications, 1998), 311 n.8.

4. Janice Drakich, personal communication with the author, 2001.

5. Beverley Skeggs describes a similar processes in Women's Studies programs in Britain. See "Women's Studies in Britain in the 1990s: Entitlement Cultures and Institutional Constraints," *Women's Studies International Forum* 18, no.4 (1995), 475–485.

6. Rinehart, "Feminist Education," 174.

7. Linda Christiansen-Ruffman and Marilyn Porter, *Report of the External Reviewers of the Gender Studies Programme: St. Thomas University* (Spring 2003), 3.

8. Sandra Bell and Jane Gordon, "Scholarship — The New Dimension to Equity Issues for Academic Women," *Women's Studies International Forum* 22, no. 6

(1999), 645–658.

9. Ibid., 647. Bell and Gordon had their own research devalued in tenure and promotion assessments. Their research was collaboratively based and involved community partners who actively contributed to the definition of the research and as well their teaching and professional activities and writings were based on feminist methodologies.

10. Claire Polster, "A Break from the Past: Impacts and Implications of the Canada Foundation for Innovation and the Canada Research Chairs Initiatives," *The Canadian Review of Sociology and Anthropology* 39, no. 3 (2002), 275–299.

11. The study entailed interviewing ten faculty and four staff members at five universities, four of which I examine in this chapter. Institutional ethnography is a field-based approach to analyzing institutional process with a focus on how action is organized as a practical matter. This is discussed generally in Dorothy E. Smith, *The Everyday World As Problematic: A Feminist Sociology* (Boston: Northeastern University Press, 1987).

12. I am describing the programs in this way in order to maintain anonymity. It is no surprise that several of the people I interviewed were concerned with being identified at a time when programs are being targeted for cutbacks.

13. Neil Tudiver, *Universities for Sale: Resisting Corporate Control over Canadian Higher Education* (Toronto: James Lorimer, 1999), 190.

14. Jenny Hornosty, "Balancing Child Care and Work," in Jackie Stalker and Susan Prentice, eds., *The Illusion of Inclusion: Women in Post-Secondary Education* (Halifax: Fernwood Publishing, 1993), 185.

15. Field notes, April 17, 2001.

16. Ibid.

17. Polster, "A Break from the Past."

18. I thank my research assistant, Monique Bourgeois, for this insight.

19. Will C. van den Hoonaard, "Is Research Ethics Review a Moral Panic?" *The Canadian Review of Sociology and Anthropology* 38, no. 1 (2001), 19–36.

20. Will C. van den Hoonaard, "Some Concluding Thoughts," in Will C. van den Hoonaard, ed., *Walking the Tightrope: Ethical Issues for Qualitative Researchers* (Toronto: University of Toronto Press, 2002), 185.

21. Having sat on a regional funding body, I am familiar with faculty who admit to no knowledge of how to conduct or evaluate qualitative research when they set out to evaluate feminist proposals based on the criteria of the biomedical model. They argued forcefully that the feminist proposals were not "tight enough to meet national standards" but backed down when they were called on what they were doing.

22. Field notes, April 18, 2001.

23. Field notes, March 16, 2001.

24. It is worth noting that the Women's Studies faculty had a rather large death rate due to breast cancer in the earlier years, losing five faculty and one PhD student. One faculty explained that the stress due to unstable funding, high committee

work and large student numbers was extreme. It is common knowledge that breast cancer survivors identify stress as a major factor in becoming ill. "Stress May Not Trigger Breast Cancer," *The Globe and Mail,* 14 June 2002, A10. While women themselves say stress is related to the onset of breast cancer, researchers are not able to find a way to verify this. Hence the title of the article! It is distressing that newspapers see it this way.

25. Paul Phillips and Erin Phillips, *Women and Work: Inequality in the Canadian Labour Market* (Toronto: James Lorimer, 2000), 85.

26. CIHR Presentation, Fredericton, NB, May 10, 2001.

27. St. Thomas's Response (draft, November 2002) to "Towards a New Brunswick Innovation Strategy," written by Dr. Alan B. Cornford.

CHAPTER 7

Intellectual Property, Higher Education and Women's Inequality:
Exploring Connections /
Proposing Solutions

Claire Polster

THE DEVELOPMENT AND EXTENSION of intellectual property laws and regulations is a dry and complex matter that most of us would rather leave to the lawyers and legislators. In this chapter, I argue that to do so is a serious mistake, as we all have much to lose from, and have already lost much to, the ongoing privatization of previously public knowledge. Perhaps more than any other group, it is women who have the most to lose from the development and extension of intellectual property regimes (IPRs). From the ability to feed our children to our reproductive autonomy, women's already limited control over the conditions of our lives is further threatened — and promises to be threatened further still — as various forms of knowledge are converted into the private property of individuals and corporations.

While the harmful impact of intellectual property (IP) rights on some aspects of women's lives has been attracting increasing scrutiny and concern, the implications of IP rights for others have not.[1] This chapter focuses on one such neglected area by exploring the implications of IP rights for women's or feminists' ability to work in and through the university to advance women's interests and needs. To set the context for a discussion of how intellectual property in the university may compromise women's particular interests, I first address the general implications of intellectual property for the future of the liberal university, defined as a publicly supported institution charged with the production and transmission of a broad range of knowledge in the public interest. Following a discussion of this chapter's central concern, I conclude with some thoughts on how to resist the privatization of knowledge in and through the university as a means of protecting both the feminist project and the public interest more generally.

WHERE IT ALL STARTED

Over the last twenty years, and particularly in the last decade, universities in Canada and elsewhere have become increasingly implicated in the production and exploitation of intellectual property. This involvement stems from two analytically separate, but related, developments. The first is the corporatization of the university, which is the result of efforts on the part of industry and governments in several countries to harness academic resources to national projects to enhance economic competitiveness.[2] As universities have become progressively involved with — and indeed have become more like — businesses, they have increased both their infrastructural support for, and actual involvement in, the privatization and commercialization of knowledge.[3] The second source of the university's involvement in IP is what I call "the global knowledge grab," which stems from the development and extension of national and particularly international intellectual property regimes through forums such as the GATT and the World Trade Organization. As the scope of intellectual property rights and the consequent privatization of knowledge have increased, knowledge producers in both private and public institutions are attempting to develop and appropriate as much intellectual property as possible, as both a defensive strategy to sustain their knowledge production capacities and an offensive strategy to maintain or to gain a competitive edge.[4]

INTELLECTUAL PROPERTY AND THE DEMISE
OF THE LIBERAL UNIVERSITY

I do not dispute that the university's involvement in intellectual property has benefited particular individuals and corporations. However, I argue that IP is undermining the liberal university's ability to reproduce itself in at least two ways. On the one hand, IP is eroding the university's ability to draw on and to replenish the commons of knowledge, that is, the pool of freely available public knowledge, which is one condition of its survival. On the other hand, intellectual property rights set into a motion a number of dynamics which prevent the university from fulfilling its public service mission. This may undermine public support for the university, which is a second condition of its survival. Taken together, these mutually reinforcing dynamics produce a vicious spiral that puts the university's future at serious risk. As this chapter is not uniquely concerned with the general impact of intellectual property on the university, I do not discuss these two dynamics in detail; however, I do provide some examples to illustrate how they work.[5] In presenting these examples, I distinguish between what I call private and public academics, the former being those academics who are involved in the production and/or exploitation of intellectual property (for example, through research alliances with industry, through exchanging preferential access to their research for the right to use private knowledge, or through entrepreneurial activities of their own), and the latter being those academics who are not.

Depleting the Commons of Knowledge

Whether they are "private" or "public," the ability of all academics to replenish the commons of knowledge is being curtailed by intellectual property rights. Private academics are less involved in replenishing the commons of knowledge because the results of their work are increasingly being privatized or withdrawn from the intellectual commons. Private academics are also less involved in replenishing the commons because their contribution to public-knowledge production is progressively limited, both by obligation and by choice. To a growing degree, private academics are either explicitly prohibited or are refraining from informally discussing their work with colleagues. They are also limiting their participation at or in academic conferences and slowing the pace at which they share the results of their research through other vehicles, such as scholarly journals.[6]

In a number of ways, public academics are also less able to replenish the intellectual commons. The development and extension of intellectual property regimes are limiting their access to important resources they need to do their work. These include freely accessible knowledge, research funds (which are increasingly targeted towards privately oriented knowledge production),[7] and research collaborators, many of whom are becoming private academics. Another resource in increasingly short supply for public academics is time. As more and more knowledge is privatized, public academics are spending more time keeping informed of what IP rights are granted to whom in order to avoid infringement; negotiating special access to private knowledge (such as through agreements for experimental use); or finding ways of working around the obstacles to their research thrown up by IP rights.[8] Further, as entrepreneurial research becomes more highly valued both by universities and governments, the ability of public academics to obtain institutional rewards that may facilitate their work, such as release time, is also eroded, particularly relative to (and in part because of) the ability of their privately oriented counterparts to reap such rewards. It seems likely that as public-knowledge production becomes increasingly difficult or dissatisfying for them, many public academics will be tempted to join the ranks of their privately oriented colleagues. As well as further depleting the intellectual commons, this will redouble the hardships faced by those academics who remain steadfast in their public orientation.

Impeding the University's Public Service Mission

Intellectual property rights are also impairing the ability and willingness of academics to serve the public interest. For a number of reasons, such as confidentiality agreements, private academics are increasingly less able to share the results of their research and their knowledge with a variety of publics in a variety of forums. They may also be prevented from protecting the public from harm, as was the UCSF professor who was unable to disclose the fact that the company for whom she did work was gouging the public on its drug prices.[9] Private academics (and university administrators) may even harm the public interest either inadvertently or knowingly, such as when they grant exclusive licenses to academics' inventions in order to advance institutional goals such as generating funds or cultivating valuable corporate allies. Among other things, these exclusive licences may damage the public interest by inflating the prices of consumer goods and/or by limiting scientific or economic development, as was the case when Stanford University granted an exclusive license on its oligonucleotide machine.[10]

Intellectual property regimes do not simply limit the ability of academics to *use* the knowledge they produce to serve the public interest, but may also reduce their ability (and/or willingness) to *produce* knowledge that responds to a variety of social needs. Private academics who work with corporate partners may be less able or willing to work in the future with or for groups with other or opposing interests. This may be for a number of reasons, ranging from fears of compromising their personal financial interests (if they have a stake in the company) to fears of being sued for infringing on the company's IP when working for these groups.

On the other hand, declining funding and institutional rewards for alternative knowledge production, that is, knowledge not aimed at the production of IP, makes it more difficult for public academics to do research that responds to a diversity of social needs. As well as becoming more difficult, alternative knowledge production may also become more risky as IP becomes more important to the university. Indeed, there is growing anecdotal evidence of universities suppressing the production of alternative knowledge that threatens their or their partners' commercial interests, such as by failing to support grant applications for such potentially "dangerous" research or failing to renew the contracts of academics who engage in such research.[11] It stands to reason that as more academics become less responsive to the needs of the general public, and as confidence in academics' impartiality and reliability wanes, public support for higher education will decline, as will the public funding on which universities in most countries still heavily rely. This will set into motion a vicious cycle through which the universities' dependence on, and subservience to, private sources will only continue to grow.

It is worth emphasizing that these two threats to the future of the liberal university — namely, the erosion of the university's ability to replenish the commons of knowledge and to fulfil its public service mission — are inextricably linked and mutually reinforcing. Together, they will make it increasingly difficult for the liberal university to continue on as it has. While intellectual property is not likely to produce the physical destruction of the university, it is very likely to produce a fundamental, and likely irreversible, transformation of it. From an institution that produces a broad range of freely available knowledge that serves a multiplicity of social needs in a variety of ways, intellectual property regimes are helping to turn the university into an institution that produces a more limited range of knowledge, to which access is increasingly restricted, and which is shared with society (and which serves society) primarily through the mechanism of the market. Ultimately, this shift is likely to dissolve most if not all of the differences between the university and any other private knowledge institution. There will remain no university dedicated to a robust conception of public service, that is, one that stems from a concern with intrinsic rather than mere utility values and one that is universalistic rather than particularistic in its orientation. And there will thus remain no university worthy of public support.

IMPLICATIONS OF THE LIBERAL UNIVERSITY'S DEMISE

Thus far, this argument has focused on the costs to the liberal university of its involvement in intellectual property. My underlying concern, however, is the cost to the general public of the loss of the liberal university. Although knowledge production and transmission in the public interest can and do take place outside of the university's walls, the existence of an institution dedicated solely to these functions is a precious, possibly irreplaceable, resource whose potential loss should be vigorously protested and resisted. And while this loss needs to be opposed by all citizens, I would argue that it should be protested and resisted even more by members of disadvantaged groups, particularly women.

As is the case when other public institutions are destroyed, it is women who will be disproportionately harmed by the liberal university's demise. Be it because they are less able to afford the escalating costs of higher education (which are intimately related to the university's involvement in IP),[12] or less able to have their research needs addressed by academics, or less able to access the knowledge, services and products whose creation their tax dollars subsidize, women's inequality will be intensified by the liberal university's demise. It is not only the costs of the destruction of the liberal university to individual women that need concern us, however — even though, in and of themselves, they are sufficient cause for concern. For the impacts of IP will also cost women collectively in that they will undermine the university's effectiveness as a tool to advance the feminist project. In the following section, I address some of the potential threats to the feminist project that are posed by the university's increased involvement in intellectual property.

Threats to the Feminist Project

It is indisputable — and an understatement — to say that the liberal university has not always effectively or willingly served women's interests and needs.[13] Nonetheless, the university has been a very useful tool in advancing the feminist project, particularly in two respects. First, it has furnished feminists with the opportunity and space within which to develop a knowledge base that is vital to supporting and sustaining our movement. Second, the university has served as a site in and through which to build links among women that support and sustain our movement. The university's involvement in IP will dramatically reduce our ability to produce and sustain both the knowledge and solidarity that feminists need to advance our project. While this is unlikely to destroy our project outright, it will, nonetheless, deal it a serious blow.

Eroding the Feminist Knowledge Base

Above I suggested that the development and extension of IPRs both within and outside the university will put increasing pressure on all academics to become private academics, that is, to become involved in the production of privatized knowledge. While feminist academics might be more philosophically or politically opposed than most to becoming private academics, they may also be more pressured than most to become private academics. Because feminists are disproportionately marginalized and vulnerable in the university, the greater research opportunities and institutional rewards that accompany privately oriented research may be harder for them to pass up. This is not simply for personal or professional reasons, such as the legitimate desire to protect or enhance one's career. This may also be for political reasons based on the beliefs that it is better to do private research than no research at all (due to funding shortages); or that it is possible to squeeze one's own research agenda into a larger private research agenda; or that it is important that feminist perspectives be at least represented in, rather than completely marginalized from, private research initiatives.

Notwithstanding the good intentions that often lie behind them, such strategies of accommodation to intellectual property in the university may cause considerable damage to the feminist project.[14] While feminists who become private academics may protect their careers and thus their places in the academy, they will do so at the cost of eroding the feminist knowledge base, both in terms of the research that they do and do not do. In that the results of their research will be private rather than public, these researchers will directly erode the feminist knowledge commons. They will also slow down other feminists' work, as the knowledge the latter need to do their research will no longer be freely available and may actually be unaffordable or otherwise inaccessible. It is worth further noting that in working on projects oriented to producing intellectual property, feminist researchers may be investing their talents and energies in projects that are not directly useful to women or that are less useful to women, such as developing expensive drugs to cure diseases as opposed to working on preventative approaches to diseases. In the sense that they waste or fail to maximize precious resources, private feminist academics again diminish our knowledge base.

Further, as more feminists become private academics, those who remain public in their orientation will face increased difficulties in their research work. They may have less access to free knowledge, face higher research costs, and have more constraints on their research time. They may also have even fewer collaborators with whom to work, or even to consult, which is already a serious difficulty faced by feminists in many research fields. In the present university context, which is characterized by both a serious reduction in support for publicly oriented research and a growing obsession with performance indicators, one may predict that many public feminist academics will be caught in a vicious spiral of declining productivity, worsening track records, reduced institutional rewards and intensified workloads. Be it because they give in to pressures to engage in private research, or fail to get academic promotions, tenure or tenure stream appointments, or abandon the university in disgust and/or despair, the public feminist knowledge base will be further diminished to the detriment of our movement.

Fragmenting Feminist Community

Equally damaging to the feminist project are the multiple ways in which intellectual property may divide feminist communities, severing many of the links that sustain or unite our movement. As implied above, intellectual property regimes may fragment the feminist research community by reducing the formal research interaction between feminist academics (at conferences, through journals and so on) as well as the informal interaction (in university hallways, over coffee, etc.) between them. It seems likely that IP will also divide feminist researchers by producing a number of destructive tensions and resentments between them. These hostilities may compromise, in turn, various of the hard won gains in the university that feminists solidarity has made possible, such as the establishment of feminist institutions, resources and practices on campus, thus further weakening the bonds among women/feminist workers and students in the university.

The development and extension of intellectual property regimes may also strain relationships between women inside and outside the university, particularly between feminist academics and activists. In the past, and still today, feminist research in the academy has directly and indirectly supported the work of feminist activists. In return, feminists outside the university have championed feminist academics and feminist studies in a number of ways. As intellectual property transforms the university, this mutually supportive relationship may be disrupted with the result that feminists are perceived to be, and actually end up, abandoning one another to their mutual disadvantage.

For example, as private feminist academics become involved in research oriented to the production of IP, both their research time and the results of their research will become less available and/or accessible to the feminist community. For a number of reasons, including various obligations to their private research partners or sponsors, these private feminist academics may also be less able and/or willing to serve the feminist community in other ways, such as by speaking at public forums, writing for the popular media or serving as expert witnesses for the community. While this silencing of private feminist academics may last only so long as do the private research projects in which they are engaged, it also has the potential to become permanent. As implied earlier, there have been cases in which researchers have been sued for supposedly divulging private information acquired in one research project in the course of working for or with other groups.[15] The mere threat of being hit with a lawsuit in retaliation for their activism may be enough to silence some private feminist academics permanently. This silencing of private feminist academics will further separate them from the wider feminist community, undermining the latter's strength and further eroding their support for private feminist academics and/or feminism in the university more generally.

The ability of public feminist academics to serve the women's movement may also be compromised in a number of respects. As their working conditions and status in the university deteriorate, they will have fewer resources to devote to the growing research needs of the feminist community. They may also be less tolerant of the many complexities and tradeoffs that this kind of work frequently involves. And although they will be free — in the sense of being allowed — to serve the feminist community in various other ways, they will have less time and energy to do so, against straining the bonds between women inside the university and those outside it. It is worth noting that their increased vulnerability within the university, which is both cause and consequence of their separation from the broader feminist community, may also put a chill on public feminist academics' activism. For example, as their institutional security and community support erode, public feminist academics may be increasingly reluctant to challenge questionable or even harmful private research being conducted in their own or other universities for fear of jeopardizing their jobs. Yet the more they retreat from such activism, the more they will be seen as letting the women's movement down, and the more the distance between women inside and outside the university will grow.

The university's involvement in IP may not only weaken the feminist knowledge base and the strength of our movement in the short term, but also, and perhaps more so, in the long term. This is most clearly illustrated by considering ways in which IP may transform the nature of feminist academics' relationships with their students. For instance, as private feminist academics get progressively more research support than do public feminist academics, they will take on a larger share of graduate student training, particularly in the hard science fields. This may erode the feminist knowledge base in the long term, as the training the next generation of feminist researchers will receive will not necessarily be directed toward serving feminist priorities nor involve feminist research methods and practices. Moreover, as public feminist academics are likely to be penalized for their relative lack of productivity by being assigned heavier teaching loads, there will be a greater number of students being serviced by a smaller number of overworked feminist professors. This too has the potential to weaken our movement in the long term by reducing the number of women studies students, the amount of feminist activism on and off university campuses and ultimately the number of women and men who identify with and work to advance the feminist project.

RESISTING INTELLECTUAL PROPERTY

To be sure, the scenarios discussed in the previous section are only possibilities, not yet realities. Nonetheless, we should not underestimate how easily they may materialize. The dynamics set into motion by intellectual property are sweeping over the entire university, not only the feminist enclaves. As such, situations like those described above may develop far sooner than we expect. They may also be more difficult to resist than we might imagine. For feminists, there is a thin silver lining to the cloud cast by intellectual property over the university, however. It is that the battle against it is not ours alone; it belongs to all people committed to the liberal university. In concluding, I offer some thoughts on how we might all work together to resist intellectual property and its harmful effects on the university, the feminist project and the public interest.

Above I noted that the ongoing transformation of the liberal university is being driven in large part by dynamics that originate outside it. Although the university is increasingly implicated in the global knowledge grab, it is clearly beyond the university's ability to stop it single-handedly. In the long term, it seems to me that the most effective strategy to protect the liberal university is for its supporters to ally with the many other social groups — farmers, Indigenous organizations and others — working to halt the development and extension of IPRs, both directly (at the level of national and international law) and indirectly (through various local and global acts of resistance).[16] In the short term, however, there are some less ambitious but potentially worthwhile strategies that we can and should pursue.

The main strategy I advocate to protect the liberal university in the short term is for feminists and others to seek broad exemptions for academics from intellectual property rights. These exemptions could be sought on the basis that they are crucial to the survival of the liberal university, which, in turn, is vital to the feminist project and to the broader public interest. It is conceivable that both the general public and even the private sector could be convinced of the merits of granting exemptions from intellectual property rights to the university. However, for this to happen, at least one condition would have to be satisfied. In order to be granted IP rights exemptions in the name of the public interest, universities would have to work solely in the public interest. This means that the university's involvement with private knowledge producers would have to cease, as would academics' involvement in commercial activities of their own. Failure to meet this condition would destroy any chance of the university being granted IP rights exemptions, as it would afford both universities and their allies an unfair market advantage.

Even before campaigns to convince the public and industry to grant IP rights exemptions to the university could be undertaken, support for this proposal would have to be cultivated within the academic community. While it might be difficult to convince entrepreneurial academics of the merits of severing corporate ties as a precondition for an exemptions campaign, other academics might be more easily persuaded, particularly once their less self-serving concerns are allayed. For example, the fear that a ban on entrepreneurial activities might produce a "brain drain" from the university to the private sector may be dispelled, as we remember academics' long history of forgoing financial rewards in exchange for others such as professional autonomy and the opportunity to work in a stimulating environment (two benefits that are being destroyed by the university's involvement in IP). Fears that cutting corporate ties will further aggravate universities' dire financial situations may also be quelled, once the multiple costs — to universities, students and the general public — associated with producing and sustaining corporate links are fully brought to light.[17]

In addition to persuading academics of the feasibility — and necessity — of withdrawing from private knowledge production, there are some additional measures that those seeking to preserve the liberal university could adopt to help advance their goal. First, as a means of building public support for IP rights exemptions and of rejuvenating both the commons of knowledge and the university's public service mission (three mutually reinforcing conditions), we could launch campaigns to encourage academics — feminist and others — to voluntarily sign over to the public the IP rights to their work. Another possibility is the development of "knowledge collectives" in which various academics pool their intellectual capital and use it as a lever to free up even more knowledge. For example, these collectives could oblige anyone wanting to use a collective's knowledge to share their own intellectual property with the collective. Such a strategy would reverse the dynamic through which access to knowledge is progressively limited and move in the direction of protecting and enlarging a commons of knowledge. Efforts to change university policies, such as by incorporating into university contracts clauses that vest with the public the rights to any knowledge academics produce, would also be extremely useful, if more difficult to achieve, in terms of creating conditions favourable to an exemptions campaign. So too would be efforts to resist if not reverse various government policies that promote the development and exploitation of university intellectual property, such as those proposed by the Canadian Expert Panel on the Commercialization of University Research to the Prime Minister's Advisory Council on Science and Technology, and those being implemented as a result of the recent national innovation consultations.[18]

To be sure, the above proposals — not to mention the larger campaign for IP rights exemptions which they are designed to advance — raise many sensitive and complex considerations that would have to be widely discussed by academics in our departments, faculties, unions and professional organizations. They will also have to be negotiated with a number of constituencies, including university administrations, boards of governors, government and industry leaders, various social movements and the general public. The various competing interests involved will certainly make such discussions and negotiations difficult and complex. However, the costs of failing to take up this challenge are far too high for us to shy away from it. Once again, the feminist community has a chance to be at the forefront of a struggle that is vital both to women's interests and to those of general public. I offer this chapter in the hopes that we take full advantage of this opportunity.

NOTES

An earlier version of "Intellectual Property, Higher Education and Women's Inequality: Exploring Connections/Proposing Solutions" appeared in *Atlantis: A Women's Studies Journal* 25.2, 2001 (www.msvu.ca/atlantis). It is reprinted with permission.

1. See, for example, M. Mies and V. Shiva, *Ecofeminism* (Halifax: Fernwood Publications, 1993), and V. Shiva and I. Moser, *Biopolitics: A Feminist and Ecological Reader on Biotechnology* (London: Zed Books, 1995).
2. See H. Buchbinder and J. Newson, *The University Means Business* (Toronto: Garamond Press, 1988); L.C. Soley, *Leasing the Ivory Tower: The Corporate Takeover of Academia* (Boston: South End Press, 1995); J. Currie and J. Newson, *The University and Globalisation: Critical Perspectives* (Thousand Oaks, CA: Sage Publications, 1998); and S. Slaughter and L. Leslie, *Academic Capitalism* (Baltimore: The Johns Hopkins University Press, 1997).
3. M. Bordt and C. Read, *Survey of Intellectual Property Commercialization in the Higher Education Sector, 1998* (Ottawa: Science and Technology Redesign Project, Statistics Canada, 1999). The corporatization of the university has had many other impacts on the institution and on women's experiences in it. Lack of space precludes a discussion of these here. For one excellent account see M. Krouse, "Women and the University as Corporation: A Call For Feminist Rresponse," in S. Brodribb, ed., *Reclaiming the Future: Women's Strategies for the Twenty-first Century* (Charlottetown, PEI: Gynergy Books, 1999), 215–236.
4. S. Shulman, *Owning the Future* (New York: Houghton Mifflin Company, 1999).
5. The dynamics discussed in this chapter are not developing in the same way, or even at all, in all countries, universities or academic departments. My aim here is not to deal with their variations but rather to explore broad trends and to predict how they will develop over time so that their more harmful effects may be mitigated. It is worth further noting that while most of my examples are drawn from the "hard" sciences, intellectual property rights are increasingly transforming the nature of academic work in the fine arts, social sciences and humanities. Indeed, the development and exploitation of intellectual property in these areas is a growing concern of government and industry leaders. See, for example, Expert Panel on the Commercialization of University Research, *Public Investment in University Research: Reaping the Benefits*. Report presented to The Prime Minister's Advisory Council on Science and Technology (Ottawa, 1999), 9. For more elaboration of this argument in this section, see Claire Polster, "The Future of the Liberal University in the Era of the Global Knowledge Grab," *Higher Education* 39 (2000), 19–41.
6. See, for example, D. Blumenthal and N. Causino, "Withholding Research Results in Academic Life Science," *Journal of the American Medical Association* 277, no. 15 (1997),1224–1228; M. Scott, "Intellectual Property Rights: Ticking Time Bomb in Academia," *Academe* (1998), 22–26; P. Loughlan, "Of Patents and Professors: Intellectual Property, Research Workers and Universities," *European Intellectual*

Property Review 18, no. 6 (1996), 345–351; and Editorial, "Time to Withdraw an Undesirable Privilege?" *Nature* 391 (1998), 617.

7. Claire Polster, "Compromising Positions: The Federal Government and the Reorganization of the Social Relations of Canadian Academic Research" (PhD diss., York University, 1994).

8. E. Marshall, "Need a Regent? Just Sign Here," *Science* 278 (1997), 212–213.

9. G. Vogel, "Long-suppressed Study Finally Sees Light of Day," *Science* 276 (1997), 525–526. The case of Dr. Nancy Olivieri and the Hospital for Sick Children in Toronto is relevant here as well.

10. J. Cohen, "Exclusive License Rankles Genome Researchers," *Science* 276 (1997), 1489.

11. K. Strosnider, "Medical Professor Charges Brown U. with Failing to Protect His Academic Freedom," *Chronicle of Higher Education* 43, no. 45 (1997), A12.

12. E. Negin, "Why College Tuitions Are So High," *Atlantic Monthly* (March 1993), 32–44.

13. See N. Aisenberg and M. Harrington, *Women of Academe: Outsiders in the Sacred Grove* (Amherst: University of Massachusetts Press, 1988); A.I. Dagg and P.J. Thompson, *MisEducation: Women at Canadian Universities* (Toronto: Ontario Council on Graduate Studies, 1988); H. Bannerji et al., *Unsettling Relations: The University as a Site of Feminist Struggle* (Toronto: Women's Press, 1991); Chilly Climate Collective, ed., *Breaking Anonymity: The Chilly Climate for Women Faculty* (Waterloo: Wilfrid Laurier University Press, 1995); and J. Stalker and S. Prentice, *The Illusion of Inclusion: Women in Post-Secondary Education* (Halifax: Fernwood Publishing, 1998).

14. For an extended critique of academics' strategies of accommodation to the trans-formation of the liberal university, see J. Newson and C. Polster, "Reclaiming Our Centre: Towards a Robust Defense of Academic Autonomy," *Science Studies* 14, no. 1 (2001), 55–75.

15. R. Stone, "The Perils of Biotech Consulting," *Science* 263 (1994), 1079.

16. The work of Indian activists, such as Vandana Shiva, to have natural and cultivat-ed seeds designated as community property so as to prevent their privatization and commercialization by private corporations is one such kind of resistance. See M. Barlow, "Seed Keepers," *Canadian Perspectives* (Winter 1999), 12.

17. Indeed, as much feminist public policy analysis reveals, the tangible and intangible costs of corporate links with many public institutions are generally far greater for the majority of citizens, and particularly for women, than are the benefits derived from them. See, for example, L. Ricciutelli, J. Larkin and E. O'Neill, eds., *Confronting the Cuts: A Sourcebook for Women in Ontario* (North York: Inanna Publications and Education Inc., 1998), and D. Broad and W. Antony, *Citizens or Consumers? Social Policy in a Market Society* (Halifax: Fernwood Publishing, 1999). See also Claire Polster, "An Ounce of Abstention Is Worth a Pound of Cure," *The Third Degree* (Spring 1998), 34–36.

18. Expert Panel on the Commercialization of University Research, *Public Investment in University Research*.

CHAPTER 8

GENDER AND HERDING CATS:
WOMEN AND MEN IN
ACADEMIC ADMINISTRATION

A. Marguerite Cassin

ACADEMIC ADMINISTRATION IS A perilous business for everyone who
engages it. It is, of course, described by insiders as the work of "herding
cats." Many things are implied by such an account. In the metaphor,
"cats" refers to the faculty. The metaphor is apt in that it stresses the
individuality and independence of "power professors" and their aversion
to being administered. A deft hand, insider knowledge and the co-
operation of the faculty is required to administer in the university
setting. In view of this, and in view of the profoundly gendered character of the university, it is interesting to look at just how women are doing
at "herding cats."

UNIVERSITIES ARE CHANGING

Universities in Canada are changing. These changes involve changes to
relationships within the universities and relationships between universities and business, government and communities. The changes are being
driven by forces from inside the universities and by external shifts in
public policy, government–business relations and public governance.

These changes are felt in the working and learning lives of staff, faculty, administrators and students. They are also are embedded into programs and degrees in the universities, into the labour force and into relationships within organizations. Overall universities are becoming more active in situating themselves in local, national and international contexts. At the same time, communities, business and government are coming to view universities as economic and social resources within policy frameworks. This is an important shift in orientation to and thinking about universities because it places the teaching and education as well as research activities on the public policy agenda. Universities as knowledge producing and knowledge disseminating institutions are thus brought into the active realm of politics, economic positioning and strategic development.[1]

In the anecdotal realm, we can see the shift expressed in the work of university presidents and more generally in the management of universities. In addition to their traditional and engaging work with the internal politics of the university and the world of fund raising, university presidents now concern themselves with raising the public profile of the university and making sure it is on the public policy and public finance agenda of provincial and federal governments. University administration now includes a presidential office equipped with strategic and policy staff whose job it is to know the contexts and environments necessary for growth and to develop strategic directions locally, nationally and internationally. To use the language of the (business) street, universities are "open for business." Their business is knowledge.

These shifts are clearly evident in four current university trends: program markets, university finance, student debt and university governance. In some respects, these trends are innocuous and simply part of university life as it moves along in a changing society. In other respects, these trends are lived out with sharp contradictions. Central to these contradictions is the ideal of universities as places of expansion, inclusion and pluralism in discovery, learning, knowing and teaching as they transform into public and business-like institutions concerned with market positioning, economic trends, labour force development and public policy agendas. Of course, the two characterizations are not mutually exclusive and are not entirely new. It is important to understand that this is happening within universities as a consequence of the trends that we can identify and as important to discover where those trends might be leading us.

Universities are profoundly gendered organizations and institutions. The gendering involves the usual matters of workforce, organizational systems and structure. It also involves the knowing, recognition and authorization of knowledge and teaching. In this respect, only the family as an institution can challenge the social significance of universities in creating, promoting and maintaining unequal gender relationships. Whatever their origins and motivations, the changes that are taking place in universities are fed into this profoundly gendered domain, one in which changes related to gender equality have nothing more than a tiny foothold.

GENDER AND THE UNIVERSITY: A MATTER OF MIND

From the perspective of women, universities are historically most notable for the absence of women as learned members. This is not to say that women have not contributed to universities and to the development of knowledge. They have. It is to say that women have not been present as women in the creation of knowledge within universities. The implication and impact of this simple matter is profound in both university and human history.

As the university developed into an institution that creates, authorizes and teaches knowledge, women were notably absent as authoritative members. They have, therefore, been absent in the creation of the modern disciplines, fields of study, methods of investigation and in determining what counts as knowledge. What we take as knowledge has been largely produced by and for men and on the basis of the experience of men. In many respects, it is the absence of women and what they can bring to the production of knowledge that is most profound and in most need of remedy in modern universities and scholarly disciplines. This absence of women as scholars in the creation of knowledge and in the conduct of the disciplines has established particular forms of gender relations and gender inequality in universities in general and in Canadian universities in particular.[2]

Twentieth-century feminism has begun to open up a pathway for change in the presence and influence of women within universities. In North America, the broadening participation of both men and women in post-secondary education and the related expansion of universities in the 1960s brought women into the universities as students. In doing so, universities, being what they were and are, and university education gave young female students the experience of being the "other." This experience of being the "other" (as both professors and students), of course, has provided and continues to provide the fertile ground for critique, rebellion and desire for change among academic women.

Feminist studies has established gender as a core social practice.[3] There are two key points in the conception of gender: the first is the focus on the relationship between men and women, and the second is the recognition of gender inequality as institutionalized within objectified relationships of authority and control in organizations, policy and more generally governance.[4] At the present time, both women and men appear in universities as staff, students and faculty. But, as noted above, women are relative newcomers. The absence of women throughout most of our universities' history speaks to us of an institution whose design and development has presupposed the life situations of men and not of women. We know that rules, policy, tradition, authority and even hierarchy arise from and are practised from a material base and become abstracted into disembodied principles over time as they change in organizational form.[5]

In this most general way, then, the university is gendered in its foundations. This speaks to the need for changes in policy, procedure and daily practice that would bring more balance in the participation and contribution from men and women in all domains of university life. We can see some institutional changes: women are entering the academy and gradually being promoted and some are entering administration; employment equity is forcing accounting and auditing of gender as part of the federal Contractor's Program; and women academics are pursuing research programs. We can also see in the other chapters in this book that these changes are of indeterminate value in creating remedies for more balanced gender relations in the university. The fragility of the gains made by women and the limited change in gender relations can be used to direct our attention to how we might usefully think about the university in a way that has the possibility of giving us some direction for more progress.

One way to see the university is to think about what it is from the inside. I think the university can be usefully seen to be about "mind."[6] It has gathered, created and taught knowledge from its inception and created an accepted version of "mind," which investigates and establishes the topics taught in the university. Being "a mind" is a particular way of being, living and knowing. If we think about this further we can see that all academics (men and women) have some initial experience of learning about "mind" in the university. My own came in a particularly embarrassing experience of being the "other" at the hands of a much admired woman professor and her male colleague at an academic party early in my own graduate education. The three of us were visiting, doing "party talk" when at some point the conversation shifted to a discussion of some sociological topic of interest to them both and at the outset also to myself. As I tried to add my comments, they talked over me by saying, "Excuse me Marguerite, but I just need to say ..." As I write this I can easily bring back the sense of acute humiliation, yet it is not the humiliation I am objecting to here. This experience is simply part of life's lessons in the growth of our consciousness. What I want to do is show something of what I learned from the experience. In my own personal history this event was a profound "aaaaha" moment. It made me realize that I needed to learn how to "display mind" if I was going to be in the university.

In practical terms the "display of mind" means using appropriate vocabulary, engaging in topics without emotion and learning how to play "have you read" in order to demonstrate that "you know" the literature seriously and rigorously. However, "displaying mind" well is not enough since in addition to "displaying mind" one has to be seen and heard to be "doing mind" by professors, graduate colleagues and students. This social and interactional domain of the "establishment of mind" underpins classroom performance, grading of papers, recognition of work and ultimately degrees. It also underpins the conduct of work in academic departments, appointments to the professoriate, advancement, teaching authority and academic administration, which is the topic of interest here.[7]

The social and interactional domain of "mind" is profoundly gendered. We have a lot of evidence about this.[8] Some time ago, Dorothy Smith pointed to the practices of interaction and conversation through which women are excluded, are made invisible and are deliberately unseen within the university. Ursula Franklin points to women in science who find their careers glorious and life fulfilling but have to struggle for visibility and recognition in the academic community.

Similar issues exist for women students. This is not to say, of course, that men as individuals do not have to strive to be heard within the university and have not had the experience of being left out of the game; they do and they have. However, the point is that this situation does not arise for them because they are men, but because they are individuals in relationship with another identity. Being seen and heard to be doing "mind" as a woman requires serious work, and the results are uncertain at best.[9] This is because the first level of attention we receive is as a woman.

Beyond this core issue of whether women can routinely be "minds" are the surface issues related to gender in the university. Women are participating within the university. Participation rates of women students have risen and are rising at all levels of education and in almost all disciplines and professions.[10] Leaving aside the gendering of occupations, which remains a persistent issue in the labour force, women make up a goodly proportion of staff within the university. The participation of women in the professoriate has grown (marginally) and women are gaining promotion within the ranks.[11] To my knowledge, comprehensive surveys of professional and job satisfaction among women professors do not exist (but it is a good idea). Should one exist, I would hazard a guess that it would point out that while women are likely to be quite happy with their knowledge work, they are generally unhappy with the university as an employer and the place in which they build their career. While the university offers professors a work environment with a good deal of individual control (relatively), it has been slow to provide supports to women that might help them attain family-work balance, slow to explore the gendered character of merit and its implications and largely silent on issues of gender in student–professor relationships. As an employer, the university is neither progressive nor well informed on issues of gender.

The changes taking place within the university are negatively affecting the situation of women, particularly in small universities where intense competitiveness and the status of seniority appointments marginalize women's chances of career development. Finally, there are long-standing myths about male and female solidarity. Women and men are not all the same. Women coming into the university as professors do not necessarily want to champion "women's issues"; they want to work as professors, teach their students and pursue their research and publishing. At the same time, the ongoing gendering means that women (and men) are often called upon to politicize their working life in order to make gains or support other women. University unions and the national unions have gender on their agendas. It would be useful to examine how the gender issues have been politicized within university unions.

The key point, then, is that the university is a gendered domain. At the core of gendering is the issue of practising "mind" (which I use here to mean the practice of knowing, displaying and being recognized as an intellectual authority in an academic discipline). This is an issue of mind as a normative order (that is how it is practised and recognized) and how it is institutionalized into university programs, teaching, assessment of performance, scholarly work and research. The changes being made within the university today are feeding into these relationships.

THE ACADEMY: ACADEMIC ADMINISTRATION AND GOVERNANCE

Some years ago, I was working with the advisory board for my school (composed of deputy ministers from two levels of government) on a matter that involved university governance. The chair of our board leaned over the table to his colleagues and said in a reverent and confidential tone, "They do not do things the way we do; how they do things is a mystery." His comment conveys the most important things to be known about university administration. It is not like other institutions and how it works is mysterious, even to insiders.

At the core of the university's organization is the idea of the "academy," which is derived from the institution's monastic roots and which means a self-governing body of scholars interested in the creation of knowledge. How the "academy" is constituted differs widely in universities across Canada, but the basic "academy" is composed of those (tenured) faculty and academics who hold teaching and administration positions. Collectively and through administration units, faculties and a university senate, this group of academics governs and controls academic matters within universities through a series of rules, which include

- the selection, tenuring and promotion of professors
- the creation, design and implementation of curriculum
- the admission of students and requirements for degrees, including course requirements, pass levels, grading
- the operation of committees at levels of academic units, faculty and university

- the review of academic units, appointment of department heads, directors, deans, academic vice-presidents, and
- the influence on the appointments of university presidents and all associated academic matters.

It has been and is common to describe the professoriate within the university as the academy of scholars and refer to them as the "gowns." The "gowns" govern matters of mind in the institution. They do so from the authority drawn from their discipline-based knowledge. The easiest way to see this is in the two titles faculty members hold. The title of doctor, which comes from their PhD designation, and their membership in their discipline or profession. Their title of doctor designates their rank in a particular university as an organization and institution, holding the doctorate is a condition of being a professor. The governing of academic matters within the university rests both on the academic appointment to the university and on the authority vested in the terminal degree and in associated scholarly research and publication. This is also the authority to teach.[12]

As universities have expanded and grown, particularly since the 1960s, two definite and different organizations have emerged. These are the academic ("gown") side of the university, which is conducted through hierarchical collegiality, and the operational business side of the university, which is increasingly organized through management orientations. Modern, large-scale organizations are managerial in character; they are characterized by and structured and conducted through management systems that focus the teleology of the particular organization.[13] Work and prerogatives around action within managerial organizations are systematically circumscribed and embedded in a definite hierarchy and authority structure. In this way, individual initiative, knowledge and action are focused on organizational matter.

Academic administration, in contrast, is hierarchical, collegial, rule oriented and normative. It is not managerial.[14] In daily action it depends upon a deft hand, knowledge of the participants and their histories, and respect for reputation for many different prerogatives. Were it not a huge insult to the institution of home and family, we might say that the academic administration is very domestic. The point being that professors hold a great deal of authority within the framework of academic administration, most of which is exercised tacitly and is generally not experienced as power or authority but as the obligation and responsibility to defend their turf.

The organization of academic administration fosters ongoing tensions among professors, departments and faculties. The duality in the organizational form of the university also fosters tensions between academic administration and the more management-based operations side of the university. This is intensified as the comptroller takes a more prominent place in the universities (driven by public sector reform) and as managerialism seeps into academic administration.[15] As in all organizations, key areas of tension are those that focus on the allocation and expenditure of resources. Financial management and administration typically sit in the business and operations side of the university. This indicates both epistemological and ontological differences with academic administration. These tensions and the general framework of the academy form the domain in which academic administration gets done, and these tensions also feed the relationships among faculty as they govern the academy.

DOING ACADEMIC ADMINISTRATION

Doing academic administration poses challenges for both men and women. In truth, at some point in a term of office, doing academic administration brings out the best and worst in each person. It is a challenge not because of the work itself but because of becoming engaged in the process of doing the work.

The training ground for academic administration is university committee work, and a professor's first position in academic administration is as the head, chair or director of an academic unit. These positions are held for limited terms, the appointments are collegial and there is often a small stipend for doing the "job" added to the professor's basic pay. On the face of it the job involves simple administrative activities — negotiating and allocating resources, staffing courses and committees and maintaining relationships with students and other university administrators. While there are varying views about these administrative posts, the most general one is that departmental administration is a necessary evil and a distasteful interruption of the more serious career-based academic work of research and teaching. The head of an academic unit is often seen to be in a "caretaker" position, which should be undertaken once a career has been established, relationships with colleagues consolidated and when "taking a turn at administering" will be helpful to their department.

Those who do stints as chairs, heads or directors do so most successfully if they are seen to be undertaking the role as a necessary evil in service to their colleagues. If they are seen to be seeking or conducting the position ambitiously, they will almost certainly be scorned and face ridicule as a hapless fool with no scholarly career and thus an interest in administration. If they are seen to be taking up power over and in relation to their colleagues, they place themselves in a perilous position and possibly face ostracism and revolt. Tacitly, the job is understood as a part-time activity charged with protecting and preserving the academic unit and if possible extending its influence within the faculty. The value in the position lies with the tacit value (reputation, influence) of the unit in the faculty and university.

Perquisites of academic administration lie in abilities to respect and gain co-operation from colleagues while in these temporary (limited term) and poorly paid appointments. The key control (over heads) in the relationship is that these administrators return to their academic positions and thus to the collegiality (or not) of their colleagues. The metaphor of herding cats is apt. It is possible to herd cats, but only if they agree to be herded, and even then the risk to life and limb is ever present.

TENSIONS BETWEEN ACADEMIC WORK AND ADMINISTRATION

Academic administration functions on the basis of persuasion, influence, knowledge of and reliance on the normative order of units, faculties and universities. The collegiality of the academy means that academic administrators need to be able to depend on the respect of their own academic and intellectual careers as well as on the common history and crony relationship with their peers.[16] The administrative role also involves constantly mediating the demands that are made by different levels of the organization. The two key functions in achieving this are allocating resources and satisfying colleagues' needs as they conduct their careers. The latter is the more critical of the two.

In their academic work, professors teach, research and perform university service (committee work and associated service). There are, needless to say, inherent tensions among these three dimensions. On the face of it the issues seem to be simply a matter of balance. On the one hand, academic research and publishing are key to developing an academic career and to gaining influence and respect within professions and the university. On the other hand, teaching assignments are important services to the ongoing work of the university. It is, however, more than a matter of balance — managing the relationship between teaching and research is an ongoing struggle for professors and is at the core of decision-making within the administrative units.

Obviously, a professor's teaching workload influences just how much time she or he can allocate to research. The number and level of courses and the proximity of courses to a faculty member's scholarly interest greatly affect the amount of time teaching workloads take up. It is, therefore, a matter of considerable sensitivity and a part of the politics of all units. This has been and continues to be an issue for women since typical patterns of career development (tenure and promotion) have actually assumed the life patterns of married men.[17] Teaching workloads are becoming more contentious with the advent of the corporatization of universities. Increasingly, resources are being allocated to units on the basis of student enrolment (in keeping with provincial grants processes). Obviously, then, offering a curriculum with interesting choices and that covers the elements of a discipline or field is also of major importance in attracting students and funds. One implication of this is the expectation that faculty members will maintain high levels of teaching effort throughout each of their academic years as well as throughout their careers.[18]

Heads of academic units, therefore, must manage the joint tensions between offering a curriculum that sustains or increases enrolment and the competitive relations among faculty who are struggling to control their teaching workload in order to augment their research, which often results in the loss of collegial harmony within academic units. For women this can be particularly difficult. If they are mothers, female faculty will usually carry a larger share of child-related family responsibilities. Because they often have to take time out to deal with these responsibilities, their academic responsibilities are weighted on teaching and service over a longer period of time. This limits their research output.

Shifts in research are also affecting how academic administration is done and how faculty members are relating to one another. Increasingly, research "counts as research" when faculty members have brought research moneys into the university in the form of grants or contracts.[19] This is in stark contrast with previous conditions under which university appointments afforded faculty resources, time and flexibility to pursue their research in a variety of ways. The shift to grant-based research is driven in part by the corporate directions taken by the national research funding bodies, and in part by the increased workload of professors, which has been the outcome of conditions of university funding over the past fifteen years.[20] Professors seek funded research to buy their way out of teaching workloads and to provide resources to help them attend conferences where they can present their work and find out more about the current topics in their fields. Thus, the preparation of grant proposals and being awarded grants and contracts have become important components of a faculty's research and publishing career. This, in turn, increases the competitive relationships among professors and focuses their efforts on landing grants, securing teaching release time and fighting for preferred courses and levels of courses, particularly in relation to the larger service-oriented courses. These conditions also place more stress on male–female collegial relationships, especially given the fact that men and women are only beginning to learn to work together as academic colleagues.

FINANCIAL CONSTRAINTS AND ADMINISTERING ACADEMIC UNITS

The long-term effects of funding restraints and the shifting strategies that are bringing new monies into universities through designated funding or direct funding for research compound the problems of administering academic units, and often begin to affect the overall governance of individual universities[21] and the relationship between universities. In contrast to the broadening participation in the management and governance of institutions in the private, volunteer and public sectors, universities are becoming less collegial and democratic. Changes in the composition of university senates are an important indicator of such a shift. Another important effect is the downloading of costs onto students. This is in turn increasing the students' consumerist attitude towards their education. As a result, they demand more services for their money, which unfortunately detracts from the value of learning. As universities compete for students and attend to their consumer needs rather than their educational needs, the quality and standards of education begin to diminish.

These have been times of change. These are times during which heads of units have been and are being asked to mediate between the long-term effects of underfunding and the current conditions. They need to increase the faculty's teaching appointments (thereby increasing workload), to improve educational delivery, to update curriculum and course delivery and to motivate (often exhausted) faculty to generate research funds. These demands are compounded by the issues facing new hires and managing fairness for academics who work part-time. These conditions create difficult administrative experiences for both female and male faculty.

At the best of times, the head of an academic unit is engaged in mediating, cajoling and pleading in order to do their job. As one colleague in this position put it to me, "I use the few levers I have to make the place work." The current conditions bring out unrestrained individualism among the faculty and intensify student demands. In addition, chairs and heads of units have the contradictory job of conferring with faculty while attempting to embed the new corporate regimes into academic programs and research. This is particularly difficult since, as discussed earlier, academic administration depends heavily upon normative order rather than on managerial systems of authority.

WOMEN DOING ACADEMIC ADMINISTRATION

Administering academic units is challenging for everyone. Experience as head of a unit usually discourages most faculty from taking on future administrative positions and is the graveyard of many a career and collegial relationship. It has been particularly challenging in the recent past and even more challenging in the current climate, and it is particularly challenging for women. As women have gained seniority in academic work, they have had greater opportunities of becoming heads and chairs. They often have their first opportunity when the unit is in difficulty or when no one else wants the position.

The culture and character of the academy and of academic units require that the head of a unit have the support of her or his colleagues to be successful. That support is secured from past experience, reputation and prestige. It is often more difficult for women to secure strong reputations and prestige that will see them through the normal difficulties of administering academic units. This is where the issue of "mind," discussed above, comes into play. Women are seen as "members" in the academy through their scholarly work. Moreover, this is connected to more gender-based interpretive practices and expectations of women's behaviour (which are under-examined in the literature on working relationships between men and women).

While there are variations within the culture of the university, it has been normally expected that heads of units will protect their colleagues and keep administration as far away from teaching and research as possible. Under current conditions, this is largely impossible. The changes being fed into academic units are and have been altering work and working relationships. Under these conditions, women can and often do have much more difficulty gaining the co-operation and accord necessary to administer units successfully, and they are less able to call upon past associations for assistance. Neither men nor women colleagues accord women administrators the respect of office once pressing difficulties, which affect working life, arise. Both men and women faculty tend to personalize the decisions made by female heads, and are less willing to accept their decisions and more willing to attribute poor judgement and partiality to the head's understanding of situations.

The reliance upon normative order and the significance of corridor-based patterns of opinion-making on particular issues, which is combined with the more general culture of academic prestige as the basis of respect, is gendered. In practical terms this means that women can very quickly lose the willingness and co-operation of colleagues to do their share of the work, which they are seldom able to recover. As this happens they lose their ability to mediate issues and conflict. At this point conflict focuses on the unit head herself and university-based issues, such as gender bias, disappear.

Gendered Patterns of Conflict

When men and women come into conflict in administrative and faculty settings, a gendered pattern of treatment and a gendered perception of the conflict become visible. This unfair treatment has long-lasting effects on the motivation, participation, productivity and well-being of everyone involved, and results in a "downward career pattern" for women. Here are the typical components of a gendered pattern of conflict:

- Men and women have different and largely unrecognized expectations of women in administrative positions. For example, they rely upon women to ease tensions and "look after things."[22]

- When conflict or difficult decisions arise, women heads are blamed personally and their decisions are seen to be the result of inexperience at best and incompetence at worst.
- Both women and men faculty withdraw their co-operation.
- Women heads tend to work harder and take on more responsibilities in these circumstances and often seek support and guidance from senior members of administration.
- Faculty take for granted the work of women administrators and see them as siding with university administration.
- The issues become further gendered as the head is criticized for being disorganized, not working well with faculty, not sharing authority and decision-making, not managing students, being unfair and not working well with support staff.
- Under these circumstances, women heads are isolated by their colleagues and lose access to corridor-based information.
- Faculty members criticize women heads to students and encourage student disrespect and tacitly encourage student revolt.
- As women unit heads work harder and become more isolated, gossip increases and rumors of impropriety arise. For example, she is looking for a better job in administration; is engaged in sexual impropriety; or is ill.
- Members of faculty seek audiences with deans, associate deans, vice-presidents and presidents as well as unions to complain about their unit head.
- Women administrators become increasingly stressed and "lose it" in some fashion, which suggests they are in personal difficulty. The incident is interpreted as an indication of incompetence and unsuitability.
- Faculty members form a unified opposition force (which their individuality and competitiveness prevents them from doing under other circumstances). No one can remember that issues are about workload, course allocation, routine administration and research. They focus on the unit head and see her as incompetent, badly intentioned and lacking in student support. Faculty members claim that she is harming students.[23]
- Typically these criticisms are raised at times of reappointment but can also be raised in the middle of a term.

- Women who quit in the middle of a term or are denied reappointment under these circumstances are ostracized by colleagues, suffer severe stress and damage to their self-esteem, all of which works to undermine their careers.

It is interesting that neither men nor women see these as gendered patterns when they are engaged in opposing a women head or chair. Indeed, faculty who draw attention to these gendered patterns of conflict become marginalized and excluded. Women administrators who raise gender issues surrounding their treatment are seen as playing the "gender card" and seeking special treatment. Gendering is part of how we put our world together. We all engage in creating gendered relationships, and it is not necessarily the case that this is or has to create inequality. At the same time, inequality is created when difference is singled out and made relevant in ways that "count."[24] Gendered patterns, including expectations and judgements, are being made "to count" in decision-making conflicts in academic administration. However much we recognize gender as an important dimension of institutions at a theoretical level, we seem unable to see that we all hold gendered notions and expectations and that in university settings, practising them creates inequality. Moreover, we seem unable to recognize the inherent sexism of such behaviour when it takes place in our own work settings.

PROSPECTS FOR WOMEN HERDING CATS

As more women become senior academic faculty, more women will have the opportunity to be heads of academic units. At the same time, the corporatization of the university is affecting academic units and introducing greater competition and more conflict among faculty. Women who encounter difficulty as heads of their units cannot hope to enter into more senior administrative positions. The methods of appointment preclude those who do not have adequate support behind them. This current practise marginalizes senior women and at the same time tacitly strengthens the gender dimensions of the university culture and its normative order. A key issue is whether more gender balance and more equality can be introduced into the culture and normative order of academic units. It is essential that this happen if the academy wants to continue to function as a collegial environment.

The failure of the collegial university to take gender into account will most assuredly result in gender-based complaints being heard under human rights legislation with adjudicated solutions at some point. Decisions based in human rights currently focus on structural and systemic issues and tend to strengthen formal authority structures. The general point is that failure to address collegial relationships between men and women in the academy will tend to support the increase in managerialization of academic units. As more analyses of women in administration begin to recognize the effects of gender, the tendency will be to direct attention in favour of creating more objective and authoritative forms of decision-making that will be less open to the informality and tyranny of the corridor. There is likely to be increased tension between gender-equality seeking faculty and university administration so long as there are women senior enough to be appointed to positions as head of units. What is often not understood is the fact that the patterns we see are the expression of complex processes. They involve, for example, the history and structure of universities; assumptions about men and women; assumptions about men and women and "mind"; expectations of women and men; and expectations of women and men in positions of authority and collegiality. In truth, we are only at the beginning of learning how to create collegiality between men and women in the academy. We (both men and women) know very little about how to work with women in positions of authority and decision-making.

This is an area that would benefit from both case studies and more generalizing forms of research. It would be useful as a basis for understanding these issues more deeply and for learning how to address them. It is important to seek balance and to understand the key significance of how faculty see themselves and how they see the role of the university. We need conceptualizations for change that work for all of us and that allow us to better understand our professional relationships so we can make constructive changes. Women and men have not worked together as colleagues within the university for very long. We need to recognize that women's experiences continue to be challenging ones, and that the gendered way in which collegiality and academic administrations works is a key component of that challenge.

NOTES

1. An accessible and informative display of opinion is offered in *Policy Options* 23, no. 8 (September 2003), 10–61, which focuses on universities. Prominent Canadian professors and university administrators discuss university education, market relationships, public policy, research, teaching and university funding. For early discussions, see David M. Cameron, *More than An Academic Question: Universities, Government and Public Policy in Canada* (Halifax: IRPP, 1991), 473; "Equity and Purpose in Financing Universities: The Case of Nova Scotia," *Canadian Public Administration* 43, no. 3 (Winter 2000). There is also an interesting discussion of tenure in the context of public policy in *Policy Options* 22, no. 10 (December 2001), 6–13.

2. Dorothy E. Smith, *The Everyday World as Problematic: A Feminist Sociology of Knowledge* (Toronto: University of Toronto Press, 1987), 244; *The Conceptual Practices of Power: A Feminist Sociology of Knowledge* (Toronto: University of Toronto Press, 1990), 235; *Texts, Facts, and Femininity: Exploring the Relations of Ruling* (Toronto: University of Toronto Press, 1990), 247; *Writing the Social: Critique, Theory and Investigations* (Toronto: University of Toronto Press, 1998), 307.

3. By this I mean that feminism has drawn attention to gender relations as critical dimensions of how the social world is constructed, known and organized. It is only with feminism that gender is recognized as a matter to be studied rather than assumed. As such, the study of gender relations has entered most disciplines (from biology to literature) and most fields (from architecture to public administration). See, for example, Iris Marion Young, *Justice and the Politics of Difference* (Princeton: Princeton University Press, 1990); Deborah Tannen, *You Just Do Not Understand: Men and Women in Conversation* (New York: Ballantine Books); Dale Spender, *Man Made Language* (London: Routledge and Kegan Paul, 1980); Nicole Morgan, *The Equality Game: Women in the Federal Public Service, 1908–1987* (Ottawa: Advisory Council on the Status of Women, 1988); and Catharine A. MacKinnon, *Only Words* (Cambridge, MA: Harvard University Press, 1993).

4. The are, of course, other important aspects of the conception. These are the dimensions useful to this chapter. A number of feminist theorists have seen this point in different ways. I find Dorothy Smith particularly useful. In both *The Conceptual Practices of Power* and *Texts, Facts, and Femininity*, she demonstrates the features of objectified social relations as general properties of the relations of ruling in capitalism. She draws her analysis from her reading of Karl Marx. Here I just want to draw attention to these relations as properties of the institutional relations of gender in universities. Smith and others have developed a method of investigation for the relationship of institutional relations and everyday life, which she takes up in *Writing the Social*. Her discussion in "From Women's Standpoint to a Sociology for People," in Janet L. Abu-Lughod, ed., *Sociology for the Twenty-first Century: Continuities and Cutting Edges* (Chicago: University of Chicago Press, 1999), 65–82, explores the method and politics of the approach.

5. This is, of course, what law, public policy and organizational policy is. See Smith, *The Conceptual Practices of Power* and *Texts, Facts, and Femininity*; A. Brooks

A. Marguerite Cassin

"Regulating the Politics of Inclusion: Academic Women, Equity Issues and the 'Politics of Restructuring,'" *International Review of Women and Leadership* 4, no. 1 (1998), 49–60; and Catharine A. MacKinnon, *Feminism Unmodified: Discourses on Life and Law* (Cambridge, MA: Harvard University Press, 1987), 315.

6. It is about other things as well, but I am stripping these away to make a point.

7. We all owe a debt of gratitude for this insight to a long line of thinkers and scholars in phenomenology in philosophy, ethnomethodology in sociology and, most recently, interdisciplinary post-modernism. It is key to see that this gendering is cumulative. That is, existing rules and institutional policy and practice rest on earlier practical ground and so conditions existing practice. This is why, for example, a change in policy can have almost no effect on everyday behaviour in organizations. There is also the important and influential works by Dorothy Smith on how women are excluded and which points to how the international domain and the "structural" domains are part of the same processes within universities. See Smith, *The Conceptual Practices of Power* and *Texts, Facts, and Femininity.*

8. Smith, *The Conceptual Practices of Power,* 122; Ursula M. Franklin, *The Real World of Technology* (Toronto: Anansi, 1999), 209; Ursula M. Franklin, *Will Women Change Technology or Will Technology Change Women?* (Ottawa: CRIAW, 1985), 46; and Catharine A. MacKinnon, *Toward a Feminist Theory of the State* (Cambridge, MA: Harvard University Press, 1989), 330.

9. At the risk of looking too closely at this in a personal way, I would report I have a colleague whose attention wanes as soon as I begin to speak. He gets coffee, straightens his papers and signals me with the "time out" sign when he thinks I should stop talking in school meetings. Students, being much better schooled in observation than we are, brought his behaviour to my attention.

10. CAUT, *Annual Report,* 2002. See also A. Marguerite Cassin with G. Morgan, "The Professoriate and the Market-Driven University: Transforming the Control of Work in the Academy," in Linda Christiansen-Ruffman, Raymond F. Currie and Deborah Harrison, eds., *Fragile Truths: Twenty-five Years of Sociology and Anthropology in Canada* (Ottawa: Carleton University Press, 1992), 22–41.

11. The participation of women in the university as professors does not match improvements of women in management in the public sector and is about even with the private sector, showing the university to be the most intransigent of institutions. Part of this is accounted for by the lack of growth-based hiring over the past decade, market supply and the gendered character of merit in the university, which has yet to be rigorously explored. Nadya Aisenberg and Mona Harrington in *Women of Academe: Outsiders in the Sacred Grove* (Amherst: University of Massachusetts Press, 1988) offer wonderful accounts of women's experiences of finishing their PhDs in the 1970s and 1980s and the process of entering into and being "deflected" from academic life.

12. It is generally the case that terminal degrees are the only qualification for tenured positions in Canada. The general point is, however, that the authority to govern academic matters involves two dimensions: the profession and the institution.

13. Management systems include accounting and finance, operations, human resources, marketing and information. They are a particular development of the

twentieth century and have their immediate origins in the building of the American railways. The account of the rise and place of management in capitalism and the account of the railways is offered in Alfred Dupont Chandler, *The Visible Hand: The Managerial Revolution in American Business* (Cambridge, MA: The Belknap Press, 1977). It is key to see that management systems are not neutral; they propose a particular way of doing things, which depends upon and organizes particular ways of thinking, seeing and being. See A. Marguerite Cassin, "The Routine Production of Inequality: A Study in the Social Organization of Knowledge" (PhD diss., University of Toronto, 1990).

14. Management in the sense of managerial organizations means systems of organization, including accounting, marketing, information, personnel and operations/production. See Chandler, *The Visible Hand*, 137–284; and J. Hearn, "The Critical Study of Men Managers in Universities," in D. Cohen, Lee J. Newman et al., eds., *Winds of Change: Women and the Culture of Universities Conference Proceedings* (Sydney: University of Technology, 1999).

15. The encroachment of managerialism into the management of professors and university administration is a topic in itself and is only alluded to here. The elements which provide the basis of a more systematic management are being put into place and include student course evaluation and financial formulas to allocate resources. See, for example, William G. Tierney, *The Responsive University: Restructuring for High Performance* (Baltimore: The Johns Hopkins University Press, 1998).

16. Herman Bakvis and David Cameron, "Post-Secondary Education and the SUFA," *Policy Options* (May 2000), 46–48.

17. Career arrangements assume life conditions and are gendered. For example, teaching assignments tend to be heavier at entry level when faculty members are junior and become lighter with experience, seniority and acquisition of research funding (which is used to buy time out from the teaching workload). This pattern is problematic for younger women who may be starting families and beginning their careers, thus they have to meet the conditions of tenure and promotion at the same time as having children. The point is that we need more flexibility in models of career progression and measures of performance. There are beginning to be interesting discussions of this. For example, see Margret Allen and Tanya Castleman, "Fighting the Pipeline Fallacy," in Ann Brooks and Alison Mackinnon, *Gender and the Restructured University: Changing Management and Culture in Higher Education* (London: Open University Press, 2001), 151–165; and Robyn Munford and Sylvia Rumball, "Managing Innovatively," in Brooks and Mackinnon, *Gender and the Restructured University*, 137–150.

18. This varies across universities and across faculties within universities. The most affected universities are the smaller teaching universities which are primarily focused on providing undergraduate education. They are in the most competitive position in relationship to both provincial funds and students. They are also in the least competitive position in relationship to research if for no other reason than the critical mass of faculty.

19. This has been true in the sciences and applied sciences and professions for some time. It is currently true in the social sciences and is becoming the case in the humanities.

20. Claire Polster, "Compromising Positions: The Federal Government and the Reorganization of the Social Relations of Canadian Academic Research" (PhD diss., York University, 1994), 335.

21. It is important to understand that new money coming into universities is not coming in as increases to regular university funding but as direct funding for specific research projects, funding chairs and so on. It should be understood that the funding is being shaped and affected by private contributions to universities. This growing reliance on private contributions will shift the public-oriented culture of universities over time.

22. The tacit basis of gendered expectation, interpretation and responses to conflict in these settings are important to understand.

23. Notice that competence issues are raised at the end of the conflicts.

24. It is not difference itself that creates inequality but how difference is made relevant. In the movement for women's equality (and other social identity movements), the practices of making differences count has been politicized. In practical terms, this politicizes everyday life, which has been effective in raising issues. At the same time, once everyday matters are politicized, it makes it difficult to make change routinely.

EMPLOYMENT AND EDUCATIONAL EQUITY IN THE CORPORATE UNIVERSITY

CHAPTER 9

COLLEGE "EQUITY" CENTRES AND WOMEN'S STUDIES FACULTY: REGULATION OF FEMINISM?

Diane Meaghan

IN THE MID-1980S, the phenomenon of political correctness emerged within departments of American and Canadian universities. Employing anti-discrimination and harassment legislation, governments attempted to suppress workplace speech that was thought to be "offensive" and workplace behaviour deemed to be harmful to individuals within the domain of public institutions. Although departments and ministries of education may have been committed to establishing "equitable educational outcomes," their policies had far-reaching implications for transforming post-secondary educational institutions into instruments of government policy that served a political agenda. While forms of bigotry such as sexism and racism can never be justified, defining harassment as making someone feel uncomfortable created a potential for arbitrary and discriminatory enforcement that was not limited to curtailing threats and insults. In view of the fact that one person's discussion can be interpreted as harassment to another person, and that faculty have reported that students frequently feel uncomfortable in entertaining innovative ideas as part of the intellectual process of growth, a shadow of orthodoxy was cast over the academic environment.[1] Government legislation directed at university administrators, who were sensitive to the perils of policing language in consideration of academic freedom and freedom of speech, actually curbed numerous forms of speech. Inventive "human rights" legislation enabled university administrators to castigate faculty for political remarks, religious debates, humour, verbal irrelevancies and art in the name of political correctness.[2]

THE POLITICAL INCORRECTNESS
OF THE "POLITICALLY CORRECT" AGENDA

Under the guise of promoting equity and protecting human rights, college administrators targeted faculty as part of a methodology that sought to monitor and discipline through the circumvention of traditional forums for academic debate and trade union defense. The requirement that, in order to be offensive, speech had to be severe, pervasive or simply offensive to a reasonable person disappeared and was replaced by an interpretation in anti-harassment policies and practices (of unduly restrained speech in order to prevent an "abusive environment") that resulted in chastisement and repression of faculty for uttering isolated comments and statements. These workplace regulations seriously undermined due process and human rights for those accused, revived some of the orthodoxies of the past and reversed some of the earlier achievements of progressive social activism.[3]

What began with the noble idea of addressing equity and inclusion as part of the educational mission of colleges became a cloak to disguise disputes concerning relations of institutional power. In 1994, for example, the Ontario government introduced the Antiracism and Ethnocultural Equity Policy, together with guidelines and policy initiatives in a document entitled *Framework Regarding Harassment and Discrimination in Ontario Universities and Colleges*. These framework documents established the government's "zero tolerance" policy (a phrase borrowed from the Reagan-era war on drugs) and inaugurated procedures to monitor conduct on Ontario university and college campuses.[4] In the words of the college administrator who suggested the parameters for the Ontario framework, the intent was to "cleanse the culture of the college of unwelcomed/unwanted, offensive, intimidating, hostile or inappropriate comments and conduct."[5]

With the introduction of these new speech codes, the charter rights of professors as citizens were swept away in the workplace and, as a result, colleges became more extensively monitored and regulated than most other public institutions.[6] Some administrators established practices steeped in intolerance to relentlessly scrutinize every aspect of the educational experience. Censorship and, more lamentable, self-censorship had the effect of curtailing free speech and academic freedom.

EQUITY CENTRES AND THE NEW BALANCE OF POWER

The introduction of Equity Centres intensified a relationship of power between management and faculty when equity centre staff were appointed by college administrators during the mid-1980s to introduce constraints and disciplinary mechanisms directed towards faculty words (and deeds). Determining if a complaint would be investigated and establishing rules of evidence for ascertaining "guilt" (for rarely were individuals found "innocent") was subject to managerial discretion, and thus procedurally and substantively compromised. To acquire a judgement of guilt, the mere filing of a complaint and suggesting (justifiably or not) the "feeling" of being uncomfortable or offended was usually sufficient to establish the defendant's culpability. In many instances, students baseless allegations would not have initiated an investigation without the imprimatur of the Equity Centre. Single incidents based on subjective attitudes, misreported or falsely reported allegations were given new status by the Centres (absorbed with the issues of the complainant while often demonstrating complete indifference or even manifest contempt for the rights of the defendant) that transformed picayune disputes into formal adversarial altercations which required the intervention of the equity "experts" (a word used by Equity Centres).

College policies and practices were transparently ideological in intent when using procedures that lacked due process and natural justice. The aim was to use the Equity Centre as a innovative arm of management with which to circumvent the collective agreement, thus establishing a culture of constraint. In some Equity Centres, personnel simply did not have the academic or legal expertise to conduct a proper investigation that conformed to the norms of quasi-judicial procedures or human rights tribunals. Nonetheless, the personnel functioned in the capacity of investigator, prosecutor and judge, building cases in secrecy in which it was claimed they were not compelled to provide full disclosure. Thus, the defendant might not know the identity of (much less cross-examine) the complainant, and the accused might not be privy to know the offense she or he was alleged to have committed, nor be made aware of the standards of investigation or be engaged in an exchange of evidence. Corroborating evidence for the plaintiff could be constructed, while exculpatory evidence and testimony for the defendant could be suppressed or ignored. Investigating allegations that were motivated by personal animus, remedying injustices for the falsely accused and instituting procedures concerning false or frivolous accusations were, for the most part, absent in the historical practices of a number of Equity Centres in Canada.[7]

In the early history of Equity Centres, men were more likely to suffer harsh and retributive administrative action and unjust discipline. A few case histories present some of the struggles of both political activists and apolitical faculty. In one case, Professor A (male) was accused of anti-Semitism. Charges were filed based on the "evidence" produced by Mr. W., a member of management who alleged he heard the comment. Professor A denied making such a remark and hired a lawyer who sought to discover the rules of procedure. When college officials suggested that they "would make up the rules as they went along," Professor A's lawyer advised him not to participate in the investigation that predictably found him guilty. After eleven days of heated testimony at the Ontario Labour Relations Board, the college offered to settle in exchange for Professor A's resignation. Anxious to clear his name and utterly disillusioned with the college, Professor A went on to an important federal judicial appointment dealing with refugees.[8]

In another case, Professor B (male), while awaiting delivery of a textbook for his class, distributed reading material written by Hobbes, Locke, Rousseau, J.S. Mill, Marx and Weber, wanting to expose the students to some famous commentaries on human nature and social institutions. A woman in the class told her friend, an ambitious student who curried favour with senior administration and became a student representative on the board of governors, that she had been asked by Professor B to read material by Karl Marx. The ambitious student approached management and accused the professor of "preaching communism." Several senior managers met secretly in a "star chamber" to compose Professor B's letter of resignation, without offering him the opportunity to testify that he was "not then nor never had been a member of the Communist Party." They ordered Mr. Y to sign the letter (Professor B's immediate supervisor); when he refused, he was relieved of his duties and subsequently resigned. Professor B continues to teach at the same college and on occasion refers to the work of Marx in his classes.[9]

In a third case, Professor C (male) taught mathematics to a class that included many special-needs students. One of them complained that he had not been given the extra time he required to write an examination and another, who failed the course, complained that Professor C had "deceived" him by encouraging him when he had expressed concern about his ability to do the work. Despite the fact that the examination of both students was written in Professor C's absence in the Special Needs Office, the complaint in the first case was upheld by the Equity Centre. The complaint in the second case was dismissed but appealed to a college review board and upheld, despite the complainant's inability to state the basis of his complaint. This led to Professor C's conviction of insensitivity and inappropriate behaviour as a professor. As a result, he was compelled to take "sensitivity training" while continuing to teach at the college.[10]

Some college Equity Centres have become large-scale operations where administrators claim authority to speak for all on campus. As a consequence, complaints have spiralled in numbers and faculty have been caught in administrative crosshairs as charges are levelled against them for creating a "poisoned environment" (rude, intimidating and aggressive speech) — an environment in which free speech is subordinated to values of etiquette, comfort, purity and self-esteem and often with little evidence of "harassment" in either the legal or common-sense meaning of the term. Administrative action is frequently prompted by its opposition to the ideals and actions of trade unionism and anti-racism that is expressed particularly among senior faculty who are most likely to possess the experience and confidence to address such matters on behalf of the faculty. Although academic activists receive disproportionate attention from the Centres, few faculty are exempt from having false charges brought against them. Even when charges of harassment and discrimination are unproven, harsh penalties may be imposed. Events often linger for years, rumours persist, reputations are sullied and the unfairly accused often remain under a cloud of suspicion without effective means of redress. In the meantime, apprehension about antagonistic encounters, trepidation about tackling contentious topics and consternation about challenging cultural conventions with students and colleagues alike stifle creativity and intellectual growth.

THE PERSONAL *Is* POLITICAL:
GUILTY WITHOUT HAVING TO BE PROVEN GUILTY

In November 2001, I became one of those faculty members against whom the Equity Centre acted when a complaint was lodged against me by one male student who was a Roman Catholic and two female students who were Muslim. They were complaining about remarks I allegedly made in one of my Women's Studies classes.[11] The incident took place during a class presentation in which I detected cheating and plagiarism involving two of the students. When the male student "organized the girls" at the end of the class to complain about his mark to my acting chair, he was joined by a friend and a female student involved in the incident. Although college policy advocates mediation as a first-level intervention, this process was interrupted when the students' complaints were transformed by the Equity Centre into fifteen separate allegations of harassment, discrimination and poisoned environment. Despite the fact that the male student's attendance had been extremely poor and the two female students had equally poor concentration and note-taking abilities, their complaints were saturated with dozen of verbatim quotes I allegedly made over the course of the class, some of which dated back several months.

In his accusation that I was "closed-minded," the male student ironically referred to a class which had focused on the transformation of matrilineal culture into patriarchal culture (in a section of the course which dealt with ancient women's history) as a disturbing example of my "rude" ideas concerning violence against women. He also suggested that in this discussion I was "brainwashing" students by telling them that "Christianity is man-made," "Christmas is a fake date that is really in February," "men are bad people" and "men are responsible for all the evils of history." The two female students complained about my ineptness as a teacher as well as my inability to understand the Q'uran because I was not a Muslim. As well, they misunderstood integral aspects of the curriculum and were critical of topics under discussion which they considered to be foreign to their value systems and expectations — abortion, premarital sexuality, arranged marriage, polygamy and homosexuality.

The Equity Centre failed to investigate my claim (as is required in the Harassment and Discrimination Policy) that these frivolous and vexatious allegations stemmed from the incident of cheating and plagiarism, as well as from weeks of student misconduct that included laughing, talking and answering a cellular telephone in class (regulations against which are set out in the Student Rights and Responsibility Policy). At no time did the students approach me or speak about their difficulties, nor did college administrators enforce the long-standing practice that required initially bringing concerns to the professor's attention. Nor did the investigating officer deal with issues of academic weakness (that resulted in the male student being asked to leave the college by a promotion committee and one of the female students placed on academic probation), lateness, failure to attend class and take examinations and one incident of hostility which was displayed by using an offensive epithet ("fucking bitch").[12]

When I *was* questioned by the investigating officer (whose previous job as support staff was to deliver the audio-visual equipment to my classroom), he asked me if I had used the following phrases in class: "if women ruled the world," "Christmas is in February" and "old and new testicles (testaments)." He set aside my explanations that I had briefly spoken to the class about a controversy among feminist theologians with respect to the birth of Jesus Christ occurring in February, 7 B.C., and a discussion about the old and new "testaments" of the King James version of the Bible. The extensive documentation I submitted — concerning refutation of the misstated, trivial and redundant allegations; detailed discussion of what transpired in class; descriptions of academic expectations from the course outline; examples of sexist advertising and language on the college walls and in administrative discourse; as well as student notes, marks and midterm examination results (including those of the complainants and other students) — was also ignored.[13]

I also submitted a variety of scholarly articles that addressed the pedagogical basis for Women's Studies, the "chilly climate" in postsecondary education for feminist academics along with articles that addressed issues of academic freedom, the complexity of world religions in different historical eras and cultures and psychological studies indicating the use of speech as an unreliable index of conversation recalled. My union representative (a human rights lawyer who took over my former position as vice-president of equity for the union) raised concerns about substantive issues such as procedural fairness, investigative methodology, witness selection, credibility and academic freedom. Although his analysis was later substantiated by Clayton Ruby (one of Canada's leading human rights lawyers), it was discounted by the president of the college who turned the matter over to the arbitration process. My exemplary teacher ratings, the letters of support from university colleagues (who attested to the soundness of my curriculum and scholarship) and a list of character witnesses were also dismissed. Instead, the uncorroborated opinions of three disgruntled students trumped the evidence of approximately ten thousand students I have taught without a formal complaint; the stellar administrative evaluations I have accumulated in a twenty-seven-year teaching career; and the results of a survey conducted in all five sections of my courses (in which I used the verbatim statements of the complainants), which did not reveal a single student who substantiated the complainants' allegations. (In addition, between the onset of the investigation and the delivery of an adverse finding, I was elected as the faculty representative on the Board of Governors, designated a visiting scholar in the Centre for Women's Studies at OISE/UT and appointed to the external research funding committee of the Status of Women Canada.)

In the legal exegesis of the Equity Centre's final report prepared by my representative, he emphasized a number of errors that had been made: college policy was misinterpreted and misapplied; the investigation was inadequate and incomplete; the process of fact finding was flawed; the selection of witnesses was prejudiced; the questioning of witnesses was incompetent; the assessment of the reliability of witnesses was deficient; the proof of discrimination was "seriously lacking consistency"; the provision of a proper context of behaviour was absent; and the conclusions (which excluded scrutiny of the witnesses' evidence for credibility, bias and consistency) were in error. He confirmed that "the failure to include the voluminous exculpatory evidence in the investigator's discussion strongly suggests either partiality on the part of the investigator in his selection of evidence or gross negligence that invalidates any conclusion he has arrived at regarding discrimination on the part of Dr. Meaghan."[14]

Invoking my right to exercise "academic freedom," I was exonerated on fourteen of the allegations by the Equity Centre. After eight months of investigation and $30,000 of taxpayers' funds spent on college expenses ($23,000 in expenses to date for myself), a trace of guilt was left to sully my reputation while the punishment was kept below the radar line of the collective agreement. Even though the Ontario Human Rights Code recognizes women as a group who are oppressed and anticipates the need to protect women from harassment and discrimination, I was found guilty of discrimination against a male for allegedly stating "he's a man and he should know" (allegation #14). I did not, however, make this comment. The statement I did make to the male student occurred in the context of his class presentation when it appeared to me that he was cheating. At that moment, I instructed the female student (one of the complainants) to whom he was speaking to "let *him* answer" the question. In addition, the male student did not complain about this remark, nor was it corroborated by other students in class, nor did the investigating officer think it important enough to provide me with a written allegation (as required by college policy) or to question me about it.

My representative wrote to the vice-president of human resources to point out that allegation #14 could not be substantiated in an analysis of the evidence. In the Centre's final report, the investigator referred to section 5(e) of the policy but actually quoted section 5(d), namely, that "discrimination is based on treating an individual unequally or differently" on the basis of sex (in the refusal to provide a benefit or a service), and that as a result of such differential treatment the individual suffers a negative effect concerning her or his academic status. My representative noted that normally a negative comment constitutes harassment rather than discrimination. The Ontario Human Rights Code defines harassment as "engaging in a course of vexatious comments or conduct"; an isolated remark is not sufficient to amount to harassment. Thus, the legal concept of *de minimus non curat lex* ought to have taken effect since "the law is not concerned with trifles, nor with trivial acts ... nor with inconsequential breaches."[15] The investigator, however, chose the category of discrimination which does not require more than one act, even though the comment and circumstances did not meet the requirements for discrimination.[16]

Despite meeting three out of four criteria in the policy concerning the right of an appeal (the fourth was irrelevant), my appeal was denied.

Although a number of allegations ("doesn't put notes on the board"; "doesn't have facts to back up statements") did not constitute violations of the Ontario Human Rights Code and were never presented to me in investigative interviews or corroborated with factual material, they were characterized as "improper and unprofessional behaviour" and referred to the acting chair of my division for further intervention. Shifting the grounds from "human rights" to academic administration and making use of the adulterated results of the Equity Centre investigation, meant that concerns arising from limitations of human rights complaints need not be addressed when the acting chair mandated a semester of "professional development" activities to "monitor classroom management techniques, teaching style, interactions with students, course objectives, evaluation and the validation of those objectives." Although a public board that formerly allowed deputations by employees, the board of governors ruled that personnel matters were operational in nature and would not be addressed because they may interfere with the relationship between the college and the union.

At the Mitchnick Arbitration Board hearing in May 2003, the college's counsel raised a preliminary objection of jurisdiction by characterizing my grievances of "unjust and unwarranted discipline" as part of my "professional development" activities. Although the board upheld that the college's "findings" did not constitute discipline which could be relied upon in future disciplinary action, it upheld that the college's discrimination and harassment policy was not part of the collective agreement and it was therefore outside of the board's parameters to hear the merits of the case. Currently, the case is at the stage of mediation before the Ontario Human Rights Commission.

FEMINISM UNDER ATTACK

My experience raises a number of substantive issues. The first deals with the systemic gender discrimination that permeates many colleges. As Dorothy Smith notes, social experience can be used to explicate the dynamics within an organization (which produces and reinforces unequal social relations) through the establishment of a dominant paradigm of authority that subordinates and marginalizes women. In starting with the problematic of the everyday world experience, the relations of ruling can be found to be located in ideological and structural college relations often based in the social organization of knowledge.[17]

The analysis examines college policies and procedures as part of the ruling apparatus (and as sites of political struggle) related to power and privilege. Sexism and racism are revealed to be systemic in nature and part of the power relations that give rise to specific forms of inclusion and exclusion. Although appearing to be neutral, equity policies and practices are developed to justify and support the status quo.[18] These policies and procedures, which are not subject to interpretation, become entrenched as "common-sense" notions of the way the world is and ought to be.[19] At the same time, the interactions of teachers, students and administrators as gendered and racialized subjects can also be explored as socially constructed through these administrative apparatuses of ruling, rather than being thought of as "natural" and therefore unalterable.[20]

The second issue is that gender continues to make a difference in educational settings. To paraphrase Somer Brodribb in her article "Apolitical Correctness in a Period of Reaction," this is a climate where the prosecution of a feminist professor who allegedly offends a male student is condoned rather than confronting sexism on Canadian campuses.[21] Several studies have documented the ongoing domination of classroom discourse by male students. Male students are more likely to be assertive, not out of malice but simply as an expression of socialization; they are also more likely to resort to gender stereotypes, make sexist comments, interrupt when women speak and create an inhospitable environment for women. Some of the criticism of Women's Studies courses that Nancy Porter and Marlene Eileenchild encountered in their study "became personally directed toward some of the instructors," the group that bore the burden of single-handedly remedying systemic sexism. Carol Krupnick found that strongly sex-typed men who thought in terms of gender stereotypes were more likely to focus on gender when interacting with women and were more likely to "put a woman down" with a sexist remark.[22]

Anne McIntyre defines sexist classroom behaviour "as a form of sexual harassment poisoning the learning environment and undermining self image and the career aspirations of women."[23] The Status of Women Committee of the Canadian Association of University Teachers (CAUT) states:

> Gender harassment or the "poisoned work environment" usually arises from the holding of stereotyped views of women. It may also result from the acting out of stereotyped expectations in an effort to re-establish the

traditional roles of men and women, or prevent women from achieving equity in rank and status. In its milder and more common form, gender harassment consists of negative comments about the general unsuitability of women for the professional work in which they are involved or the status to which they aspire.[24]

Yet a common stereotype of Women's Studies courses is that they are engaged in "male bashing" and "feminist teachers can face some of the same problems as women students in class."[25] Distinction occurs partly because women are evaluated by different and harsher standards than that of their male counterparts. Male standards are often imposed on women who are then rejected by men because they are not "feminine enough," or they do not advocate a traditional feminine position. Jane Gordon suggests that women's "lack of authority makes it harder to change negative decisions."[26]

The "chilly climate" for women in post-secondary education that was first documented two decades ago still exists for women on college campuses today. In both the 1982 seminal work entitled *The Classroom Climate: A Chilly One for Women?* and the 1995 publication *The Chilly Climate for Faculty Women,* patterns of discrimination against women students were documented and identified as a lack of adequate career advisement, a paucity of appropriate female role models, a failure to engage females in classroom discussions and a decline in career aspirations of women faculty.[27] The continuing need for Women's Studies is evident when college practices continue to contribute to the subtle and not-so-subtle marginalization and exclusion of women. College administrators are often curiously silent about feminist accomplishments when they speak about activities on campus.[28] As Linda Briskin comments, women experience "otherness" and they suffer the consequences of being perceived as outsiders. She observes that women are marginalized in academic institutions when it comes to acquiring power to make decisions and to specify who sets the agenda.[29] Jane Gordon has commented that the difficulties women face take several forms, including a lack of participation; exclusion from centres of authority; under-representation of women's concerns; difficulty in establishing themselves as serious scholars; devaluation of feminine pedagogical styles; and a failure on the part of the administration "to recognize and provide appropriate support systems including women's studies programs, women's centres and recreational facilities."[30]

A third issue involves the intricate relationship between women's rights and religious and cultural imperatives. The subject of Women's Studies focuses on the institutional and attitudinal roots of social, economic, political, cultural and religious discrimination against women. Forms of discrimination against women (and other oppressed groups) are the basis for the establishment of women's rights and the enactment of human rights codes to protect these rights.[31] The distorted and overly simplified inference of the male student ("men are responsible for all the evils of history") suggests that a teacher pointing out facts (that men have been in positions of power and in some instances have perpetuated injustices) in a classroom discussion creates a poisoned environment for individuals who subscribe to patriarchy and the unequal status of women. While the student in question should be allowed air time to express his opinion, the individual should not be accorded the right of censorship in a classroom setting. Even though patriarchy and its practices are now considered anathema to societies governed by human rights codes, the finding of guilt based on discrimination suggests that the male student was within his rights (claiming harassment and discrimination based on sex) by arguing that my Women's Studies lectures were offensive. Such a claim makes a mockery of the Canadian Human Rights Code and the resulting censorship that prevents a classroom discussion of women's rights is an egregious violation of freedom of speech and interferes with the proper role of the teacher.[32]

Given that feminism is about choice, I provided the two Muslim women with opportunities to discuss their concerns when they demonstrated that they were having difficulties with the curriculum. At the same time, it was important to discuss the rigid belief system that considers the subordinate status of women as a sacrosanct and unassailable good and to explore how this belief system is manifested. One woman argued, for example, that all men in Canada ought to have four wives as prescribed by her religion because the population of women exceeds that of men. Resorting to cultural explanations of women's devalued status reasserts conceptual gender biases and invokes defensiveness and combativeness rather than logic and reason. According to McIntyre, "[A]ntifeminism is overtly contemptuous of feminists, feminist research is labeled unscholarly, feminist comment is dismissed as propaganda and ... feminist teachers are described as unqualified."[33] The renowned religious historian Karen Armstrong points out that in fundamentalist religious dogma (which adheres to a deferential position for women), the "women's liberation movement fills fundamentalist men and women alike with terror."[34]

Claims for an exemption from women's rights on cultural grounds exacerbate the difficulty in moving towards women's full equality. While cultural sensitivity is important, it is also critical to acknowledge that cultural practices have subordinated women's rights (particularly in light of the co-existence of multiple levels of oppression) while disguising the universality of a masculine determination of power and privilege. Departure from gender-based tradition is framed as a challenge to cultural propriety, yet a critical reading of culture exposes its ideological nature in the realm of social relations that is crucial to the establishment of hegemony and to circumscribing women's lives.

As a fourth point, to appropriately deal with the rights of all people, women's rights must be understood to be human rights. This will require a transformation of prevailing concepts that define traditional formulations of human rights based on a male model as "normative."[35] Few governments have committed to equality as a basic human right, thus the separation of women's rights from human rights perpetuates the secondary status of women. Human rights discourse and jurisprudence are constructed to give primacy to civil and political rights that protect men in public life and in their relationship with government.[36] Operations within public spheres of commerce, government and the workplace (areas traditionally associated with men) speak to male political life, given that half the "persons" addressed by such rights have little power in their community. Since most of women's experiences of human rights abuses are gendered, and human rights principles and practices have not fully integrated gender-specific abuses, there is inherent bias against women.

According to Harriet Charlesworth, "human rights are men's rights inasmuch as women's freedom, dignity and equality are persistently compromised in ways that men's rights are not." Statements of neutrality, objectivity and universality that are exclusionary of women serve as part of a system of relations of ruling that regard the concerns of men as human concerns and those of women as a distinct and limited category.[37] In Charlotte Bunch's words, "Male oriented biases have tended to recognize only the gender component of certain cases ... whose victims are male."[38] Traditional rules concerning civil and political rights of state responsibility obscure structures of women's universal subordination because they do not define violations against women as human rights infractions; rather, they deal with the harm done to women as a "private" matter and do not respond to injuries women sustain on a continuous basis.

The fifth and final point deals with issues of academic freedom and free speech. For the most part, colleges, unlike universities, do not have clauses in their collective agreements with respect to academic freedom, although some Equity Centres allege to use the concept set against the responsibility not to engage in discrimination.[39] Academic freedom reflects the social cultural context of the college, premised on an exchange of differing perspectives to propose revisions to prevailing wisdom. Such rights empower members of the academic community rather than imposing restrictions as one side of a "politically correct" debate. It provides a forum for the innovative and provocative, ensuring that faculty are free to critique the college and are protected from institutional censorship. Academic freedom applies almost exclusively to faculty who advocate change to the status quo and is rarely applied to those who uphold the maintenance of the system.[40] For feminists, academic freedom encourages the pursuit of cutting-edge teaching, learning and research that challenges androcentric and ethnocentric ideas.

One test of the civil culture of a college is to use the model developed by Women's Studies — the paradigm of knowledge that eliminates older philosophical traditions and distinctions between subject and object. According to Catharine MacKinnon, restrictive practices that limit a faculty's work transform the conventional meaning of academic freedom from protection to exclusion that reinforces social inequalities.[41] In terms of feminism, freedom of expression and equality cannot be separated. When the Universal Declaration of Human Rights advocated freedom of speech, it was the intention "never to allow the barbarous acts which outraged the conscience of mankind [*sic*] to be repeated through the deliberate silencing of voices."[42] The Canadian Charter of Rights and Freedoms is premised on the notion of offering protection to all persons with respect to equality, freedom of speech and democratic rights. The Charter explicitly acknowledges a compelling relationship between individual freedoms and equality provisions, and Western courts have traditionally balanced freedom of speech against other rights and values such as equity.[43] Similar to other grounds of discrimination in defence of a "bona fide occupational requirement," balance must be struck between the fundamental value of free speech and the freedom from discrimination.[44] This provision anticipates that, in limited employment situations such as education, free speech is a necessary qualification and one of the highest purposes of the college in a democratic society.

NOTES

1. Linda Hurst, "Politically Correct? Think Before You Speak," *The Toronto Star*, 7 August 1991, A1, A12. In Ontario, in 1994, the Antiracism and Ethnocultural Equity Policy was announced, together with guidelines and policy initiatives in a document entitled *Framework Regarding Harassment and Discrimination in Ontario Universities and Colleges* (Ontario Ministry of Education and Training, 1993). These framework documents established the government's "zero tolerance" policy (a phrase borrowed from the Reagan-era war on drugs) and inaugurated procedures to monitor conduct on university and college campuses. See also Alan Kroker, Marilyn Kroker and David Cooke, *Panic Encyclopedia: The Definitive Guide to the Postmodern Scene* (New York: St. Martin's Press, 1989).

2. For further discussion of ideas raised here, see Jack Granatstein, "Political Correctness and Free Speech," *The Toronto Star*, 14 April 1999, A12; Canadian Civil Liberties Association, "Submission to the Honorable Dave Cooke, Minister of Education and Training for Ontario, Re: Framework Regarding Prevention of Harassment and Discrimination in Ontario Universities" (Toronto, March 15, 1994); Alaina Stuart, "Truth, the State and Democracy: The Scope of the Legal Right of Free Expression," *Canadian Journal of Communication* 17 (1992), 343–360; Alan Borovoy, "Campus Thought Police Give Substance to Phantom," *The Toronto Star*, 1 February 1993, A18; Elaine Shills, "The Idea of a University and the Right to Academic Freedom," in Patricia Alcoach, ed., *International Higher Education: An Encyclopedia*, Vol. 1 (New York: Garland Publishing, 2000), 1–22; Cyril Talpade Mohanty, "Dangerous Territories, Territorial Power and Education," in Leslie Roman and Linda Eyre, eds., *Dangerous Territories: Struggles for Difference and Equality in Education* (New York: Routledge 1997), 66–78; Sheila Slaughter, "Dirty Little Cases: Academic Freedom, Governance and Professionalism," *New Directions for Public Education* 88 (Winter 1998), 59–87; and Michael Horn, "Canadian Universities, Academic Freedom, Labour and the Left," *Labour/Le Travail* 46 (Fall 2000), 439–468.

3. See, for example, Reg Whitaker, "The Cutting Edge of Ontario's Bad Law," *The Globe and Mail*, 6 January 1994, B4; Susan Warson, "BOG Rejects Harassment Policy," *Dalhousie News*, 30 March 1998, 3; Janice Drakich, Martha Taylor and Janice Bankier, "Academic Freedom *Is* the Inclusive University," *CAUT Bulletin: Status of Women Supplement* (1994), 2–3; Sara Devine, "Report on an Allegation

of Harassment under the University of Victoria Harassment Policy and Procedures" (Office of Equity Issues, University of Victoria, July 28, 1994); Arthur Nelson, "A Complaint Against Professor Ken Westhues in Accordance with Policy 33" (University of Waterloo Faculty Association, March 24, 1994); Francis Bula, "Gender War in UVIC Department Created Cruel Climate Report Says," *Vancouver Sun*, 24 January 1994, A2; and Clare Sommers, *Who Stole Feminism? How Women Have Betrayed Women* (New York: Simon and Schuster, 1998).

4. Ontario Ministry of Education and Training, *Framework Regarding Harassment and Discrimination in Ontario Universities and Colleges* (Toronto: Queen's Printer, 1993). See also David Cooke, Minister of Education and Training, Letter to Universities and the Media, February 9, 1994; Brian Linewood, "Tolerance for Zero Tolerance," *The Toronto Star*, 26 October 1994, D6; and Kroker, Kroker and Cooke, *Panic Encyclopedia*.

5. Ontario Council of Regents Task Force, *Guidelines for Centres of Equity* (Toronto: Queen's Park, January 1994), 41.

6. See Paul Clark, "Canadian Public School Teachers and Free Speech: Part I–An Introduction," *Education and Law* 8, no. 3 (1998), 295–314; and Patricia Lamay, "Offenders, Victims and Academic Freedom," *Society* (May 1997), 9–11.

7. There are exceptions, as in the case of Humber College in Toronto that has a single campus office and one investigator, who acknowledges being able to mediate the majority of the cases referred to the Equity Centre and who prides himself on the fact that he has never initiated a formal investigation process.

8. Howard Doughty, "A History Lesson," Memo to All Faculty of Seneca College, November 15, 2002, 3.

9. Ibid., 3–4.

10. Ibid., 4.

11. One feminist professor teaching at an Ontario university pointed out that "I recently received a rude and angry note from a male student who had been exceedingly respectful all year, until I gave him a low grade on his term paper. The student's message seemed clear to me. He had agreed to collude in the pretense that I was the one in charge until I dared to claim that position in a way that crossed him; at that point, I was to be crushed." See Susan Heald, "Pianos to Pedagogy: Pursuing the Educational Subject," in Himani Bannerji, Linda Carty, Kari Dehli, Susan Heald and Karen McKenna, eds., *Unsettling Relations: The University as a Site of Feminist Struggles* (Toronto: Women's Press, 1991), 129–149.

12. By way of examples of the students' complaints, I cite the following. The male student claimed that he was not wanted in class because of his gender. Part of the evidence he submitted was the fact that when he walked into the middle of a class (some three weeks after classes commenced), impertinently drawing attention to himself by saying "hello," he was "offended" when I indicated that he should unobtrusively take his seat. He was unique in his complaints among the male and female students who took my class in the fall of 2001 (including another male student in the same section), as well as female and male students in the past. I submitted to the Equity Centre investigator lecture topics, text and videos that

offered gender inclusive material, as well as a demonstration of the way I model equity and encourage the validation of all student voices by taking turns speaking. One of the female students objected to my approach to teaching, stating, "I am not paying for her to come to class and tell us her opinion about women in society." In my response to the Equity Centre, I cited the fact that I had established and taught an Introduction to Women's Studies course (as well as nineteen other college-level courses) over a twenty-seven-year career. I noted that I had taught at Durham College and had guest lectured at OISE/UT, York and Ryerson Universities. It was stated that the course reflects my doctoral work in Women's Studies and experiential knowledge gleaned from three and a half decades in the women's, labour, peace and anti-racist movements. The course also incorporated concepts and examples from the work of various professors with whom I had team taught the course, feminist scholars who are among colleagues and friends and feminist publications that keep me current in the field and to which I had made contributions in a rather extensive research career.

13. At the writing of this chapter, the documentation is between 400 and 500 pages, which I jokingly measure by the pound.

14. Stanley Gershman, "Amended Submission on Behalf of Dr. Diane Meaghan Regarding Discrimination and Harassment Complaints" (Toronto, Ontario, Seneca College, March 14, 2002), 6.

15. Gerald Gull, *The Canadian Legal System*, 2d ed. (Toronto: Carswell, 1983), 261.

16. Adelyn Bowland, *The 2001 Annotated Ontario Human Rights Code* (Toronto: Carswell, 2001), 61. My representative concluded that "there is no virtue in allowing the Human Rights office to tarnish the reputation of Diane Meaghan with a finding of a Human Rights violation against one of her students in order to justify the onerous and dilatory investigatory process that was undertaken in this matter. Nor is there any virtue in allowing the Human Rights office to settle this case by granting the male complainant any justification by finding him to be the victim of an act of discrimination" (Gershman, "Ammended Submission ...," 2).

17. Dorothy E. Smith, "An Analysis of Ideological Structure and How Women are Excluded: Considerations for Academic Women," *The Canadian Review of Sociology and Anthropology* 12, no. 4 (1975), 353–369, and *The Everyday World as Problematic: A Feminist Sociology* (Toronto: University of Toronto Press, 1987). Smith suggests that the social organization of knowledge can be used to challenge how the social and historical exist in everyday lived experiences at the point of disjuncture with conceptual practices of power within institutions. A materialist historical understanding treats experience as part of an interpretative relation rather than valorizing any individual or group experience as a repository of "truth." It discloses the ideological character of a discourse that objectifies and dominates while providing a means by which to actively acquire knowledge. See Smith, *The Everyday World as Problematic* and *The Conceptual Practices of Power: A Feminist Sociology of Knowledge* (Boston: Northeastern University Press, 1990).

18. Feminist scholars have challenged the claim of neutrality in the theories, structures and institutions constructed by men. While one of the students who challenged my authority in class was male as was the Equity Centre investigator, acting chair

of my department and president of the college, it is important to point out that not only have I been supported by feminist friends and colleagues but I also experienced exceptional assistance and advocacy from my union representative, a number of colleagues and a human rights lawyer, all of whom are men.

19. Smith, *The Conceptual Practices of Power.*

20. Issues such as the gender and race of both the professor and student influence classroom interactions. Ellen Kashak found that women students rate their female professors equally with male professors on such variables as effective/ineffective, concerned/unconcerned, likeable/not likeable and excellent/poor. Female students did not discriminate on the basis of sex, except to choose to take a course from another female professor. Male students, however, assigned higher ratings to male professors on these variable regardless of the subject matter. See Ellen Kashak, "Sex Bias in Student Evaluations of College Professors," *Psychology of Women Quarterly* 3, no. 3 (1998), 235–241.

21. Somer Brodribb, "Apolitical Correctness in a Period of Reaction," *CAUT Bulletin: Status of Women Supplement* (1994), 5.

22. Nancy Porter and Marlene Eileenchild, *The Effectiveness of Women's Studies Teaching* (Washington, DC: National Institute of Education, 1990), 37; and Carol Krupnick, "Women and Men in the Classroom, Inequality and Its Remedies," *On Teaching and Learning* 1, no. 2 (May 1995), 18–25. See also Cheris Kramarae and Pat Treichler, "Power Relationships in the Classroom," in Susan Gabriel and Ila Smithson, eds., *Gender in the Classroom: Power and Pedagogy* (Urbana: University of Illinois Press, 1990), 41–59.

23. Anne McIntyre, *Teaching Women's Studies: Feminist Theory/Feminist Activism* (New York: Routledge, 1998), 239.

24. Jane Gordon, "Experiencing Academic Life: A Review Essay," *CAUT Status of Women* (Ottawa: Canadian Association of University Teachers, 1998), 2.

25. Kramarae and Treichler, "Power Relationships in the Classroom," 51–53. Professor Mary Hart of the University of Wisconsin described what happened to her when a small group of neo-conservative students ganged up on her in class. "They made a point of ignoring me, avoiding eye contact and disrupted the class with loud sighs and talk among themselves. Once disrespectful behavior such as this gets started, it can escalate, drawing in other students including some women and ruining the course" (Krupnick, "Women and Men in the Classroom, Inequality and Its Remedies," 24).

26. Gordon, "Experiencing Academic Life," 2. See also Anne Dagg and Patricia Thompson, *Miseducation: Women and Canadian Postsecondary Institutions* (Toronto: Ontario Institute for Studies in Education/University of Toronto, 1998), and Huana Zhu, "The Testimony of Women Writers: The Situation of Women in China Today," in Julie Peters and Andrea Wolper, eds., *Women's Rights, Human Rights: International Feminist Perspectives* (New York: Routledge, 1995), 96–102.

27. Roberta Hall, *The Classroom Climate: A Chilly One for Women?* (Washington, DC: Project on the Status and Education of Women, Association of American Colleges, 1982); The Chilly Collective, *The Chilly Climate for Women Faculty*

(Waterloo: Wilfrid Laurier University Press, 1995); and Frances Maher and Mary Kay Thompson Tetrault, *The Feminist Classroom: An Inside Look at How Professors and Students Are Transforming Higher Education for a Diverse Society* (New York: Basic Books, 1994).

28. See, for example, Renee Priegert Coulter, "Introduction," *CAUT Status of Women* (Ottawa: Canadian Association of University Teachers, 1998); and Carolyn Green, "Issues Within Female Intensive Disciplines," *CAUT Status of Women* (Ottawa: Canadian Association of University Teachers, 1998), 8.

29. Linda Briskin, "A Feminist Politic for the University: Beyond Individual Victimization and Toward a Transformed Academy," *CAUT Status of Women* (Ottawa: Canadian Association of University Teachers, 1998), 10. According to Statistics Canada, the enrolment of females within Ontario community colleges increased to 54 percent of the college population. These data suggest that the education of women is a central task of the colleges and the nature and quality of that education ought to be assessed with respect to its suitability. Statistics Canada, "Learning for Self-Direction in the Classroom: The Pattern of a Transition Process," *Studies in Higher Education* 1, no. 1 (1998), 5–72.

30. Gordon, "Experiencing Academic Life," 2.

31. Stanley Gershman, "Amended Submission," Report to Nimmi Pitt, Vice-President, Human Resources (Toronto, Ontario, Seneca College, July 26, 2002), 2.

32. Ibid.

33. McIntyre, *Teaching Women's Studies,* 7.

34. Karen Armstrong, *The Battle for God* (New York: Ballantine Books, 2000), xi. Armstrong cites a female Roman Catholic leader of the U.S. Moral Majority as stating that "feminism is a disease and the cause of all the world's ills." One can only speculate as to what an Equity Centre would do if a small Taliban Madrassah (study group) were established on campus (where male students, the only kind, are taught fundamentalist tenets concerning the treatment of women), and a feminist professor insisted on teaching the class, in which she or he suggested that women should be equal with men in educational, employment, economic and healthcare matters as well as in the family and in sexual matters. Gershman, "Amended Submission," 8.

35. Julie Peters and Andrea Wolper, "Introduction," in Peters and Wolper, eds., *Women's Rights, Human Rights*, 2.

36. Harriet Charlesworth, "Human Rights as Men's Rights," in Peters and Wolper, eds., *Human Rights, Women's Rights*, 103.

37. Ibid., 103, 105.

38. Charlotte Bunch, "Transforming Human Rights from a Feminist Perspective," in Peters and Wolper, eds., *Women's Rights, Human Rights*, 15.

39. Academic freedom is commonly understood to apply to post-secondary educational institutions where differences in views and values are respected and protected. As an exclusive right of the academic and scientific communities, it is

taken to mean that faculty in particular are protected against interference and retribution by society when they advance knowledge that may be at odds with extant
policies and procedures of the state (Marilyn Dietz, "The Exclusion of Inclusion,"
CAUT Status of Women Supplement [Ottawa: Canadian Association of University
Teachers, 1994], 9). It is applied almost exclusively to faculty who advocate
change to the status quo and rarely pertains to those who uphold the maintenance
of the system (Drakich, Taylor and Bankier, "Academic Freedom *Is* the Inclusive
University"). "Since the concept of academic freedom is fundamental to the structure and philosophy of the modern college," Lynn Menard argues that problems
arise for such institutions that cannot entertain conflicting ideological and political views ("The Future of Academic Freedom," *Academe* 8 [May/June 1993], 12).

40. See Thelma McCormick, "Politically Correct," *Canadian Forum* (September
1991), 8–10.

41. Catharine MacKinnon, *Only Words* (Boston: Harvard University Press, 1993), 78.

42. Lisa Ashworthy, "Citizenship Revised," in Nira Yuval-Davis and Pnina Webner,
eds., *Women, Citizenship and Difference* (London: Zed Books, 1979), 7.

43. Drakich, Taylor and Bankier, "Academic Freedom *Is* the Inclusive University," 10.

44. National Association of Women and the Law, *Human Rights Legislation: How It
Can Work for You* (Ottawa: NAWL, 1998), 10.

CHAPTER 10

AGENTS OF CHANGE?
A STUDY OF EQUITY PRACTITIONERS
IN CANADIAN UNIVERSITIES

Carol Agocs, Reem Attieh & Martin Cooke

DURING THE 1980S AND 1990S IN CANADA, many universities appointed staff specialists in response to the rapid growth in the diversity of
student populations, pressures from faculty and students concerned
about discrimination and, most important, the requirements of the Federal Contractors Program that took effect in 1987. These new equity-
related occupations deal with employment equity, human rights, race
relations, sexual harassment, the status of women and services to
Aboriginal people and to persons with disabilities who work or study in
universities. In theory, an affirmative action or employment and educational equity program is an exercise in large-scale organizational change.
As such, an organization may employ equity practitioners whose expertise and efforts could help to bring about change in the organization's
policies, practices and culture in order to remove discriminatory barriers
and create a more inclusive environment that better meets the needs of
women, racialized minorities, persons with disabilities and Aboriginal
people.[1] In some organizations, equity practitioners might be considered
to be "change agents," at least from the perspective of equity policy and
the disadvantaged groups that such policies are designed to assist.

This chapter analyzes the responses of sixty-nine equity practitioners from thirty-one Canadian universities who participated in a national survey in 1998–99.[2] The survey was conducted to assess the likelihood of the practitioners being able to function effectively as agents of transformative change on behalf of marginalized groups within their university organizations. The analysis focuses on the tensions and contradictions inherent in equity practitioners' relationships with the organizations in which they work. It examines (1) their identities and personal commitment to equity; (2) the degree to which their mandates focus on organizational issues as opposed to assistance to individuals; and (3) the placement of their roles within the structure of power and influence in universities.

The survey responses demonstrate a high level of commitment to values and actions that are supportive of equity-related change among equity practitioners, most of whom are women, Aboriginal persons or members of racialized minorities. However, many equity practitioners appear to be hindered in their desires to bring about transformative change by the limitations of their mandates and positions within the university's power structure. Those few equity practitioners who have organization-wide mandates and some access to power are best positioned to function effectively as organizational change agents. These findings point to the central importance of commitment and support for equity-related change from administrative and academic leaders, as well as the broader strategic context of change that includes political pressures from advocates of marginalized groups and effective enforcement of government equity regulations.

EMPLOYMENT AND EDUCATIONAL EQUITY INITIATIVES

Available data demonstrate both the increasing diversity of the population of university students and the ongoing lack of diversity among faculty in Canadian universities. In 1998, women earned 59 percent of bachelor degrees and first professional degrees, and 35.5 percent of earned doctorates; 49 percent of PhD students were women. In 1996, the most recent data available at this writing, 34.4 percent of the university faculty workforce were women: this workforce included anyone who worked in this occupation between January 1, 1995 and May 11, 1996, whether full time or part time, and may be regarded as the

AGENTS OF CHANGE?
A STUDY OF EQUITY PRACTITIONERS IN CANADIAN UNIVERSITIES

academic availability pool.[3] Yet in 2001–02, only 25 percent of tenured full-time university educators were women, while 39 percent of tenure-track and 42 percent of non-tenured full-time faculty were women.[4] A rapidly growing proportion of the student population, and of holders of doctoral degrees, are immigrants or members of racialized minorities. Thirteen percent of university graduates in 1999–2000 were "visible minorities," and over 40 percent of immigrants of working age who arrived in the 1990s had university degrees as of 2001. Young adult immigrants were more likely than the rest of the population to attend university in the 1990s.[5] While no current data are available regarding the proportion of Canadian university faculty who are members of racial minorities or immigrants, there are indications that these groups are poorly represented among the faculty in most fields of study.[6] Canadian census data for 1996 showed that 18.7 percent of the workforce of those having earned doctorates were visible minorities. Indeed, 38.5 percent of doctorates in engineering and applied sciences, and 46.4 percent of doctorates in engineering and applied sciences technologies and trades, were held by visible minorities.[7] However, only 12 percent of the workforce of university professors were visible minorities. Data on visible minority representation among people employed as full-time university educators have not been available.

Aboriginal people and persons with disabilities are increasing in number as students, although they are still under-represented in comparison with their representation in the Canadian population. Universities are being challenged to become more accessible to prospective Aboriginal and disabled students and to accommodate their needs and aspirations. In 2000–01, 3.3 percent of first year students were Aboriginal, and 5 percent were persons with disabilities.[8] As of 1996, 0.3 percent of the workforce holding earned doctorates and 0.5 percent of working university professors were Aboriginal. Their representation among students and full-time university educators is unknown, and there are no recent data on people with disabilities who are students, who hold doctorates or who are employed as university professors. The lack of current information regarding the representation of racial minorities, Aboriginal people and persons with disabilities among Canadian university faculty and holders of a doctorate is a significant problem in itself, and is symptomatic of the institutionalized inequality and discrimination in university employment.

The environment in which the positions of equity practitioners have emerged has been a politicized one. Among the pressures on universities have been legal liabilities arising from human rights complaints on grounds including sexual and racial harassment. Whether settled informally or by decisions of administrative tribunals or courts, such cases have led to negative publicity and financial consequences for universities. In some universities (Queen's, for example), equity clauses have been negotiated in collective agreements between faculty unions and the administration, leading to a need for specialized equity-related expertise. In the 1970s and 1980s, advocacy by student and faculty organizations representing women, Black students, Aboriginals and other groups brought political pressures on university administrations to make the university more accessible, to create more inclusive curricula and to employ more members of under-represented groups. However, such advocacy was met in the 1990s with fierce resistance that transformed pro-equity arguments and initiatives into "politically correct" acts carried out by "thought police" seeking to destroy the rule of merit in the university.[9] Overall, universities have responded cautiously and conservatively to these countervailing pressures. While a few institutions have made fairly significant commitments to equity programs, many others have done only what is required to satisfy the lenient standards of the Federal Contractors Program compliance review.

Government regulation and legislation in the mid to late 1980s was the dominant influence on Canadian universities that committed resources to equity. The Federal Contractors Program (FCP) is one of two federal policy instruments under which employers are required to implement employment equity for women, visible minorities, Aboriginal people and persons with disabilities (referred to as the "designated groups" under Canadian employment equity policy). The FCP requires organizations that employ 100 or more people, and that receive federal grants or contracts worth $200,000 or more, to implement employment equity programs and be subject to compliance reviews. The FCP requirements include (1) conducting an employment equity census and maintaining data on the representation of women, visible minorities, Aboriginal people and persons with disabilities in the organization's workforce; (2) preparing an annual report to the FCP, which is not required to be available to the public; (3) setting goals and timetables for improving the representation of under-represented groups; (4) implementing "special measures" to remove barriers and accommodate diversity in order to encourage the full participation of these groups in employment; and (5) permitting FCP staff to review the university's compliance with FCP requirements from time to time.[10] Canadian universities are not required by legislation or regulation to implement affirmative educational equity programs, but are covered by human rights codes prohibiting discrimination in relation to provision of services as well as employment.

There is evidence that Canadian employment equity policy has had small positive effects on increasing the representation of visible minorities and decreasing occupational segregation in participating organizations. Furthermore, some characteristics of employment equity programs, notably degree of formalization — including formal written goals, plans and timetables, a formal administrator and regular audits — demonstrate significant correlations with more representative hiring of racial minorities.[11] The complex and changing environment in which equity programs are implemented in Canadian universities, and the fact that most larger universities are FCP participants, makes it difficult to systematically evaluate the results of the FCP and the work of equity practitioners as change agents. Penni Stewart and Janice Drakich found that strong employment equity strategies made a difference in the recruitment and rank distribution of women faculty in seventeen Ontario universities from 1980 to 1990.[12] Such strategies included affirmative searches and advertising for faculty positions and peer monitoring of the hiring process at the departmental level — measures intended to ensure fair and merit-based hiring.

In the late 1980s, the province of Ontario provided incentive grants to universities to establish staff positions for employment equity practitioners. Since that time, 46 percent of Canadian universities, including nearly all the larger institutions, have become participants in the FCP and have established various kinds of staff positions for equity practitioners. However, these positions have undergone a variety of changes over the past decade as universities and provincial governments have provided and then withdrawn funding, and commitment to equity has waxed and waned with the rise and fall of political support. The 1990s were also a time of shrinking financial support for universities from federal and most provincial governments. As a result, numbers of full-time faculty decreased by 11 percent between 1992 and 1997 and hiring of new faculty and staff declined, as did resources committed to equity.[13] This financial squeeze has undermined efforts to improve the representation of women and minorities on faculties.

While there have been improvements in the representation of women among new appointments to faculty positions in universities in Canada,[14] patterns of gender inequality have been persistent and well documented.[15] There has been little research on under-representation and other issues of inequality faced by women and men who are members of racialized minorities, Aboriginals or persons with disabilities in Canadian university employment.[16] However, the conclusion suggested by the existing literature on universities is that inequality on the basis of gender and race is a persisting issue that continues to require significant efforts to bring about organizational change.

OVERVIEW OF THE RESEARCH ISSUES

In our survey, we focused our research questions on the personal characteristics of equity practitioners, their roles in the organization and the position of these roles in the context of power relations within the university. Each of these areas of enquiry pose a tension or contradiction that arise from the complex political and organizational environment within which equity practitioners work.

Personal Characteristics and Values

To what extent do equity practitioners demonstrate personal characteristics and claim values that are consistent with a commitment to equity-related change? One might assume that an organization, particularly a university, that creates and maintains positions for human rights or equity officers would seek to staff them with individuals who have personal commitments to equality and past experience in working or advocating for equity for disadvantaged groups.

However, perhaps in creating positions for equity professionals, universities are not seeking organizational change but, instead, are fulfilling the letter of a regulatory requirement or responding in a visible but minimal way to political pressures from marginalized groups and their advocates. If this is the case, one might expect that universities would not staff equity-related positions with committed and effective advocates for change, since such individuals could become irritants to decision-makers whose priority it is to maintain the status quo and the organization's public image. Our analysis examines whether or not there is coherence or fit between the personal values and past experience of equity practitioners and the expectation that they function as agents of change on behalf of disadvantaged groups.

Equity Practitioners' Roles and Mandates

To what extent are equity practitioners given a mandate to act as agents of organizational change? On one hand, we might expect that an equity practitioner's role or job description would entail activities intended to bring about change in the university's policies, practices, programs, culture and human resources mix, so that the organization would better meet the needs of a more diverse population. On the other hand, it is possible that the primary function of the equity practitioner's role is to defuse pressures for organizational change. The equity practitioner may serve to buffer administrators against pressures for change, or assist individual members of disadvantaged groups to live with discrimination or change themselves in order to survive in or conform to the organization as it is. Universities may appoint equity practitioners primarily in order to fulfill the technical record-keeping and reporting requirements of the FCP, or to support such traditional human resource management functions as employee relations and training.

Our analysis seeks to understand the degree to which the scope and mandate of equity practitioners' roles, and the activities on which they spend their time, are directed towards organizational change or towards changing individuals who are members of groups that have suffered exclusion and discrimination in universities. Their orientation towards either organizational or individualized change may be attached to their organizational roles, be rooted in personal value commitments or be a combination of values and mandate.

Situating Equity Practitioners' Roles in the Context of Power Relations

Where do the roles of equity practitioners fit within the organizational structure of power and influence in the university? They can be considered boundary roles in that they deal with transactions between institutionalized university structures and programs and members of under-served or under-represented groups who have been disadvantaged by those traditional structures in terms of access to employment or study. In practice, their ability to bring about organizational change from a position of marginality within the organization's structure depends upon their access to the power and resources that are the levers of change. Previous research and theory suggests that in order for equity practitioners to function as effective agents of organizational change, they must have power — defined by Rosabeth Moss Kanter as "the ability to mobilize resources to get things done."[17] Kanter proposes that this kind of power comes from supportive ties with people at higher levels in the hierarchy, access to information on which organizational politics and decision-making is based and access to resources, notably, budgets and time. Kanter also notes that power is enhanced by visible success in managing problems that are considered priorities by organizational decision-makers.

THEORETICAL PERSPECTIVES ON THE ROLE OF THE CHANGE AGENT

Most published research on large-scale organizational change deals with the private sector and with change undertaken to promote efficiency, effectiveness or productivity in order to maximize profit or market share. Published discussions of roles of change agents tend to describe the exploits of corporate leaders or to discuss projects undertaken by external consultants hired by top management to carry out a change strategy on its behalf.[18] While a few studies address internal change agents' roles,[19] literature on change agents tends to focus on their personal characteristics rather than situating them within the structure and culture of the organization.[20]

In a survey of 1,500 organization development (OD) practitioners in the U.S., Allan Church, Janine Waclawski and Warner Burke found tension between personal beliefs in the value of transformative organizational change and "surviving the mire of corporate politics."[21] This tension was particularly evident for internal OD practitioners as compared with external consultants. In an earlier study, the same researchers found that while 38 percent of external consultants considered their primary client organization to be quite flexible and open to change, only 17 percent of internal practitioners described their employers in these terms — a significant difference.[22] Thus most internal change practitioners appear to be faced with the reality that transformative change is unlikely, whatever their personal values may be. Moreover, there is survey evidence that corporate OD practitioners are more likely to be involved in technical projects and individual or small group interventions than in system-wide or strategic change.[23] Noel Tichy's early study of change agents working as external consultants in a variety of organizations found a lack of congruence between the progressive values to which OD practitioners were personally committed and the efficiency and output goals of the organizations that hired them.[24]

Much of the literature on organizational change agents reflects an OD frame of reference, with the shortcomings for which this perspective has been criticized. These include managerialist assumptions and inadequate analysis of the structural, political and power-related dimensions of organizational change and the change agent's role.[25] Much of the OD literature views organizational change as a process that is initiated from the top in order to realize senior management's agenda, which conforms to the typical pattern of corporate organizational change.[26] Within this frame of reference, resistance to change is manifested by those in middle and lower ranks whose interests are counter to the top-down change program. The role of the external consultant or the internal change agent is to "manage" this resistance and to facilitate the realization of top management's program — not to initiate or advocate for change that is proposed by, or designed to benefit, relatively powerless and disadvantaged groups of employees or clients.[27]

Equity change in universities is intended to benefit present and prospective employees and students who are members of groups that have been marginalized and under-represented in the past by identifying and removing barriers to their full participation and impediments to their learning. The issue of interest is to understand how policy that is transformative in its intent is implemented within the organizational setting by focusing on the individuals who are given responsibility by the organization to engage with the equity policy framework. We approach our enquiry with the assumptions that the equity change agent's role is strategic and political, in that it exists within a context of countervailing pressures from multiple stakeholders having conflicting interests and varying in their access to power. We also assume that the equity practitioner's role is designed and staffed by the organization's decision-makers to achieve their purposes. Hence both its location in the structure of power relations and the organization's expectations of the change agent's role, which are reflected in its mandate and job description, are significant influences on the degree to which the equity practitioner can facilitate change.

THE EQUITY CHANGE AGENT IN THE UNIVERSITY

Although there is a body of research literature on inequality in universities, there is very little on the roles of equity change agents or the kinds of organizational change that may be effective in bringing about more equitable working and learning environments.[28] Employment equity in Canada, in theory, is a large-scale organizational change project that has the potential to challenge traditional values, practices and routines, and it clearly provokes significant resistance from those privileged by the status quo.[29] As mentioned previously, the role of the equity practitioner is a boundary or marginal role that exists in a state of tension between "insiders" and "outsiders."[30] The equity practitioner must maintain credibility with disadvantaged groups as their advocate in the organization, while maintaining her legitimacy with organizational insiders so that they will accept her and be open to her influence. Yet the equity practitioner's role is inherently quite powerless, since in most instances she is a member of the administrative staff within a two-headed organizational structure and culture where staff tend to be powerless and invisible, while faculty are powerful, valorized and protective of their privileges.

Because of their marginality, their mandate, their newness and their lack of clear career ladders or even locations within the academic or staff structure or culture, equity practitioners' occupations are anomalies within the university. Furthermore, their work, to the extent that it involves organizational change, requires confronting powerful groups and individuals who resist challenges to their established privileges and to traditional assumptions about how the university should operate. Challenging the systemic racism and sexism that is embedded in customary organizational practices is part of the equity practitioner's job. For these reasons the legitimacy of equity programs and those who work in them is frequently attacked, particularly as resource limitations generate heightened levels of conflict.[31] The equity practitioner usually lacks the protection of tenure or job security, and is often silenced by rules or norms of confidentiality and may be unable to effectively defend herself when challenged. If senior academic administrators are unwilling to stand up for equity principles, programs and practitioners, people in these positions may be highly vulnerable. Indeed, there is evidence that equity practitioners experience a high rate of turnover and job restructuring, and the occupational culture of the equity practitioner is rich with stories of the casualties of equity change in universities.[32] Some individuals who were on the original contact list for our survey and who have since left their positions did not leave voluntarily.

The equity practitioner's position as an insider may be doubly complicated if she is a woman or a member of a group that is under-represented and disadvantaged within the university. As a result, many equity practitioners may also experience the discrimination that their occupations exist to address.[33] Dorothy Smith theorizes a distinctive standpoint for women as a gender-based mode of experience in the university, viewed as an institutionalized structure of relations of ruling. Smith notes the contradictions inherent in women's participation in decisions and practices that they had no part in creating, and may indeed loathe, as over time they learn how "to be a subject alienated in an objectified mode."[34] Patricia Hill Collins points out that Black women's position of marginality in academic settings has been both a source of alienation and oppression, and a wellspring of creative insight arising from the standpoint of the "outsider within."[35] Debra Meyerson and Maureen Scully use the term "tempered radicalism" to connote the ambivalence and tension lived by those who identify with and are com-mitted to the organization that employs them, while at the same time they are committed to a value or action framework that is at odds with their organization's dominant culture. Such individuals may be engaged in the dilemma of working within the organization and being successful on its terms, and at the same time trying to change it.[36]

Even though the equity practitioner may not have a secure position as an organizational "insider," from the standpoint of "outsiders" (who include some members of disadvantaged groups), the very existence of the role may be viewed as a form of co-optation, a mechanism for mar-ginalizing and containing pressures for change. This impression may gain strength as the equity practitioner struggles to maintain her legiti-macy as an insider in the face of powerful insiders' resistance to the kinds of change she represents.

We would expect that under these circumstances, equity practi-tioners who have a mandate and a personal commitment to work for organizational change are most likely to survive and be effective if their role provides access to a degree of power within the organization. Kanter has suggested that "change masters" are most effective when they have access to productive power which is based on access to resources (including a budget), information and support from key people. Access to power is mediated and facilitated by formal and informal network ties that link the change agent to others who are within the organization and external to it, as has been demonstrated by research on organizational networks in change.[37]

SURVEY FINDINGS AND DISCUSSION
Personal Characteristics and Values

The survey included several items intended to elicit equity-oriented values that are strongly held — values to which the respondent indicates public commitment or the expenditure of personal time and effort. For example, half the equity practitioners had served as volunteer leaders in organizations representing or advocating for disadvantaged groups. Table 1 shows that nearly half had participated in collective action on behalf of such groups and most practitioners claimed to identify themselves publicly as feminist or anti-racist, or both. Those who endorsed feminist or anti-racist values were most likely to have volunteered in organizations working for disadvantaged groups and to have participated in collective action in their behalf. These responses suggest a high level of commitment to values and action supportive of equity-oriented change, as one might expect among equity practitioners. Half of the survey respondents mentioned a desire to work on behalf of designated groups in response to an open-ended question about why they had accepted their position as an equity practitioner.

Table 1: **Responses to "Statements About Yourself"**

	STRONGLY AGREE	AGREE	NEUTRAL	DISAGREE	STRONGLY DISAGREE	MISSING
I identify myself publicly as a feminist	25 (36.2%)	21 (30.4%)	9 (13.0%)	2 (2.9%)	7 (10.1%)	5 (7.2%)
I identify myself publicly as anti-racist	33 (47.8%)	20 (29.0%)	7 (10.1%)	1 (1.4%)	2 (2.9%)	6 (8.7 %)
I am an active participant on collective action in behalf of disadvantaged groups	14 (20.3%)	18 (26.1%)	15 (21.7%)	11 (15.9%)	4 (5.8%)	7 (10.1%)

As for the designated group characteristics of equity practitioners, responses to the survey indicated that 84 percent were women (of these, 74 percent were able-bodied white women), 12 percent were members of racial minorities, 10 percent were of Aboriginal ancestry and 7 percent were persons with disabilities. By way of comparison, of the Canadian workforce of administrators at the middle-management level in post-secondary education in 1996, 50 percent were women, 6 percent were visible minorities and 1.5 percent were Aboriginal.[38]

Personal experiences may motivate commitment to change: 56.5 percent of respondents strongly agreed or agreed that they had experienced discrimination in an employment or educational setting on the basis of gender, 14.5 percent on the basis of race and 20 percent on the basis of cultural background. Table 2 shows that respondents were likely to have experienced discrimination on the basis of their designated group identity.

However, it is perhaps surprising that as many as one-third of the respondents did not publicly identify themselves as feminist and one-quarter did not publicly identify as anti-racist, and half were not motivated by a desire to assist designated groups when accepting their positions. Only 38 percent of the respondents had done equity-related work in their previous job. An index of equity commitment with values ranging from 1 to 11 was constructed using survey items on degree of commitment and action on behalf of disadvantaged groups. The respondents showed considerable variability on this index, with about 40 percent scoring below the midpoint of the scale. No statistically significant relationships were found in an analysis of correlations among equity-related reasons for accepting the equity practitioner's position and past job, designated group status, experience of discrimination, volunteering, collective action and feminist or anti-racist values. This suggests that equity practitioners accepted their positions for a variety of reasons, aside from a desire to work on behalf of disadvantaged groups. It is important to recognize that individuals end up in equity-related jobs in universities as a result of hiring decisions by the organizations that are based upon considerations known only to the decision-makers. We do not know whether universities prefer or avoid hiring committed activists into equity-related positions, or whether the most active and committed equity practitioners were among the respondents to our survey.

Table 2: **Experience of Discrimination by Designated Group Membership of Equity Practitioners**

| | PERSONAL IDENTIFICATION | | |
	WOMAN	RACIAL MINORITY	FIRST NATIONS	PERSON WITH A DISABILITY
Strongly agree or agree:	N=56	N=8	N=5	N=5

"I have experienced discrimination in an employment or educational setting on the basis of"

	WOMAN	RACIAL MINORITY	FIRST NATIONS	PERSON WITH A DISABILITY
Gender	68%			
Race		75%	40%	
Cultural Background		75%	40%	
Disability				80%

In general, our findings suggest that equity practitioners in Canadian universities have change-oriented personal values and commitments, although they may have had a variety of reasons for accepting their positions. Only one-fifth of the respondents indicated that they intend to be working in the equity field five years from now; most were uncertain as to their future field of work.

Equity Practitioners' Roles and Mandates

We will now assess whether equity practitioners might be hindered in their desires to bring about transformative change by the limitations of their mandates and positions in the structure of power within the university. The survey results demonstrate that equity practitioners differ as to mandate and responsibilities, and that Canadian universities vary widely with respect to arrangements for staffing equity-related positions. The distribution of specialities is shown in table 3. Many equity practitioners are responsible for a broad range of responsibilities and relatively few are specifically specialized in the issues of a single designated group. Eighty-two percent of equity practitioners worked full time, and 18 percent worked part time.

Table 3: Equity Practitioners' Areas of Specialization

Equity, Human Rights, Diversity (general)	24 (34.8%)	Human Resources (general)	7 (10.1%)
Sexual Harassment	10 (14.5%)	Status of Women	2 (2.9%)
Disability	9 (13.0%)	Anti-racism	2 (2.9%)
Ombud, Complaints	5 (7.2%)	Gay, Lesbian, Bisexual	1 (1.4%)
Aboriginal People	6 (8.7%)	Student Services	2 (2.9%)
International Students	1 (1.4%)		

Based on the job titles and descriptions provided by the survey participants, four job categories were created and ranked (table 4). The duties associated with these positions, in addition to administrative tasks, included developing and implementing projects and policies,

Table 4: Job Categories, Titles and Descriptions by Number of Respondents (N=69)

JOB CATEGORY	JOB TITLES	JOB DESCRIPTIONS	NUMBER OF RESPONDENTS
Director	Director, Manager, Chair of Council and Associate VP Equity	Design & implement programs and policies, advocate on behalf of designated groups	20 (29.0%)
Officer	Equity, Sexual Harassment, Human Rights Officers, Ombudsperson	Administer university policies	11 (15.9%)
Co-ordinator	Co-ordinator, Counsellor	Provide services and programs for designated groups	21 (30.4%)
Advisor	Advisor	Assist in resolving problems, mediating complaints, and providing information	17 (24.6%)

advocating on behalf of the designated groups for changes at the university, raising the awareness of faculty, staff and students of various equity related policies and procedures, mediating complaints and providing information.

Survey respondents were asked to characterize the roles that best described their jobs, using a Likert scale. Fifty-six percent indicated that they were often or always a change agent, 34 percent were sometimes, and only 8 percent were rarely or never change agents. The caseworker role was always or often claimed by 38 percent, and rarely or never true for the same proportion.

The examination of equity practitioners' mandates assessed the degree to which each respondent's primary activities focused on organization-wide networks and strategic activities, as compared with primary casework and services to individuals (see table 5). The indicator of an organizational mandate was time spent in meetings with a variety of stakeholders, including designated group representatives, administrators, union representatives, equity committees and other committees, and time spent on the Federal Contractors Program requirements. A primary focus on casework and assistance to individuals was indicated by time primarily devoted to investigating complaints or dealing with concerns of individuals, primarily students.

Table 5: **Number of Respondents by Percentage of Time Spent Monthly on Key Activities**

PERCENT	MEETING WITH KEY STAKEHOLDERS	FCP REQUIREMENTS	INVESTIGATION OF COMPLAINTS	INDIVIDUAL REQUESTS & CONCERNS
0 or no answer	7 (10.1%)	7 (10.1%)	26 (37.7%)	10 (14.5%)
Less than 15	11 (15.9%)	41 (59.4%)	37 (53.6%)	34 (49.3%)
15 to 25	16 (23.2%)	11 (15.9%)	5 (7.2%)	13 (18.8%)
25 to 50	31 (44.9%)	6 (8.7%)	0 (0%)	11 (15.9%)
More than 50	4 (5.8%)	4 (5.8%)	1 (1.4%)	1 (1.4%)

The data suggest that most equity practitioners were extensively involved in meetings with key stakeholders, suggesting an organizational focus to some extent. They also spent more time dealing with individual requests and concerns than on FCP requirements. Some practitioners were more focused than others on providing service to individuals, but most were involved in some mix of organizational and individually oriented activity.

Situating Equity Practitioners' Roles in the Context of Power Relations

The survey occurred at a time of turbulence in the equity field resulting from changes in the political environment. The fact that a fairly large number of persons contacted about the study had left their positions as equity practitioners is indicative of the high degree of change that was taking place in this field. Generally speaking, the occupation of equity practitioner in Canadian universities dates back to 1987 when the Federal Contractors Program began. Only 9 percent of survey respondents' positions predated 1987, 12 percent were created in 1987–88, and the remaining 79 percent were created since then. Twenty-five percent of respondents had been in their jobs for two years or less, and only 45 percent had held their jobs for more than four years. Two-thirds of respondents were the first occupants of their positions. The relative newness of equity practitioners' positions and their short tenure may hinder their ability to influence organizational decisions.

A central interest of this analysis is the position of equity practitioners in the structure of power and authority in the university. Their reporting relationship is one indicator of their proximity to administrative power. Nearly 40 percent of respondents report to the most senior administrators in the university: 26 percent of respondents report to the president or principal and 13 percent report to the vice-president or assistant/associate vice-president. Other respondents reported to the director of human resources (17 percent), the director of equity or equivalent (20 percent), an academic dean (6 percent), or others (10 percent). Proximity to those in authority may have provided access to powerful individuals and some inside information and visibility, but did not necessarily confer power on the equity practitioner herself.

About two-thirds of the respondents had managerial responsibilities in relation to other managers, clerical or administrative assistants, students or volunteers. However, one-third had no managerial role and only 9 percent of respondents had direct reports who were managers. Of the 69 respondents, 29 percent had no budget and 9 percent administered less than $10,000 annually, while 32 percent were responsible for budgets of more than $100,000. However, of those who provided information, 41 percent said that their budgets had decreased over the past five years and 41 percent have had constant budget allocations. Only 18 percent reported a budget increase over the past five years. This variety of managerial and budgetary responsibilities, as well as the differing job categories reported in table 4, suggest that equity practitioners' positions differ considerably in authority and influence.

Among those who worked full time, a wide range in gross annual salary was reported, from $30–39,000 (6 percent) to greater than $80,000 (8 percent), with a median salary category of $50–59,000. At least one graduate degree was reported by 57 percent of the respondents, while 27 percent held only an undergraduate degree and 16 percent did not hold undergraduate or graduate degrees. Only thirteen respondents had doctoral degrees. The educational and salary indicators suggest that few equity practitioners possess the markers of high status in the university.

A composite measure was developed to examine the degree of power and authority that the equity practitioners had within the university, their status in the hierarchy and their access to resources. Those who placed lower on the power index had less power to effect organizational change within the university. The composite power indicator was constructed by combining scores on the following variables: managerial authority as indicated by positions of those who report to the respondent (.520), rank in the organizational hierarchy as indicated by positions of those to whom the respondent reports (.329), job category (.523), annual budget (.712), salary (.759) and the sum of a nine-item scale that measured the degree to which respondent felt as an "outsider" or "insider" within the university (.405). The composite power indicator had a roughly normal distribution, and the Spearman's rho coefficients, shown in parentheses above, indicate the strength of the correlation between each variable and the power indicator as a composite measure. The scores were converted to standard scores for purposes of analysis.

Cross-tabulations using chi-square showed a statistically significant association between designated group membership and the power indicator (dichotomized), with members of racialized minorities and Aboriginal persons tending to have lower power scores. The power and focus indicators have a Spearman's rho of 169, which indicates that they are only weakly correlated and therefore are to some extent measuring distinct phenomena.

The power and organizational focus scores of all equity practitioners were examined in order to determine whether there were differences based on designated group membership. Equity practitioners who identified themselves as racial minorities, Aboriginals or persons with disabilities were few among respondents with high power and organizational focus ratings, and tended to have lower power ratings and an individualized focus and mandate. This may reflect a tendency of universities to hire minorities to deliver services to other minorities, but less frequently to manage the organization's generalized equity programs.

A combination of higher power scores and an organizational focus was more common among equity practitioners who were white women. It is important to recall that the higher end of the power measure is relative to variation within the population of equity practitioners: it is not an indicator of absolute position in the university's power structure, and does not imply access to significant power or resources. A minority of equity practitioners had staff or significant budgets to manage, and salaries were far from high, at best, relative to salaries in the university as a whole.

A statistically significant relationship was found between composite indices of practitioners' power and authority and their involvement in a mandate focussing on strategic organizational change (Pearson correlation=.426, sig..01). This suggests that equity practitioners whose mandate focused on organizational rather than individual issues were more likely to have access to organizational power and influence. Furthermore, a statistically significant positive relationship was found between practitioners' power and their universities' support for the equity practitioner's role (Pearson correlation=.343, sig..01). University support was measured using a composite index, including enlargement of the equity position's scope, increase of the practitioner's budget, supportive policies and commitment by university leaders and absence of resistance and harassment directed towards the practitioner.

Those equity practitioners who had organization-wide mandates and networks and some access to power were best positioned to function effectively as agents of organizational change. Yet their proximity to power in the university does not necessarily mean that they had influence on key decisions made by those who held administrative power in the organization. In general, values on the power index clustered towards the lower end of the ten-point scale, indicating that the majority of equity practitioners had relatively little organizational power. Many respondents indicated that their roles always or often (18 percent) or sometimes (25 percent) involved being a buffer or apologist for the administration.

FACTORS THAT FOSTER AND IMPEDE EQUITY-RELATED CHANGE

What are the implications of our findings concerning the personal characteristics, roles and power of equity practitioners? Given what we know, what is the likelihood that equity practitioners will function effectively as agents of transformative change within their organizations? What organizational conditions would assist them to be effective as change agents? Equity practitioners play diverse roles that contribute in important ways to the access, success and development of marginalized groups within the university. However, few of these positions have access to the power and strategic mandate that are necessary to effectively champion change at the organizational level unless their efforts are supported by significant commitment and assistance from administrative and academic leaders. It is the mandate and location of equity practitioners' positions within the organizational structure, not merely their personal traits and values, that makes it possible for them to function effectively as agents of equity-related organizational change.

We have presented a preliminary and primarily descriptive analysis of responses to a survey of equity practitioners in Canadian universities, a relatively new occupational group. The data paint a picture of a diverse group, most of whom are committed to equity-oriented values and see themselves as change agents within their universities. However, some equity practitioners were hired into their positions with little relevant work experience or personal commitment to equity-related change, and indicated that they accepted the job entirely for career-related reasons. This suggests the need to review the institutions' reasons and criteria for creating and staffing these positions — likely a challenging task for the researcher. It also suggests the desirability of involving informed representatives of the designated groups in making decisions regarding the design of equity practitioners' positions and in the recruitment and selection of their incumbents.

Some equity practitioners have access to power, as indicated by the status, resources and authority available to them, as well as having a role that is focused on strategic activities and connections at the organizational level. These practitioners may be positioned to function effectively as agents of organizational change. Other equity practitioners' roles are focused primarily on services to individuals, and this, in combination with a lack of access to power, may make them unlikely to function as change agents. Our data suggest that many equity practitioners focus on providing support and services to the individual members of under-represented and disadvantaged groups, often with the objective of influencing these individuals to change so that they are able to survive and succeed within the organization as it is.

Equity practitioners delivering services to individuals through providing information, counselling and casework are in a position to make an essential contribution to the survival and success of members of under-represented and disadvantaged groups once they gain access to the university. But these professionals probably do not command the power or possess the mandate to significantly affect decision-making concerning access to the university or organizational change that might address the systemic barriers that contribute to the problems faced by members of disadvantaged groups within the university. Like battlefield medics, these practitioners can alleviate suffering and even save lives, but they can rarely stop the conflict that created the injuries in the first place.

The survey findings concerning power relations point to the importance of developing strategic alliances with more powerful supporters inside and outside the university, as a means of counteracting the powerlessness of their roles and their frequently narrow mandates. The support, sponsorship and legitimacy that they receive from more powerful decision-makers within the university is particularly important, since without a supportive context there is little likelihood of equity-oriented organizational change. Both survey and focus group data also point to the importance of pressures towards change from advocates within and external to the university community that represent the interests and concerns of the designated groups. These advocates play an essential role by strategically critiquing organizational practices and decisions while working collaboratively with equity practitioners who are attempting to bring about changes that will benefit the designated groups. The regulatory context in which universities are situated also has a significant influence on the equity practitioner's effectiveness in working for change. The experience with the FCP reported

Carol Agocs, Reem Attieh & Martin Cooke

by equity practitioners suggests that the compliance review process in the universities has no teeth, and that filing the required report — with little demonstrated action towards equity — is sufficient to pass the compliance audit. The threat of an unfavourable review is one of the equity practitioner's primary means of persuading image-conscious decision-makers to make a serious commitment to equity-related change. Hence weak enforcement of the FCP is a major impediment to such change in universities.

As a conceptual tool for further research, we suggest some hypothetical roles that equity practitioners may play within their institutions, within a context of their mandate and focus (individual or organizational) and their relative power.

Professional: Practitioners with educational credentials and specialized expertise in a professional field, such as counselling, who manage programs designed to assist individual members of designated groups, delivering services to students or others.

Toxic handler: This colourful term was proposed by Peter Frost, who credits managers who "voluntarily shoulder the sadness, frustration, bitterness and anger of others" with saving organizations from "self-destructing."[39] While Frost does not mention equity practitioners as examples of these "healing" roles, they are likely to be present in universities. Ironically, their effectiveness in helping individuals to live with discrimination may serve to shield their organizations from being confronted with the necessity to change. Frost points out that those who play this role are frequently victims of severe stress.

Counsellor: Many equity practitioners deliver counselling, information and problem-solving services to individual students or employees, assisting them to cope with the system. Counsellors are also likely to be well acquainted with those who do not succeed because of unaddressed issues within or external to the university. For example, a focus group with Aboriginal counsellors in post-secondary institutions provided striking examples of the dedication of these practitioners, who spoke of taking Aboriginal students for medical care, feeding them when they were hungry, encouraging them to study and substituting for their family away from home.

· *219* ·

Technician: The FCP requires participating organizations to conduct an employment equity census and maintain a database, to set numerical goals and timetables, and to prepare annual reports. Experienced change agents know that in a university, the case for change must be made with data, for example, by undertaking surveys of the status of women faculty. These technical tasks and skills contribute to strategic change capability, but those who perform them typically have little access to power.

Radical: Equity practitioners who have a strategic and structural analysis of organizational change, and whose mandate confronts them with the need for change, often lack the power to make change happen — or to protect themselves. Anecdotal evidence suggests that the rate of involuntary turnover is high in this occupational group. The principled practitioner may face the same risks as the whistle-blower who identifies and opposes organizational injustices or errors and those in power who are responsible, thus exposing the gap between the organization's purported values and its actual practices. Managerial attempts to discredit or destroy the whistle-blower are likely to be particularly fierce when she "points to systemic abuses in the organization's way of doing business."[40]

Incremental reformer or "tempered radical":[41] An organizational change strategy pursued by many of the equity practitioners who have been in the field for some time is to use their influence and limited resources, and especially their credibility earned through job performance, in support of small change projects that, over time, make a difference.

Administrative ally: Access to a relatively higher level of power and a mandate to deal with organization-wide issues may mean giving priority to the interests of senior administration, not to those of disadvantaged groups, with the result that these resources may not serve as a foundation for change.

Strategic change agent: A few Canadian universities stand out as settings for innovative employment or educational equity initiatives. These institutions tend to have well-resourced and experienced equity staff who have access to the senior administration. It would be of interest to examine the relative influence of the change agent's position and power, commitment to equity on the part of organizational leaders, legal or political activism and other factors that the literature suggests may be significant in effecting organizational change.

*

The survey results depict large-scale changes over the past decade, including creation and elimination of positions, redesign of jobs to include changing combinations of duties and reassignment of reporting relationships. A significant trend has been the loading of a variety of new duties onto the existing workload of equity practitioners. For example, many positions were expanded to include all prohibited grounds of the Human Rights Code rather than being dedicated to one area, such as sexual harassment, while other positions were reduced to part time. Some respondents referred to a declining emphasis on employment equity in their jobs as other duties were added on. Only 65 percent of respondents reported that they devote 80 percent or more of their time on the job to equity work. Continuous changes in the number, definition and nature of these positions have meant that as researchers, we pursue a moving target.

Tensions and dilemmas are inherent in continual changes and restructuring imposed on equity-related positions, and in the lack of resources and commitment to equity on the part of the administrative leadership and academic decision-makers in many universities. Under the best of conditions, equity practitioners lack the power to bring about transformative change in Canadian universities, although they can and do implement incremental change and provide significant support to individual members of disadvantaged groups that contribute to their survival and success in the university.

NOTES

The authors gratefully acknowledge the support of a Research Grant from the Social Sciences and Humanities Research Council of Canada, and the helpful comments of the anonymous reviewers of an earlier version of this chapter.

1. A detailed discussion of employment equity as an organizational change project is found in Carol Agocs, Catherine Burr and Felicity Somerset, *Employment Equity: Cooperative Strategies for Organizational Change* (Scarborough: Prentice Hall Canada, 1992).

2. The population for this study consisted of equity practitioners working within thirty-one Canadian universities that are participants in the Federal Contractors Program (FCP). The survey was limited to staff of FCP universities in order to include the largest institutions and those covered by a common policy framework, while eliminating universities that may not be comparable because of size, resources and absence of external equity regulation. Each FCP university was contacted and asked for the names of university administrative staff who perform equity functions related to the focus groups covered by the FCP, as well as services to gays and lesbians and international students. The survey was sent either by regular or electronic mail, and contained structured and semi-structured items. A total of 185 questionnaires was sent out in 1998–99, and 87 completed questionnaires were received, while 25 practitioners had left their positions. Of the 87 responses, 69 were included in the analysis reported here, which examines equity practitioners employed in universities covered by the FCP. Of the respondents excluded from this analysis, seven held positions that did not fit the criteria of an equity practitioner based on their job description and list of duties (e.g., administrative assistant, instructional personnel), one completed only a small portion of the questionnaire, and ten were from non-FCP universities. The larger study also includes individual interviews with former equity practitioners and focus group interviews with equity and human rights officers, sexual harassment officers and co-ordinators of services to Aboriginal people. Analysis and reporting on these data will occur later, and these interview materials are referred to only in passing in this discussion.

3. Statistics Canada data cited in Canadian Association of University Teachers (CAUT), *CAUT Almanac of Post-Secondary Education in Canada* (Ottawa: CAUT, 2003), 24–25; Human Resources Development Canada (HRDC), Labour Branch, Data Development Section, unpublished data, 1996 Census of Canada (20% sample data) (December 1998), Table 5; HRDC, Labour Standards and Workplace Equity, Data Development Section, *1996 Employment Equity Data Report*, Release No. 2, Manual (June 1999), 40.

4. Statistics Canada data cited in *CAUT Almanac of Post-Secondary Education in Canada*, 13.

5. Ibid., 15; Statistics Canada, *2001 Census: Analysis Series. Education in Canada: Raising the Standard* (Ottawa: Statistics Canada, March 11, 2003), 15.

6. Frances Henry, Carol Tator, Winston Mattis and Tim Rees, *The Colour of Democracy: Racism in Canadian Society* (Toronto: Harcourt Brace Canada, 1995), 195–205.

7. HRDC, Labour Standards and Workplace Equity, Data Development Section, *1996 Employment Equity Data Report.*

8. Statistics Canada data cited in *CAUT Almanac of Post-Secondary Education in Canada*, 15.

9. For statements in this vein, see John Fekete, *Moral Panics: Biopolitics Rising* (Montreal: Robert Davis, 1994); Janel Gauthier, ed., *Political Correctness in Academia,* Special Issue, *Canadian Psychology* 38, no. 4 (1997). On the struggle against this backlash in universities, see Jacqueline Stalker and Susan Prentice, *The Illusion of Inclusion: Women in Post-Secondary Education* (Halifax: Fernwood, 1998).

10. For an explanation of differences between Canadian employment equity policy and affirmative action in the U.S., see Carol Agocs and Catherine Burr, "Employment Equity, Affirmative Action and Managing Diversity: Assessing the Differences," *International Journal of Manpower* 17, nos. 4/5 (1996), 30–45.

11. Joanne Leck and David Saunders, "Achieving Diversity in the Workplace: Canada's Employment Equity Act and Members of Visible Minorities," *International Journal of Public Administration* 19, no. 3 (1996), 316.

12. Penni Stewart and Janice Drakich, "Factors Related to Organizational Change and Equity for Women Faculty in Canadian Universities," *Canadian Public Policy* 21, no. 4 (1995), 429–448.

13. "PhDs in Academe: Myths and Realities," *University Affairs* (January 1999), 30.

14. Stewart and Drakich, "Factors Related to Organizational Change ..."

15. The Chilly Editorial Collective, *Breaking Anonymity: The Chilly Climate for Women Faculty* (Waterloo: Wilfrid Laurier University Press, 1995); Elena Hannah, Linda Paul and Swani Vethamany-Globus, eds., *Women in the Canadian Academic Tundra: Challenging the Chill* (Montreal: McGill-Queen's University Press, 2002); and Stalker and Prentice, *Illusion of Inclusion.*

16. Henry et al., *The Colour of Democracy,* 195–206.

17. Rosabeth Moss Kanter, *The Change Masters* (New York: Simon and Schuster, 1983).

18. See John Hurley, "Organizational Development in Universities," *Journal of Managerial Psychology* 5, no. 1 (1990), 17–22; Art Kleiner, "The Gurus of Corporate Change," *Business and Society Review* 81 (1992), 39–42.

19. Jane Howell and Christopher Higgins, "Champions of Change: Identifying, Understanding and Supporting Champions of Technological Innovations," *Organizational Dynamics* 19, no. 1 (1990), 40–55; and Kevin Wooten and Louis White, "Toward a Theory of Change Role Efficacy," *Human Relations* 42, no. 8 (1989), 651–669.

20. Thomas Case, Robert Vandernberg and Paul Meredith, "Internal and External Change Agents," *Leadership and Organization Development Journal* 11, no. 1 (1990), 4–15; and Esther Hamilton, "The Facilitation of Organizational Change: An Empirical Study of Factors Predicting Change Agents' Effectiveness," *Journal of Applied Behavioural Science* 24, no. 1 (1988), 37–59.

21. Allan Church, Janine Waclawski and W. Warner Burke, "OD Practitioners as Facilitators of Change," *Group and Organization Management* 21, no. 1 (1996), 48.

22. W. Warner Burke, Allan Church and Janine Waclawski, "What Do OD Practitioners Know about Managing Change?" *Leadership and Organization Development Journal* 14, no. 7 (1993), 3–11.

23. Gary McMahan and Richard Woodman, "The Current Practice of Organization Development Within the Firm: A Survey of Large Industrial Corporations," *Group and Organization Management* 17, no. 2 (June 1992), 130.

24. Noel Tichy, "Agents of Planned Social Change: Congruence of Values, Cognitions, and Actions," *Administrative Science Quarterly* 19, no. 2 (1974), 164–182.

25. W. Warner Burke, *Organization Development: A Normative View* (Reading, MA: Addison-Wesley, 1987); Allan Mohrmann, S. Mohrmann, G. Ledford, T. Cummings and E. Lawler, eds., *Large-scale Organizational Change* (San Francisco: Jossey Bass, 1989).

26. McMahan and Woodman, "The Current Practice of of Organization Development Within the Firm."

27. Carol Agocs, "Institutionalized Resistance to Organizational Change: Denial, Inaction, and Repression," *Journal of Business Ethics* 16, no. 9 (1997), 917–931.

28. See Jeffry Pfeffer, Alison Davis-Blake and Daniel Julius, "Affirmative Action Officer Salaries and Managerial Diversity," *Industrial Relations* 34, no. 1 (1995), 73–94.

29. Agocs, Burr and Somerset, *Employment Equity: Cooperative Strategies for Organizational Change*; and Agocs and Burr, "Employment Equity, Affirmative Action and Managing Diversity."

30. R. Tadepalli, "Perceptions of Role Stress by Boundary Role Persons: An Empirical Investigation," *Journal of Applied Behavioural Science* 27, no. 4 (1991), 490–514.

31. Ellen Kossek and Susan Zonia, "Assessing Diversity Climate: A Field Study of Reactions to Employer Efforts to Promote Diversity," *Journal of Organizational Behavior* 14 (1993), 61–81; Antonella Ceddia, "Hire a Pro," *University Affairs* (Aug.–Sept. 1995), 26–27; Chilly Editorial Collective, *Breaking Anonymity*; Sally Spilhaus, "What Equity Officers Really Do," *University Affairs* (Aug.–Sept. 1995), 26; and P.A. Sullivan, "The Role of Equity Officers," *University Affairs* (June–July 1995), 16.

32. Leela Madhava Rau, "Race Relations Policy Brought to Life: A Case Study of One Anti-Harassment Protocol," in Chilly Editorial Collective, *Breaking Anonymity*, 315–344.

33. Cynthia Cockburn, *In the Way of Women: Men's Resistance to Sex Equality in Organizations* (Ithaca, NY: ILR Press, 1991).

34. Dorothy E. Smith, *Writing the Social: Critique, Theory, and Investigations* (Toronto: University of Toronto Press, 1999), 47–48.

35. Patricia Hill Collins, "Learning from the Outsider Within: The Sociological Significance of Black Feminist Thought," in Mary Margaret Fonow and Judith Cook, eds., *Beyond Methodology: Feminist Scholarship as Lived Research* (Bloomington: Indiana University Press, 1991), 35–59.

36. Debra Meyerson and Maureen Scully, "Tempered Radicalism and the Politics of Ambivalence and Change," *Organization Science* 6, no. 5 (1995), 585–600.

37. Kanter, *Change Masters;* Herminia Ibarra, "Network Centrality, Power, and Innovation Involvement: Determinants of Technical and Administrative Roles," *Academy of Management Journal* 36, no. 3 (1993), 471–501; Herminia Ibarra, "Personal Networks of Women and Minorities in Management: A Conceptual Framework," *Academy of Management Review* 18, no. 1 (1993), 56–87.

38. HRDC, Labour Branch, Data Development Section, 1996 Census of Canada, December 1988, table 5.

39. Peter Frost, "The Toxic Handler: Organizational Hero and Casualty," *Harvard Business Review* 77, no. 4 (1999), 96–106.

40. Joyce Rothschild and Terance Miethe, "Whistleblowing as Resistance in Modern Work Organizations," in J. M. Jermier, David Knights and Walter Nord, eds., *Resistance and Power in Organizations* (London: Routledge, 1994), 252–273.

41. Meyerson and Sully, "Tempered Radicalism."

CHAPTER 11

THE UNTENURED FEMALE ACADEMIC IN THE CORPORATE UNIVERSITY

Linda Joan Paul

> Corporatization, commodification and privatization have been funda-
> mental principles of operation behind the globalization of the knowledge
> industry. These pressures have framed the process of restructuring that
> has dominated universities on a global basis in the past decade. Such
> changes have had a significant impact on institutional frameworks and
> bodies of knowledge. They have also had a profound impact on the
> academic self in physical, emotional and intellectual terms.
>
> — Ann Brooks, "Restructuring Bodies of Knowledge"

CONSIDERING THAT THE CORPORATE UNIVERSITY is continuing to
expand, it is surprising that so little has been written about commercialization and the issue of untenured and contract academics. Since
these are the faculty ranks that usually contain the highest proportion of
women, the issue has become an increasingly hot topic. It is unfortunate
that this is so. In this chapter, I attempt to tie together these topics. Why
is it important to link these topics? Because, as many academics believe,
the more universities corporatize, the more likely they are to employ
greater number of part-time or contract workers.[1]

After briefly outlining some of the key characteristics of the corporate university, I discuss how untenured and contract academics are

defined and how these positions relate to women in the academy. I then detail the difficult employment characteristics that women working as contract and untenured academics have to contend with in order to fulfill their professional goals. Since the hiring of greater numbers of these academics is anticipated in the future in the corporate university, I hope this chapter will help to make all academics more aware of these employment conditions. I also hope that faculty, their associations and administrators will find ways to redirect these trends. If this is not done, a larger proportion of Canadian academics will be working under frustrating conditions in the future.

THE CORPORATE UNIVERSITY

What are some of the salient characteristics of the corporate university? This topic is discussed in greater detail in other chapters of this book. For the purposes of this chapter, however, I refer to *The Corporate Campus* in which James Turk suggests, "'Commercialization' is the term most commonly used to designate the attempt to hitch universities and colleges to the corporate sector." Neil Tudiver identifies a major concern with this link in *Universities for Sale*, where he writes: "Profit derived from intellectual property is the cornerstone of the corporate university. Academics in potentially lucrative fields are encouraged to search for money at all stages of their research."[2] Bill Graham, past president of the Canadian Association of University Teachers (CAUT), expresses further concerns with the corporate approach: "Research is most useful in the long run when it is driven by the logic of the discipline rather than the need to generate short-term profits."[3]

The problem with this approach, argues Janice Newson, is that commercialization often changes the university from a public-serving to a private-serving mission, which tends to limit the pursuit of knowledge.[4] Julian Greenwood — who was instrumental in creating a now-closed sessionals list-serv in Canada — remarks that

> higher-education institutions are being sucked into a beguiling world of corporate "relationships," the results of which will be that educational efforts become commodified, packaged and sold for the profit of the corporate investors, at the cost of the gradual impoverishment of the university, its faculty, its students and the quality of education itself.[5]

Norman E. Bowie expands on this idea:

Public universities are supposed to serve the entire community and they have been traditionally designated as the appropriate institution to conduct research in the public interest — research that business will not undertake. Will the commercialization of the university undermine that traditional mission?[6]

If we look at the topic of research and its relation to gender, it becomes apparent that many of the research chairs and research projects supported by industry are in areas where men predominate — engineering, the natural sciences, health sciences and computer science. The majority of research chairs are allocated to these fields.[7] Thus, fewer women are likely to receive grants funded by industry or be given positions as research chairs. At the beginning of 2001, the ratio of women to men in Tier 1 and Tier 2 was 12:112 (11.5 percent women) and 16:29 (27.4 percent) for a total of 28:151 or 16.5 percent research chairs granted to women.[8] The disciplines and faculties where women academics abound are much more likely to be financially strapped. "Only 20 per cent of the chairs are set aside for Social Sciences and Humanities Research Council grant holders — where women make up more than 50 per cent of the researchers."[9] Corporatization of universities influences these choices.

THE UNTENURED AND CONTRACT ACADEMICS

How does corporatization relate to contract academic staff? Vicky Smallman of CAUT puts it this way:

> While we [CAUT] believe that tenure is essential to protecting academic freedom, we are also mindful of the fact that an increasing number of academics are being hired in non-tenured and, in the case of contract academic staff, untenurable positions. The exploitation of contract academic staff is one of the most dangerous aspects of the corporate university, and as a profession, we have to do something about it ... Contract appointments are being used by the administrators to gradually eliminate tenure by attrition.[10]

Who, then, are included in these professional ranks of academia? The terminology I use most often in this chapter is "contract academics." These are contract appointments of a fixed duration, which can be either full-time (and often called contractually limited appointments) or part-time (academics usually hired on a per-course basis). Both are common employment practices in the academy, and faculty who fill them are often used to teach specific courses or perform designated tasks. Academics can often hold more than one appointment at once and, when combined, can teach more than the full-time equivalent. To discourage overuse of contract academics, some university agreements limit the number of courses contract academics can teach, which can cause them financial hardship.

Across Canada, there is a variety of terminology used to identify part-time university teachers: for instance, "sessional" at UBC and Alberta; "adjunct" at Queen's; part-time instructor at Bishop's or Nipissing; sessional lecturer at Regina; part-time faculty at Concordia; and course-director/contract faculty at York.[11] Thus, a variety of terminology and conditions fall within the umbrella term "contract academic staff" as defined by CAUT. The terms casualized and contingent academics are also used to identify these university employees.

In this chapter, I also use an enlarged concept of untenured academics (or non-tenure track faculty), one which covers a slightly greater number of people than the term "contract academics." For instance, when describing a continuing, half-time instructor appointment, Smallman states, "If you're permanent ... then you're not a contract academic staff. What you are is part-time, non-tenured — part of the next, new category of exploited appointments — a problem created by attempts to provide stability to long-time contract folks who would not be able to qualify for tenure-stream appointments."[12]

GENDER, UNTENURED AND CONTRACT ACADEMICS

In August 2000, Statistics Canada reported that full-time faculty had decreased by 9.7 percent from 1992–93 to 1998–99, dropping from 37,266 to 33,665 in that six-year period. The reasons given for this decrease related to budget constraints as well as to a greater dependence on part-timers and a drop in student enrolment based on full-time attendance equivalence. During this period, only Prince Edward Island did not experience a decline in its fully-employed faculty. What was the relationship to gender? Perhaps surprisingly more male positions were lost among faculty (15.2 percent in the six-year period) dropping to 24,861. In contrast, the number of female academic staff expanded by 10.8 percent, increasing from 7,943 to 8,804. Lest one becomes complacent about this trend, it should be noted that only 26.2 percent of all faculty were women, up from 21.3 percent in 1992–93. Women were also concentrated in lower ranks, ranging from 13.7 percent as full-professors, to 29.1 percent as associates and 43.8 percent in other (read lower) ranks. (All three percentages indicate the proportion of females in their rank.)[13] To depict the ranks of female and male academics in the university is to portray completely opposite visual and actual perspectives. Both can be represented pictorially by pyramids: for women, the image looks like an Egyptian pyramid with a narrow point at the top and a wide base at the bottom; for men, the image has a wide top that narrows to a point at the bottom of the triangle. What these images tell us is that women are under-represented in full-time tenured academic positions. The largest proportion of women are found in contract academic positions. The Statistics Canada study also states that wages received by women academics are lower than men: "Despite gains through promotion, the continuing higher concentration of women in the lower ranks is reflected in their lower overall average salaries. In 1998–99, the average salary of women faculty was 85.7% that of men."[14]

Do these figures reflect corporatization? Another StatsCan study showed that, for Canada as a whole, the proportion of full-time faculty decreased in the five-year period from 1992–93 to 1997–98. At the same time, part-time faculty increased in most provinces, while student enrolment decreased by 2.3 percent. Regional differences occurred at this time as well. In Atlantic Canada, part-time faculty increased by 13.8 percent, and with heavy workloads, their full-time teaching equivalence increased by 20.9 percent. This contrasted with the decrease in full-time faculty (by 8.8 percent) and also student enrolment, by 2.7 percent. A similar situation occurred in Quebec, but statistics were taken for a shorter time period and therefore were not in a totally comparable time frame. In Ontario, part-time faculty actually declined by 6.0 percent (in contrast to other regions of Canada), while full-time professors declined by 4.3 percent, as did student enrolment (full-time equivalent students), which decreased by 4.8 percent. In the four Western provinces as a whole, the number of part-time faculty rose by 13.5 percent, a significant 43.7 percent in full-time teaching equivalence. This contrasted with the decline of full-time faculty by 7.0 percent and a decline in student enrollment by 5.8 percent.[15] Overall, the employment of part-time instructors has increased (in full-time teaching equivalence) as the full-time professorate has declined. All regions of Canada except Ontario demonstrated this trend.

What factors might affect hiring practices in the academy? Although teaching staff has increased in Ontario universities at the turn of the twenty-first century (as universities have rushed to accommodate the double cohort of students temporarily passing through the university system), this increase cannot be expected to continue indefinitely. Neither can the anticipated rush of baby-boomer retirees cause an increase in newly hired faculty in the indefinite or long-term future. Although regional differences occur, Statistics Canada shows a decline in number of Canadian births per year from 345,123 in 1997–98 (crude birth rate of 11.5) to 327,187 in 2001–02 (crude birth rate of 10.5).[16] Without immigration, either external or internal, fewer students can be expected to attend university unless a massive increase in students occurs due to the echo effect of baby-boomer children's having children. Out-migration of students from certain regions can add to depopulation. In the fall of 2003, for example, Regina's Roman Catholic and public schools were expected to have 200 and 600 fewer students respectively, which could affect university populations in the future.[17] Student population projections are important factors in university planning and hiring practices. Due to uncertain future student enrolment, universities will hire more part-time faculty, and corporatization will enhance this trend.

Is this a problem? Turk argues that in the corporate university, business management practices bring about labour "casualization and the introduction of labour-replacing technology."[18] Part-time staff are paid less, receive fewer benefits and have fewer rights. They find it more difficult to unionize, as they are often spatially scattered and hold varied teaching schedules. They also come from a variety of employment backgrounds, some working elsewhere full-time, some shuffling between jobs and family responsibilities (especially women academics). They are "an amorphous mass of varying needs and characteristics."[19] Tudiver suggests that "course delivery can be labour intensive and costly: small seminars may be productive for the mind, but don't generate huge profits for the institution" in a commercialized university.[20] The answer? Hire more contract staff at lower costs.

Another consideration is information technology — how does it relate to the corporate university's hiring of contract academics? One example is enrolment with on-line universities, which is surging in the United States. Full-time tenured teachers may be non-existent in these universities. Often, the instructors are paid limited funds to produce course materials but must sign the copyright for these materials over to the universities. In addition, they seldom receive royalties for the use of their work. This same process has been identified for on-line or distance education courses in Canada. Casual course co-ordinators who have not developed the courses may be the ones who teach the students, mark their papers and distribute course material. Roberta Morris, courses media advisor at the University of Toronto, comments that some statistics indicate that women are "now more frequent users of the Internet, and more frequently enrolled in on-line courses." She feels that we must take

> more seriously the access issues with respect to on-line education, and to nuance what seems to be a protectionist stance, lest we forget that what we are protecting is an institution dominated by able-bodied white men ... There are private companies quite happy to offer on-line education if the public universities don't, and the universities won't if the unions don't come up with a positive model. Access is one of the most important issues identified by students in on-line education. South of the border, there are some fine examples of what Canadians will want to avoid ... if [Canadian] universities can't provide the accessible education needed ... The Internet has no respect for national boundaries.[21]

If administrators do not develop a model acceptable to unions, the unions might "take a proactive stance regarding the use of educational technologies in order to protect public education."[22]

Distance education in Canada, where lectures are videotaped and sent to numerous locations, has the potential of going in the same direction. Through regional agreements like the North American Free Trade Agreement (NAFTA), the potential exists to export (and import) an education system through distance education courses. Education would then be sold as a commodity and not as a service for all citizens, suggests Sharon Taylor-Henley.[23] Information technology thus replaces labour. There are examples of distance-education instructors who have lost copyright over the course materials they have developed and taught. Since the university controls the copyright, it has the option of hiring more part-time teaching staff who can then use these ready-made materials. A high proportion of contract academics are women.

For-profit universities have the same potential. In Canada, in 2001, two privately owned, for-profit universities were officially recognized by provincial governments, one in Alberta (The DeVry Institute of

Technology) and one in New Brunswick (Landsbridge University, "a wholly Internet-based company").[24] Neither university offers tenure![25] An additional problem with for-profit universities, states Tom Booth, is that

> [p]ublic services like education are generally protected from trade agreements as long as they are provided by governments, on a not-for-profit basis, and not in competition with other providers ... Given that Landsbridge is a for-profit enterprise ... its accreditation could expose post-secondary education to the disciplines of trade agreements.[26]

In terms of not granting tenure and hiring a largely contract academic staff, some Canadian public universities are moving in the same direction as for-profit universities. Royal Roads University in Victoria employs under thirty core faculty and full-time instructors/faculty and between 300 and 400 short-term contract staff (about 75 full-time positions in any given year), many of whom are also actively involved in their professions. Royal Roads considers itself a "learner-centered and learning-centered university."[27] However, tenure is not granted. Thus, security and academic freedom are limited.

GENDER'S LINK TO THE UNTENURED AND CONTRACT ACADEMIC

Currently, the largest proportion of female academics fill the lowest ranks of academe. Not only does this affect their working conditions at the university but their devalued circumstances can also be extended beyond the ivy-covered walls. Women, because they carry more family responsibilities than men, tend to work fewer paid hours than their male counterparts, thus losing unemployment protection (EI) more quickly.[28] Is this not systemic gender discrimination? Another concern is that many academics on contract have meager pensions or none at all.

A study of the Massachusetts Institute of Technology found that female academics were treated unequally compared with their male counterparts in the areas of salary, benefits, allocations of laboratory space, research grants and in the processes of departmental decision-making.[29] This is probably a fairly generalized situation for academics. But if this is generally true for female academics, what are the implications for contract and untenured staff specifically? Julian Greenwood describes it clearly:

> [T]he part-timer phenomenon is in large part a form of discrimination ...
> on the basis of marital or family status, even where it is hard to show that

it is gender (sex) discrimination. Universities tend to deny that there is much sex discrimination involved, because the part-timer class is not heavily female. What is clear ... is that it is much more heavily female than the full-timer ranks, and particularly the higher full-timer ranks, but because the ratios among part-timers tend to be, say, 55 (female) to 45 (male) (i.e., not strongly female), the institutions are able to deny that they are engaging in sex discrimination ...

Yet all jurisdictions with anti-discrimination statutes also purport to ban discrimination on the basis of family or marital status. There is plenty of anecdotal evidence that the reason people get hired on the informal part-time track is because they are already in town.[30]

Often women cannot or choose not to leave their families. In smaller communities with a limited academic market, they often have no option but to take the jobs that are available.

In recognition of the many problems these women and other contingent faculty face, CAUT created the Contract Academic Staff executive committee and hired a professional officer to represent them. The executive committee was to focus on five key areas: inclusiveness, academic freedom, job security, fair and due process in all decision-making and elimination of all exploitation. As a result, many CAUT policies relating to this academic cohort have been revised, and the Policy Statement on Fairness for Contract Academic Staff was approved by CAUT Council in November 2000.[31]

Because good statistics on contract academics are difficult to obtain, because many universities do not respond to surveys and because contract academics are often isolated from the professoriate at large and other lecturers in their position, I contacted three networks in order to identify areas of concerns among contract academics: (1) contributors to the anthology Women in the Canadian Academic Tundra: Challenging the Chill;[32] (2) the CAUT CAUTEQ (equity) listserv available to all academics who wish to join, as well as other CAUT resources, staff and volunteers; and (3) the sessionals listserv started by Julian Greenwood for the purpose of communication among part-timers.

Areas of Concerns Identified

I identified the following issues from these networks. While some universities have addressed these problems, others have not and the issues remain widespread and unresolved for many women in contract and untenured positions. I briefly summarize each of the concerns in this section.

Funding for Research, Books and Travel

It is almost impossible for part-timers to receive research grants; SSHRC does not give research grants to part-timers. The three editors of *Women in the Canadian Academic Tundra*, of which I was one, could not access SSHRC funding and worked on this project, gratis, for over five years. Universities should recognize that contract academics conduct research! It is a myth to believe otherwise. Their valid research projects should be supported financially. As Patrick Grassick points out, most sessionals

> have respectable research track records. Sessionals know full well that if they ever hope to secure tenure-track positions they will have to produce a C.V. with a healthy list of publications. And they manage to produce such a list in conditions that are quite unsupportive of the research enterprise — insubstantial professional expense reimbursement, no access to research funds or labs [and so on].[33]

Contract academics should have the cost of course textbooks covered through examination copies from publishers or the universities themselves. College libraries should purchase class textbooks for contract teachers if they do so for tenured professors. Otherwise the students of part-time workers are disadvantaged. Susan Turner of Athabasca University, who works on a contract basis, finds that

> as an academic who has chosen to work freelance, my biggest issue is with continuous access to university library and services and benefits. I think there ought to be some mechanism available to resident academics who might not be teaching at their local institution at a given time to use its facilities.[34]

There should also be assistance for conference travel. It is in the students' interest, as well as theirs, to help keep them connected with their disciplines and colleagues, and ideally, to publish. By participating in conferences, contingent staff can disseminate knowledge to their discipline as the tenured academic can.

Merit Raises, Benefits and Bargaining Units

Receiving merit raises is another contentious issue. All meritorious academics should be recognized monetarily. A 1999 Workplace and Employee Survey (WES) indicated that women earned 80 cents to each dollar earned by men in 1999. Part of this differential relates to more women working part-time than men. Part-time jobs are often paid at a lower hourly rate than full-time jobs. In addition, "[w]omen were also less likely than men to have their earnings tied to their performance. Workers whose pay is affected by their performance may receive higher wages to compensate them for greater effort on the job."[35] Most part-time academics do not receive merit incentives.

Non-tenure-track and contingent staff should be granted sabbatical leaves after a specific length of service (full-time equivalence), and they should have access to insurance and pension plans. Contracts should be "truthful." If contract academics are hired over and over, then they are continuing employees and their contracts should reflect this. Their salaries and benefits should reflect this fact as well.[36] If they do become part-time permanent employees or senior sessionals, but not tenure-track employees, they should have the "right of first refusal." This clause would give them priority to teach courses over less-senior sessionals. Otherwise, gaining a higher status with higher pay will penalize their opportunities to teach additional classes at a rate commensurate with their status (as is the case at the University of Regina at the time of writing). If the institution expects loyalty and respect from its employees, so should academics anticipate this quality from their home universities:

> It is a fundamental rule of employment law essentially everywhere that employees have a duty of loyalty to their employers and that employers owe a reciprocal duty to be fair to those who have already demonstrated their commitment and loyalty.[37]

Marty Laurence of Wilfrid Laurier University suggests that part-timers should be certified as part of the full-time bargaining unit so the larger bargaining unit can bargain for and with them, using the leverage of the collective agreement.[38] Often setting limits on the percentage of part-timers who can teach in any one year forces the administration to hire more academics full time. In my opinion, it is important that grand-parenting clauses be in effect so that the full-time contracts come from the existing pool of part-timers. It is also necessary to have contract and untenured academics as part of the bargaining team in contract negotiations to ensure that their needs are not ignored. University of Guelph part-timers are working on this issue and on employing contract staff more fully, as Marianne Micros points out:

It is so often true in my academic departments that most part-time instructors are women. My feeling is that we are punished for having children and for wanting to live in the same place as our families. There is also the question of age-discrimination — by the time you are free to commit to your work more fully, you are too "old" to get a job.[39]

Family Responsibility and Childrearing

Carol Stoss of Laurentian University points out that seldom do universities arrange schedules and workloads for women whose responsibility it is to care for children and aging parents or relatives — another factor that may inhibit their full-time employment:

> It seems to me that women will make up the bulk of part-time workers ... since we are still the ones who are most likely to combine "outside" careers with home responsibilities ... What corporations plan their benefits or work schedules or job descriptions around the kind of timetables part-timers (women) may have to juggle? I'm thinking of before- and after-school responsibilities for young children (and even teens who may have karate, skating, etc., to be driven to and from) ... And don't forget those of us who may also now be responsible for aging parents and all that entails with doctors' appointments, etc. How many corporations are pro-active regarding job sharing? ... It's taken two women who realize that they would like to job share to work out most of the logistics and then bring the business or corporation on board.[40]

Daycare is also an issue for many younger academics, which often causes women to choose part-time over full-time academic life. How many universities provide a daycare service?

For many women who do have family responsibilities, working part-time is their only choice. However, part-time work can influence salaries. The 1999 Workplace and Employment Survey noted that men had an average of eighteen years full-time work experience compared with fourteen years for women.[41] Much of this can be attributed to women's higher part-time employment rate, or time spent out of the labour force during childbearing and childrearing. Both factors influence women's lower comparative wages. Susan Nimmo of the University of Alberta argues that her issue "has long been pro-rated benefits and some type of guarantee for long-term sessionals."[42]

Protecting Rights and Academic Freedom

Another major issue facing untenured staff is the fear of speaking out. If, for example, they speak out about contract issues, they may not be re-elected to committees;[43] they may not be offered extra classes to teach; or they may be ignored within their departments. As one academic who chose to remain anonymous put it: "Any sessional's job security (ha!ha!) is tenuous at best. The whole nature of being a sessional is so insecure." Adding insult to injury is the fact that speaking out about untenured employment concerns bores full-time academics. One tenured academic actually fell asleep when part-timers' were discussing their issues in a meeting!

All of this results in contract academics being given so little voice they are seldom heard, as I point out in "Voices: Your Voice or My Voice."[44] Many universities are based on a class system where the voices of the lower ranks (i.e., contract workers who are largely female academics) are seldom heard. Not only administrations but also individual faculties, departments and unions must learn to listen to the concerns of non-tenured staff and be willing to implement their suggestions to create better working conditions. Somehow, issues that concern untenured faculty must become a *cause célèbre* for tenured faculty.

Academic freedom is another important issue. Tenured professors' jobs are protected so that they are able to carry on research and publish results without fear of reprisals:

> [T]he guarantee of academic freedom supplied by tenure is precisely the condition which allows faculty members to take scholarly risks which high level or cutting edge research entails. It is also the condition which allows faculty members to engage their students in critical education rather than simply passing on testable skills to them.[45]

Contract academics seldom have that protection. More women academics fall into this category than any other rank of the professoriate and, as a result, face a greater risk of being silenced, or demonized if they do speak out.

Workload and Administrative Support

Workload exploitation is another concern raised and one that CAUT is addressing. Untenured academics are often given the largest classes to teach and are not necessarily given the teaching or marking assistants that regular faculty receive. They are often assigned classes in awkward and unwanted time slots — women sometimes more often than their male counterparts — while at the same time they are receiving fewer benefits and lower salaries than tenured staff.

Yet, as Anne Lavack of the University of Regina points out, untenured staff are much needed by universities: "It is financial reality at many universities that part-time and contract personnel are needed in order to manage fluctuating enrolment demands in a manner that is cost effective ... [and] to offer courses in new areas in which current faculty lack expertise."[46] Universities can help to make the work environment more attractive and welcoming for contract academics through recognizing the tremendous amount of preparation that goes into teaching a course for the first time and by providing extra stipends for first-time preparation. Help with new course preparation could be provided by long-term staff in the way of helping with textbook selections, offering prior course outlines and content and providing teaching tips and grading standards. Secretaries need to have the time to show contract academics where supplies are stored and how to use equipment like the photocopier. Contact phone numbers should be provided so that those teaching during off-hours have access to administrative assistance if problems arise.

Another problem is that contract staff often receive their teaching assignments on very short notice, making it very difficult to prepare their courses. They may also have their classes cancelled without compensation — which happened to me twenty-four hours before a class was scheduled to start. If preparatory work has been done, they should be paid for short-notice cancellation of classes.

Shannon Gadbois suggests that the goal for hiring women has to go beyond getting them to come to a university. To keep them, it is necessary to build networks and to use approaches such as reducing workloads for first-time teachers, pairing them with mentors to encourage them in research and teaching and providing them with teaching workshops. A climate survey conducted by the Status of Women Review Committee at Brandon University indicated that women had significantly higher incidence of "having their work devalued, being excluded from decision making, being ignored, being questioned about their academic abilities, and having more expected of them, because of their gender!"[47]

Isolation

One of the major problems many contract academics face is isolation. They are isolated within their own universities where they seldom meet others in their position and face anonymity from much of the rest of the university workers. Additionally, they rarely know how to or have time to contact contract staff in their wider disciplines or in academe elsewhere. "Full-time faculty and departments ... need to work harder at developing relations with contract and untenured faculty," for instance, inviting them to socials. "These efforts can provide a greater level of administrative and emotional support for part-timer instructors, to make them feel that their efforts are appreciated and valued, even if they are financially under rewarded."[48]

Expanding further on this subject, Suzan Banoub-Baddour of Memorial University remarks that even when invited to social functions and orientation days, part-timers may not attend.[49] The probable reason is that they are not paid for the time they spend at these functions. Not attending might also be an indication of their feelings of exclusion and disillusionment. Inviting them, however, demonstrates departmental acknowledgment, as is giving them copies of minutes, inviting them to department and university meetings and allowing them to vote.

Although many examples relating to poor working conditions both for women and contract academics have been identified before, seldom have they been compiled into a comprehensive entity such as I have attempted to do here. That they have been reiterated yet again from so many sources for use in this chapter suggests that many of these problems have yet to be addressed by our universities. These issues must be tackled before the expansion of corporate academe augments the problems.

If the corporate world mainly supports research that proves it has money-making potential, what happens to the many women who are more interested in people issues and less interested in creating machines, drugs or inventions to sell? What happens if corporations drop their support for women's projects in non-scientific fields? Do women stop asking to be a part of corporate grants? Will their careers be hurt, asks Geraldine (Jody) Macdonald of the University of Toronto?

> In the big universities, not to get big funding means that you will lose your voice. How can we protect the perspective of women in the academy if the corporate world is setting the agenda?
>
> The corporate university uses a business model and makes its decisions based on bottom line rather than caring. How long will it be before the university is just another corporate culture? ... Do we still have the right to spend money because we believe that it is for the greater good, or the right, just, fair decision, or will all of us be forced to cut back all that we hold dear, to meet the bottom line?[50]

Part-timers can offer so much to the university. Why doesn't the academy support contract academics so that they can bring energy, talent and commitment to their jobs now and possibly full-time in the future? In British Columbia, in some disciplines, the sessional pool is becoming "shallow," writes Stevi Stephens.[51] With the retirement of baby boomers, perhaps treating contract staff considerately will prove to be self-serving for all universities, including corporate academia, in the future. It would be good to remember that as baby boomers retire, there could be an employment crisis in the academy.

Wendy Feldberg offers another twist to the corporatization/gender/contract academic theme. In some corporatizing universities, programs such as English as a Second Language charge foreign students much higher fees than the fees charged to Canadian students. While the professors (often part-timers) are paid very little per course, the profits from the courses are then invested in the rest of the university, rather than offering development opportunities to the instructors. Universities have proposed "to act as an employment agency and to hire out their language teachers to a foreign institution," paying lower hourly rates to its part-time instructors than it would in Canada, while not protecting the courses the instructors have developed, their intellectual property.[52]

*

Working conditions for contract and untenured academic women are not ideal at the present time. Despite the many frustrating working conditions they face, these women are the prototype for the corporate university and, as it expands, they will feel increasingly excluded from the academy — to the point that even the "Illusion of Inclusion" will be lost.[53] In addition, the process of corporatization is compressing more people into the "teaching-only" ranks and the expectation of research (though many still undertake it) is diminishing. This expectation silences female academics and provides an inferior education for students, especially in smaller institutions where research is no longer part of the job requirement. Will women lose their academic voice even further? It is up to those of us within faculty associations and university administrations to strengthen these contract and untenured academic positions. In doing so, women's interests in the corporate university will be better protected and enhanced.

NOTES

1. See, for example, Ann Brooks and Alison Mackinnon, eds., *Gender and the Restructured University* (Buckingham: The Society for Research into Higher Education and Open University Press, 2001); James L. Turk, ed., *The Corporate Campus: Commercialization and the Dangers to Canada's Colleges and Universities* (Toronto: James Lorimer, 2000); Neil Tudiver, *Universities for Sale: Resisting Corporate Control over Canadian Higher Education* (Toronto: James Lorimer, 1999); and William Bruneau and Donald C. Savage, *Counting Out the Scholars: How Performance Indicators Undermine Colleges and Universities* (Toronto: James Lorimer, 2002).

2. Turk, *The Corporate Campus,* 4, and Tudiver, *Universities for Sale,* 59.

3. Bill Graham, "No Point to Private Universities," *CAUT Bulletin* 47, no. 4 (April 2000), 2.

4. Janice Newson quoted in "Fall Conference Exposes Commercialism Trend," *CAUT Bulletin* 46, no. 9 (November 1999), 1.

5. Julian Greenwood, e-mail to author, 27 September 2000. This quote and all other quotes from colleagues are used with permission.

6. Norman E. Bowie, *University – Business Partnerships* (Boulder, CO: Rowman and Littlefield, 1994). Posted by Ed Kent on August 30, 2000, on "University Business Partnerships #6." URL no longer available.

7. "Women Profs Charge Research Chairs Program with Discrimination," *On Campus News* (University of Saskatchewan) 10, no. 14 (March 2003), 3.

8. Judy Stanley, Wendy Robbins, Rosemary Morgan, with the assistance of Andy Siggner, "Ivory Towers: Feminist Audits. Selected Indicators of the Status of Women in Universities in Canada and Further Equity Data, 2003" on the Canadian Federation for the Human Sciences and Social Sciences Web site: <http://www. fedcan.ca/english/policyandadvocacy/win/publications.cfm>.

9. "Women Profs Charge Research Chairs Program with Discrimination," 3.

10. Vicky Smallman, e-mail to author, 27 September 2003.

11. Ibid.

12. Ibid.

13. Statistics Canada, "Part-time University Faculty," *The Daily* (August 8, 2000), 1–2. Retrieved from <http://www.statcan.ca/Daily/ English/02508/d02508b.htm>. July 1, 2003.

14. Ibid.

15. Statistics Canada, "Part-time University Faculty," *The Daily* (August 30, 2000), 1–2. Retrieved from <http://www.statcan.ca/Daily/ English/000830/d0000830c.htm>. July 1, 2003.

16. Statistics Canada, "Births and Birth Rate." CANSIM Data Base. Tables 051-0001 and 051-0004, and product no. 91-213-X1B. Retrieved from <http://www.stat-can.ca /English/Pgdb/demo04b.htm>. July 1, 2003.

17. James Wood, "Schools Face Number Drop," *The Leader Post* (Regina), 22 April 2003, B1.

18. Turk, *The Corporate Campus,* 7.

19. Linda Paul, "Dilemmas and Solutions for Part-timers," *SWC Supplement* to the *CAUT Bulletin* 45, no. 4 (April, 1998), 3.

20. Tudiver, *Universities for Sale,* 161.

21. Roberta Morris, e-mail to author, 6 June 2001.

22. Roberta Morris, e-mail to author, 7 June 2001.

23. Sharon Taylor-Henley, interview by author, Quebec City, June 2001.

24. Tom Booth quoted in "CAUT Condemns Recognition of Newest For-Profit University," *CAUT Now* 3, no. 4 (July 5, 2001).

25. Jim Turk, e-mail to author, 7 July 2003.

26. Booth quoted in "CAUT Condemns Recognition of Newest For-Profit University."

27. Estelle Paget, e-mails to author, 13 and 16 November 2003.

28. "Women Hardest Hit by Cutbacks in EI Benefits," *CAUT Bulletin* 47, no. 4 (April 2000), 7.

29. "Fighting Against Gender Bias," *CAUT Bulletin* 46, no. 10 (December 1999), 4.

30. Julian Greenwood, e-mail to author, 6 June 2001.

31. "Contract Staff Initiatives," *CAUT Bulletin* 46, no. 9 (November 1999), 1. I can attest to the thoroughness of this policy revision as I was on the CAUT Status of Women Committee for nearly six years. Policy reviews were examined by all five CAUT standing committees before recommendations were taken to the CAUT executive and CAUT general council. For the Policy Statement, see "Policy Statement on Fairness for Contract Academic Staff," *CAUT.* Retrieved from <http://www.caut.ca/english/about/fair_contractstaff.asp>. June 27, 2003.

32. Elena Hannah, Linda Paul and Swani Vethamany-Globus, eds., *Women in the Canadian Academic Tundra: Challenging the Chill* (Montreal: McGill-Queen's University Press, 2002).

33. Patrick Grassick, "A Few Thoughts about Sessionals," *CAUT Bulletin* 49, no. 5 (May 2002), A14.

34. Susan Turner, e-mail to author, 1 June 2001.

35. Statistics Canada, "Gender Pay Differentials: Impact of the Workplace," *The Daily* (19 June 2002), 1. Retrieved from <http:// www.statcan.ca:80/Daily/English/020619/d020619b.htm>. June 24, 2002.

36. Greenwood, e-mail to author.

37. Grassick, "A Few Thoughts about Sessionals," A14.

38. Marty Laurence, e-mail to author, 6 June 2001.

39. Marianne Micros, e-mail to author, 7 June 2001.

40. Carol Stoss, e-mail to author, 1 June 2001.

41. Statistics Canada, "Gender Pay Differentials."

42. Susan Nimmo, e-mail to author, 6 June 2001.

43. Linda Paul, "Voices: Your Voice or My Voice" (paper presented at HSSFC — Women's Issues Network, Quebec City, 28 May 2001).

44. Ibid.

45. Graham, "No Point to Private Universities," 2.

46. Anne Lavack, e-mail to author, 6 June 2001.

47. Shannon Gadbois, e-mail to author, 6 June 2001.

48. Lavack, e-mail to author.

49. Suzan Banoub-Baddour, e-mail to author, 6 June 2001.

50. Geraldine (Jody) Macdonald, e-mail to author, 6 June 2001.

51. Stevi Stephens, e-mail to author, 6 June 2001.

52. Wendy Feldberg, e-mail to author, 6 June 2001.

53. Jacqueline Stalker and Susan Prentice, eds., *The Illusion of Inclusion: Women in Post-Secondary Education* (Halifax: Fernwood Publishing, 1998).

THE STUDENT EXPERIENCE OF CONSUMERISM, HIGH TECHNOLOGY AND LIFE IN RESIDENCE

CHAPTER 12

GOING TO MARKET:
NEO-LIBERALISM AND THE SOCIAL CONSTRUCTION OF THE UNIVERSITY STUDENT AS AN *AUTONOMOUS CONSUMER*

Elizabeth Brulé

SINCE THE 1980S, UNIVERSITIES IN CANADA, as elsewhere, have been radically restructured according to the logic of the market. Along with severe cuts to its public funding base, Canadian universities have had to contend with a plethora of new policies that have changed the way their institutions are funded: accountability processes, standardization measures, performance indicators, benchmarking and achievement audits typify these new initiatives. Couched in terms of increasing institutional efficiency, accountability and global competitiveness, these reforms represent new administrative and managerial practices that gauge a university's performance in terms of economic gains. Seemingly innocuous, these practices and their emerging mechanisms of accountability place increasing emphasis on education as a consumable product and students as autonomous consumers. One effect of such an emphasis has been the reorientation of curriculum development and teaching practices away from the humanist liberal ideal of fostering active "learning" or "citizenship" to one focused on delivering quantifiable services and satisfying consumers in measurable terms.

This chapter provides an analysis of the key features of neoliberalism, how its discursive practices intersect with post-secondary educational policy reforms in Ontario, and its effects in constituting students as autonomous consumers. Drawing on Dorothy Smith's institutional ethnography,[1] I analyze how some students at York University in Toronto take-up consumerist arguments. In particular, I examine how "common-sense notions" of consumer relations provide students with increased opportunities to challenge course curriculum and the social relations and organization of post-secondary teaching. While there is an excellent body of literature that analyzes the impact of neo-liberal reforms on the corporatization of post-secondary institutions,[2] there is a lack of research on how students as social subjects both reflect and help shape post-secondary institutional practices and processes. This chapter reveals the ways in which one institution has responded to students' acts of resistance and the implications that their responses may have on feminist and anti-racist teaching and learning practices, as well as on larger institutional reforms.

NEO-LIBERALISM AND THE *AUTONOMOUS CONSUMER*

In the last two decades, we have seen the global adoption of neo-liberal economic policy reforms and the radical restructuring of welfare and educational institutions throughout capitalist societies. Couched in terms of *deficit reduction, fiscal responsibility, productive efficiency* and *global competitiveness*, neo-liberals have castigated welfare states as unable to maintain public institutions efficiently or effectively. Within this pro-market ideology, public institutional practices are presented as too costly and wasteful, and the clients as too dependent. As a result, the free market is poised as the inevitable and rationally superior alternative. The market is presented as fair and just: it can distribute (or even redistribute) scarce resources effectively and efficiently according to the logic of supply and demand.[3]

These prescriptive justifications for neo-liberal policy reforms, what Michael Peters identifies as a revival of classical economic liberalism,[4] are premised on the notion that individual behaviour is dominated by rational economic self-interest. By maximizing competition among service providers, it is argued that, through their economic rational choices, individuals can positively influence the quality and type of services available. Because all producers and service providers are believed to be in competition for a limited number of consumers, who, in turn, express their desires and preferences through their rational purchasing behaviour, individual consumers are considered to be in command of production. It follows that by ensuring consumers have accesses to a vast array of "choices," individuals in pursuit of their own self-interest can (and will) make the *right* economic choice.[5] Within this discourse, the self-interested, rational individual is constituted solely as a consumer — or what Peters and his co-authors identify as an autonomous chooser[6] — where individuals, in their capacity to calculate risk, are responsible for their own success or failure.[7]

In contrast to earlier forms of liberalism, where state legitimacy was premised on maintaining the conditions for "active citizenship" through the provision of social welfare and educational services, neo-liberals have favoured a minimal state whose role is to ensure the maximum conditions for a free, entrepreneurial, competitive marketplace.[8] In practice, however, rather than decreasing state involvement in the public sector, these reforms have resulted in new interventionist and regulatory mechanisms that enable neo-liberal governments to promote a public sector marketplace. Alternately referred to as New Public Management or New Managerialism, these regulating practices, adopted from managerial theories used in the private sector, involve the reorganization of institutional processes so that work activities and practices within an organization can be increasingly quantified.[9] Conceived as increasing organizational efficiency, reducing costs, improving service quality and promoting accountability, these quantifying practices provide a means for managerial surveillance and regulation over more and more aspects of public sector work,[10] resulting in what Dorothy Smith refers to (in this volume) as a regime of accountability.

It is not difficult to see how neo-liberals have extended this new managerialism to post-secondary education policy reforms. Under these neo-liberal principles, countries like Britain, New Zealand, Australia, the United States and, more recently, Canada have restructured universities according to the logic of the market. Identified "as having a crucial role to play in building a nation's or region's global competitiveness," university restructuring has "proceed[ed] in part through policies focussed on producing the right kind of workers, experts and citizens."[11] Seemingly global in their adoption, the various forms that neo-liberal practices have taken and their consequential effects have, however, been diverse and unpredictable.

In order to understand what is going on in specific settings, it is necessary to examine how particular discursive practices and the texts they embody are taken up within specific sites. As Smith argues, texts are "constituents of social relations, and hence, by exploring our own knowledge of how to operate the interrelations among them, we explicate both our own practices and a segment of the social relations in which those practices are embedded and which they organize."[12] Examining the ways in which texts are enacted and their particular effects helps us understand how practices are put into place. Such an analysis provides us with a means to respond and intervene in more informed and strategic ways in resisting the increasing marketization of post-secondary education. What follows is an overview of the federal government's post-secondary policy reforms with a specific examination of the Ontario government's adoption of neo-liberal practices, and the particular forms they have taken.

THE FEDERAL AND ONTARIO GOVERNMENTS' POST-SECONDARY REFORMS

Over the past decade, the federal Liberal government has dramatically reduced transfer payments to the provinces ($7 billion since 1993, representing cuts to education, health and social assistance), introduced corporate research partnerships, established endowed chairs and guidelines for intellectual property rights to "maximize returns to Canada [by commercializing] publicly funded research."[13] Through various new granting council requirements — such as the Canadian Foundation for Innovation, the Canada Research Chairs Program and the Tri-Council Code of Research Ethics[14] — universities are now required to have strategic research plans in place that identify research performance, priorities and objectives. Moreover, universities must now provide specialized central services that assist faculty with patents, spin-off companies, licenses and other intellectual property needs; ethics services that ensure the ethical use of human subjects; and research officers in each department to assist faculty with the new funding requirements.

With the exception of Quebec,[15] provincial governments, of all political persuasions, have followed a similar neo-liberal path in response to
the federal government's cutbacks. While operating autonomously from
one another, the provinces have collectively reduced operating grants to
universities across Canada by more than 25 percent in the last ten years.
In the past, universities typically relied on government block funding for
their operating costs along with tuition and private endowments — in
1986 these were 81 percent and 19 percent, respectively. Today, 55 percent of university funding comes from private sources.[16]

In Ontario, under Mike Harris's Progressive Conservative government (following its election in 1995), operating grants declined by more
than $400 million. This represents a 20 percent reduction in operating
grants per full-time equivalent student. It has been estimated that this
reduction could reach 25 percent following the enrolment of the double
cohort in the fall of 2003.[17] According to Statistics Canada, Ontario
provincial grants account for 47.8 percent of university revenue (the second lowest in Canada next to Nova Scotia), with student tuition fees
representing the bulk in private funding at 26.3 percent (second highest
next to Nova Scotia), and the remaining 25.9 percent representing private endowments, corporate partnerships and entrepreneurial
activities.[18] Since the 1990s, tuition fees have risen 60 percent in regulated programs and as much as 200 percent in deregulated programs like
medicine.[19] Moreover, the Ontario student–faculty ratio has risen considerably. Standing at approximately twenty students per faculty — the
second highest in the country — students now pay more for less.[20]

When the Conservative government was re-elected in 1999, it fur-
thered these restructuring initiatives by deregulating tuition fees and
introducing public–corporate partnerships, private research funding and
privatization legislation. Along with these initiatives, which directly promote private–market relations, the Conservative government also
introduced legislation that dramatically changed the way in which universities are funded: performance indicators, standardization measures,
an accountability office and compulsory best management practices by
senior administrators. Initiated in 2001, the *Accountability Act* requires
all public sector organizations, including universities, to balance their
budgets each year, publicly report their annual strategic plans, and establish and meet minimum benchmarks and performance indicators to
ensure "that transfer payment partners are providing value for taxpayer's

money."[21] Furthermore, the *Post-secondary Education Student Opportunity Act, 2002* and the *Ontario Colleges of Applied Arts and Technology Act, 2002* established a new governance system that places increased emphasis on "achievement of results."

As part of its justification for these radical reforms, the Conservative government characterized universities as out of sync with the rest of the globalizing world and in need of restructuring. Criticizing universities for being elitist, unaccountable and underperforming, the Conservatives claimed that their reforms would increase institutional excellence, accountability, student choice, global competitiveness and value for taxpayers' money. In an attempt to get tough with so-called underperforming universities, the provincial government initiated three new funding reforms in 2000 that would redistribute the operating grants to universities. These reforms entailed restructuring post-secondary curriculum — albeit at arm's-length — to better meet the needs of industry. As Diane Cunningham, the then minister of training, colleges and universities, stated: "By linking funding to performance, we are fulfilling our commitment to reward schools that do the best job of preparing students to succeed after graduation."[22]

The first of these financing reforms was the Fair Funding Grants. Introduced in April 2000, it equalized per-student funding among universities. The second, the Accessibility Fund, tied funding to increases in first-year enrolment; universities would receive funding only if they exceeded the previous year's enrolment levels. The last, and the most controversial, was the Performance Indicator Fund, which tied student graduation rates and job attrition to provincial funding.

The Performance Indicator Fund assesses a university's performance based on undergraduate completion rates after seven years of study, and employment rates six months and two years after graduation. Initially, ranked and placed into one of three categories, universities in the top category receive two-thirds of these funds, those in the second category receive one-third and those at the bottom receive nothing. As of 2001, funding is based on benchmarks of the post-secondary system's average. A university's performance that falls below 10 percent of this average receives nothing while those above are funded. These last two reforms essentially tie government funding directly to university performance — a performance that is based on garnering incoming students, graduating them and ensuring they find employment.

The significance of these accountability measures, benchmarks and performance indicators is that they gauge a university's performance solely in terms of economic gain. In doing so, they necessarily position universities as businesses and students as consumers. In positioning students as consumers, the neo-liberal discourse portrays post-secondary education as a consumable product. Following this market logic, the role of the producers (professors and universities) is to provide customer-oriented education that provides students with marketable skills that will fill a niche in the labour market. Like any other object for consumption, the social relations of education become objectified and reduced to quantifiable, standardized and rationalized skills that have exchange value in the marketplace. As McCoy argues, these accountability measures signify "documentary practices that discover and represent in calculable and comparable terms relevant administrative objects such as measurable inputs and outputs, unit costs, transaction volumes, rates of error or wastage, length of time for service delivery, customer satisfaction, efficiency."[23] These practices and processes of measurement, while seeming to respond to students' demands for more choices, objectify students and their educational experience, reducing them to quantifiable and measurable units of economic success or market performance.

Though industrial influence over post-secondary education is not new, as was revealed during the Industrial Revolution at the turn of century and in the period following the Second World War,[24] what is new is the extent to which the market processes of accountability and managerial practices are transforming it. With the increasing use of regulatory systems of accountability to determine educational "success," the learning process must also be translated into standardized, quantifiable measurements. Moreover, with performance indicators, benchmarks and departmental audits forming the basis of a curriculum's objectives and development, the work of teaching is being similarly transformed.[25]

YORK UNIVERSITY: A CASE IN POINT

At York University, more and more faculty members are being asked by administrators to relate their material to the acquisition of tangible and marketable skills. In an attempt to garner what little public funds are made available, York's administrators and department chairs — especially those in the humanities and social sciences — are restructuring programs and streamlining course offerings so as to meet the so-called market needs of students and to attract government funding. For example, York's 1999 Strategic Plan states that the University is committed to increasing the applicability of its programs to employment opportunities.[26] In the Division of Social Science, Faculty of Arts, new programs such as Business and Society have been introduced, not by the faculty or students but by the administration. In an effort to tap enrolments and target government funding, this new program now provides students with a social science alternative to the University's elite business management school, The Schulich School of Business. Furthermore, in an attempt to sell their programs, managers and administrators are illustrating how the skills acquired in arts disciplines are useful to industry. Even program evaluators are calling for departments to orient their curriculum and market their programs according to student employment needs.

In an undergraduate program review of the Social Science Division, the authors, while recognizing the Division's commitment to "interdisciplinarity, liberal education, and the promotion of critical thought," nonetheless encourage the adoption of "more vocationally specific, employment-related opportunities." To accomplish this, they suggest that upper-level courses be linked more closely with professional programs through "volunteer service in the community, work-study programs, internships, and visiting speakers from various areas in the public and private sectors."[27] While emphasizing the relevance of education to the workplace does not necessarily result in the vocationalization of a program, it does, however, put emphasis on the utility of postsecondary education for the labour market. The type of knowledge that is considered useful within this context is, as Jill Blackmore points out, "strategic knowledge," which has "immediate economic benefits to improve economic productivity over 'social' knowledge (such as the humanities or ethical and moral studies)."[28] Programs that focus on social knowledge are in jeopardy of being cut if they cannot fill their classes to capacity.

Programs in the social sciences and humanities that do not easily translate into practical or strategic skills for the market place are the most vulnerable to the narrow scope of the government funding initiatives and regulatory mechanisms. Moreover, alternative teaching practices that challenge the status quo — feminist pedagogy, anti-racist, critical pedagogy and the like — are increasingly pressured to justify their practices in terms of their practical efficacy and knowledge value.[29] For example, John Ibbitson, a journalist for Canada's national newspaper *The Globe and Mail,* writes about the 2001–02 strike between educational workers and the administration at York University:

> [T]oo many of York's research centers are devoted to "feminist research," "racial ethics," "refugee studies," "work and society" and so on. If it is humanly possible to graduate with a university degree and still be unable to find a job, these are the sorts of courses that will do it. Tory governments don't lavish cash on research in practical ethics.[30]

Ibbitson conceives anything to do with social justice issues as trivial, useless or just too costly; ironically, a luxury only the privileged can afford. As he points out in his article, York University's reputation for "ineffectual liberalism" and its emphasis on social justice issues has jeopardized its potential for further government funding. The solution, of course, is framed as a rhetorical question: "Can the university preserve its dedication to social justice in the face of more mundane student demands for a guaranteed well-paying job? Can it survive cutthroat competition from other public universities and soon-to-arrive private ones?"[31]

In juxtaposing these two questions, the author positions postsecondary education as a commodity and students as rational consumers. De-sexed, de-raced, de-classed and able-bodied, it is assumed that the student as a consumer can and will make economically rational choices. The only choices considered rational, however, are those that increase one's employment opportunities within the strict confines of the labour market. Any choices and educational objectives that are not related to increasing one's job market opportunities are construed as irrational and irrelevant; in short, useless. What's more, if students fail to make the *right* economic choice, they have only themselves to blame.

In this marketized context, it is little wonder that more and more students have come to see themselves as consumers and their education as consumable products. Though many neo-liberals view consumerist relations as forcing universities to be more accountable to students, they fail to see that rather than making universities more accountable, such actions have had the effect of diminishing student choice, our professional judgement as educators and the space for alternative learning opportunities.

In my experience as a course director at York University, I have found that students increasingly use consumerist arguments in an effort to contest particular curriculum objectives and teaching practices. Students do not readily or consistently argue in consumerist terms, however market principles nonetheless play into their demands to have the curriculum changed to reflect what they consider to be tangible, marketable skills. They typically ask me, "How marketable are these skills?" "How does this stuff have anything to do with the real world?" "Will these skills get me a job?" The normalization of consumerist ideas tend to legitimate these students' demands to learn what they perceive as appropriate and useful in getting a job. More importantly, though, students are increasingly drawing upon consumerist arguments as a means to dispute particular institutional practices that relate to service delivery and customer satisfaction.

In fact, conversations I have had with students reflect how they make use of consumerist relations as a means to assert their rights as students. For example, one student, who had been asked to submit his rough drafts for an essay he had submitted in a Women's Studies course, discussed his situation this way:

> How come I'm being asked to provide drafts of my essay? Are they accusing me of plagiarism? I would never be treated like this in the private sector. I am a consumer and I have a right to be treated and served in a way that gives me what I am here for — an education. There is no way this would happen in the business world. I have rights as a consumer and I'm thinking of getting a lawyer.

This student's comments are particularly insightful. Rather than following the process outlined in the University's rules governing suspected cases of plagiarism and speaking directly with the instructor, he sees his rights as a consumer superseding any notion of academic honesty or integrity. In doing so, he reduces the social relations of learning and teaching to particular notions of "customer service," which, ironically, do not constitute substantiating whether he has done the work himself or not. Not only does he use consumer relations as a means to assert his rights as a student but he also compares the university to a business and appeals to the judicial system as a way to enforce what he sees as his consumer rights. Educational accountability in this context is reduced to whether services have been rendered or not.

In another example at York, a group of students objecting to a course director's teaching practices and course examination were able to withdraw from the course well past the course drop-date. Although the students were primarily concerned with their mid-term examination grades, they argued that, because the course director had made changes to his course outline and the weighting of his assignments past the course drop-date, any changes made without their approval was a breach of contract. Using the process of mass petition, these students success-fully lobbied the administration to allow them to drop the course for a full refund.[32] Regardless of the pedagogical objectives that the course director's original changes may have intended, he was nonetheless required to use his original outline for the remainder of the term.

The ramifications of students using consumer relations of commod-ity exchange as a means to contest administrative and teaching practices are extensive. Since this event, and other coinciding ones described below, all teaching faculty at York University are now required to submit course outlines that detail their grading scheme, weekly schedule of readings and specifics of assignments to their respective departments well before classes begin. These are then posted on their faculty Web sites, along with the rules and regulations governing curriculum changes. The regulations stipulate that any changes made to one's course outline must be done no later than two weeks after classes begin. This new regulatory practice represents a fundamental departure from the former, more loosely defined practice that required teaching faculty to *reasonably* define course expectations before drop-dates. When I inquired as to the reasoning behind the new requirement, one adminis-trator explained to me that, because students were unable to drop courses for a full refund after the two-week period, any changes made after the first drop-date could potentially constitute a breach of contract.

These new regulations require faculty to be accountable to students by providing measurable services as stipulated in our course outlines. The more specific we are in our course outlines as to the grading scheme, assignment requirements, student expectations and penalties for late submission of work, the less likely we will encounter problems of accountability. If we fail to do so, we face possible problems with grade appeals, class petitions and administrative regulation of our classroom teaching. These changes are not necessarily bad in and of themselves, and in some respects may provide students with some recourse in situations where faculty arbitrarily change course require-ments. However, the notion of accountability here is not based on the quality of one's teaching, or the pedagogical objectives of a particular discipline or philosophy, but on narrowly defined notions of quantifiable "services rendered."

Feminist, anti-racist and critical pedagogies, which foster the decentering of knowledge and validate student experiences, subjectivity and personal agency, are severely constrained and potentially negated within the narrow confines of quantifiable and measurable "services rendered." Moreover, students' demands to have what they learn relate to strategic knowledge — and potentially enforced through the contractual obligations of commodity exchange — provide increased opportunities to call into question a professor's efficacy and capacity to teach. Students wanting to know the *right* or *correct* answer, as has been my experience, often see feminist, anti-racist and critical educational practices as a sign of a teacher's incompetence. A Black female professor attending a workshop at York University on "Power in the Classroom" stated that her alternative teaching practices were constantly called into question. Because she had encouraged students to question particular canons of knowledge and did not give them the *right* answer, they perceived her as incompetent and did not consider her to be a serious scholar.

Other important events at York University that have significantly impacted the social relations of teaching and further entrenched the notion of education as a commodity are the two class action lawsuits launched by undergraduate students against the University's administration. The first lawsuit, initiated in 1997, occurred when students lost approximately three weeks of instructional time due to a strike by York University Faculty Association (YUFA). The lawyers representing the students argued that the relationship between the University and the students was a contractual one. In allowing students to sign up for courses through the voice registration system, the University had entered into a contractual arrangement with students to provide a specified number of instructional hours for each course that students had enrolled in. The students argued that, because they had not received the full number of instructional hours paid for, the quality of their education had suffered and, as a result, they were less educated.

Although unsuccessful in illustrating that lost class time constituted material damages, the lawsuit and the emerging arguments have established a significant precedent. Mr. Justice J. Winkler, who presided over the case, determined that, while he could not pass judgement over the quality of education that the students had received, the relationship between the University and the students was in fact a contractual one.[33] Because the complainant representing the students had successfully completed his courses, graduated and found employment due, in part, to his education, no material damages could be claimed. Justice Winkler determined that York University had successfully mitigated any adverse effects of the strike through the actions it had taken in the unpredictable events of the strike and, as a result, had fulfilled its contractual obligations; in essence, it had acted accountably in rendering its educational services.

Justice Winkler's decision is an important one. Not only does it affirm that the relationship between students and the university is primarily a contractual one but it also establishes the criteria of educational accountability as being quantifiable and measurable in outcomes of services received. The subsequent lawsuit against York University further illustrates this emphasis and represents a reorientation of post-secondary education towards meeting the contractual obligations of commodity relations.

The second lawsuit began in November 2000 as a result of the strike between York University and the Canadian Union of Public Employees, Local 3903, representing the University's teaching assistants, graduate assistants and contract faculty. During the seventy-eight-day strike (the longest by educational workers in Canadian history), teaching assistants and graduate assistants identified tuition indexation as the major barrier in reaching a settlement. Tuition indexation, won in the 1992 round of negotiations, guaranteed teaching assistants dollar-for-dollar tuition rebates for any tuition increases greater than the 1992 rates. However, in a bid to clawback previous gains, the York administration attempted to quash tuition indexation, stating that there was excessive pressure from other universities and the Harris government "to get rid of it."[34]

The group leading this lawsuit, the Student Circle, while sympathetic to the workers' concerns, nonetheless drew upon the contractual obligations of commodity exchange and avoided any discussion of affordable or accessible education for undergraduate students. During various interviews with the CBC, Hooman Rowshanbin, the founder of the Student Circle, stated that students had nothing to do with the strike or the issues surrounding it. Rather, he posited that because of the strike and the fact that the administration had not done its utmost to avoid a labour dispute, the university negated its contractual responsibility in delivering its services to its students and, as such, were in breach of contract. Because of this breach, students' contractual rights had been infringed upon and they were therefore in a position to demand monetary redress.

Since the strike, the group has continued its class action suit to demand redress for a host of financial burdens the students incurred during the strike: lost summer employment due to an extended term; lost student loans and bursaries; reimbursement for courses not completed; rent incurred for the extra months of school attendance; and fee reimbursements for foreign students. By appealing to the rules and regulations of contract law and illustrating that they have suffered material damages for services not rendered, they may very well be successful in their class action suit.[35]

Although the lawsuit is still before the courts, the emerging effects can already be seen. As was mentioned earlier, rather than identifying what constitutes good teaching, administrators and managers — themselves removed from classroom practice and pedagogical concerns — are preoccupied with ensuring that faculty produce detailed course outlines, reading lists and grading schemes that ensure neo-liberal accountability practices. While such regulatory mechanisms appear bureaucratically mundane, they have the potential of further entrenching notions of education as a commodity requiring the increasing monitoring and quantification of more and more aspects of our work and our students' work. Within this marketized context, faculty's professional judgement, under the guise of quality and choice, is positioned as secondary to the practices and processes of accountability, and our students' learning experiences are reduced to the acquisition of marketable skills.

*

So how do we collectively resist a curriculum that is becoming more and more generic, depoliticized and market oriented? How do we thwart the evident infringement on our teaching practices and our students' learning opportunities? I believe we need to redefine notions of what constitutes educational quality, accountability and professionalism in our own terms. What does a quality education constitute within our various and diverse disciplines? Who are we accountable to and to what end? What does academic professionalism indicate? How is it experienced and put to work in our intellectual development, research and social contribution to students and society as whole? The ramifications of the contractual obligations of consumer relations may have the potential of further entrenching notions of education as a commodity. However, collaborative resistance with our students in identifying restrictive accountability practices and redefining the terms of what constitutes a "quality" post-secondary education may help in establishing an educational system that is based on social contribution rather than economic gain.

NOTES

While substantially revised, a version of this article entitled "Going to Market: Post-Secondary Educational Reform and the Social Construction of the Student as Consumer" was first presented at the World Congress of Comparative Education (WCCE), Korean National University of Education, Choongbuk, Korea, June 2001. I am grateful to the Office of Research Administration, York University, for providing the funding to attend the conference.

1. Dorothy E. Smith, *The Conceptual Practices of Power: A Feminist Sociology of Knowledge* (Toronto: University of Toronto Press, 1990) and *Writing the Social: Critique, Theory and Investigations* (Toronto: University of Toronto Press, 1999).

2. Janice Newson and Howard Buchbinder, "Corporate–University Linkages in Canada: Transforming a Public Institution," *Higher Education* 20 (1998), 355–379; Neil Tudiver, *Universities for Sale: Resisting Corporate Control over Canadian Higher Education* (Toronto: James Lorimer, 1999); Janice Newson and Claire Polster, "Reclaiming Our Centre: Towards a Robust Defense of Academic Autonomy," *Higher Education Policy* 7 (2000), 18–38.

3. For a similar analysis of neo-liberal prescriptive arguments for reforming post-secondary and public education, see, for example, Michael Peters, *Poststructuralism, Politics and Education* (London: Bergin and Garvey, 1996); Kari Dehli, "Between 'Market' and 'State'? Engendering Education Change in the 1990s," *Discourse: Studies in the Cultural Politics of Education* 17, no. 3 (1996), 363–376; Michael W. Apple, "Between Neoliberalism and Neoconservatism: Education and Conservatism in a Global Context," in Nicholas C. Burbules and Carlos A. Torres, eds., *Globalization and Education: Critical Perspectives* (London: Routledge, 2000), 57–78; Michael Peters, James Marshal and Patrick Ritzsimons, "Managerialism and Educational Policy in a Global Context: Foucault, Neoliberalism, and the Doctrine of Self-Management," in Burbules and Torres, eds., *Globalization and Education,* 109–132.

4. Peters, *Poststructuralism, Politics and Education*, 74.

5. Apple, "Between Neoliberalism and Neoconservatism," 60.

6. Peters, Marshal and Ritzsimons, "Managerialism and Educational Policy in a Global Context," 120.

7. Engin Isin, "Governing Cities Without Government," in Engin F. Isin, ed., *Democracy, Citizenship and the Global City* (New York: Routledge Press, 2000), 156.

8. Peters, Marshal and Ritzsimons, "Managerialism and Educational Policy in a Global Context," 121.

9. Liza McCoy, "Accounting Discourse and Textual Practices of Ruling: A Study of Institutional Transformation and Restructuring in Higher Education" (PhD diss., Ontario Institute for Studies in Education of the University of Toronto, 1999), 10–11.

10. Ibid., 11.

11. Ibid., 3–4.

12. Smith, *The Conceptual Practices of Power*, 149.

13. Expert Panel on the Commercialization of University Research, "Public Investments in University Research: Reaping the Benefits" (Ottawa: Industry Canada, May 4, 1999), 10.

14. For a detailed analysis of the impact of the increasing privatization of university research, see Claire Polster, "A Break from the Past: Impacts and Implications of the Canada Foundation for Innovation and the Canada Research Chairs Initiatives," *The Canadian Review of Sociology and Anthropology* 39, no. 3 (August 2002), 275–299.

15. Quebec is the only province that has maintained its public funding base with student tuition representing only 10 percent of its total funding. Canadian Union of Public Employees, "Ontario Universities and the Double Cohort: What Will Be the Impact on CUPE Members?" CUPE Research Report (October 15, 2002), 4.

16. Sarah Schmidt, "Governments Let Universities Down," Canwest News Service, 11 June 2003, 1.

17. In 1997 the Ontario government reformed the secondary school system reducing its five-year program to four years, thus eliminating Grade 13. Commonly referred to as the "double cohort," the implementation of the plan resulted in the simultaneous graduation of high school students in both Grades 12 and 13 in June 2003. Close to 72,000 students — double the norm — accepted offers of admission from universities across the province. CUPE, "Ontario Universities and the Double Cohort," 4.

18. Schmidt, "Governments Let Universities Down," 1.

19. CUPE, "Ontario Universities and the Double Cohort," 4.

20. Ontario Confederation of University Faculty Associations, "Ontario 2002 Budget — Post-secondary Education Provisions," Press Release, June 11, 2001, 1.

21. Ibid.

22. "Highlights of Operating Grants and Tuition Announcement," Ministry of Training, Colleges and Universities, Government of Ontario. Retrieved from <http://www.edu.gov.on.ca/eng/document/nr/00.03/spacebg.html>. March 15, 2000.

23. McCoy, "Accounting Discourse and Textual Practices of Ruling," 9.

24. Paul Axelrod, *Values in Conflict* (Montreal: McGill-Queen's University Press, 2002), 87.

25. Chris Shore and Susan Wright, "Coercive Accountability: The Rise of Audit Culture in Higher Education," in Marilyn Strathern, ed., *Audit Cultures: Anthropological Studies in Accountability, Ethics and the Academy* (New York: Routledge, 2000), 73.

26. Michael Stevenson, "Strategic Planning for a New Millennium 1999–2010," York University Academic Priorities and Planning Committee Report (May 1999), 72.

27. Pat Armstrong, Caroline Andrew, Anthony Pare and Bryan S. Turner, *The Undergraduate Program Review* (Toronto: York University, Division of Social Science, 2000), 9–10.

28. Jill Blackmore, "Globalization: A Useful Concept for Feminists Rethinking Theory and Strategies in Education?" in Burbules and Torres, eds., *Globalization and Education*, 149.

29. See, for example, Jill Blackmore, "Disciplining Feminism: A Look at Gender-Equity Struggles in Australian Higher Eduation," in L. Roman and L. Eyre, eds., *Dangerous Territories* (New York: Routledge, 1997), 75–95; Dorothy E. Smith, "Report and Repression: Textual Hazards for Feminists in the Academy," in Roman and Eyre, eds., *Dangerous Territories*, 163–178; Tina Barnes-Powell and Gayle Letherby, "'All in a Day's Work': Gendered Care Work in Higher Education," in D. Malina and S. Mastin-Prothero, eds., *Surviving the Academy* (London: Falmer Press, 1998), 69–77; Sandra Bell, Marina Morrow and Evangelia Tastsogloue, "Teaching in Environments of Resistance: Toward a Critical, Feminist, and Antiracist Pedagogy," in M. Mayberry and E. C. Rose, eds., *Meeting the Challenge* (New York: Routledge, 1999), 23–46; and Susan Prentice, "The Conceptual Politics of Chilly Climate Controversies," *Gender and Education* 12, no. 2 (2000).

30. John Ibbitson, "York U Strike All Pain, No Gain," *The Globe and Mail*, 14 December 2000, B3.

31. Ibid.

32. Stacy Lopez, "Students Fed Up with Prof," *Excalibur* (York University), 8 March 2000, A1–3.

33. *Ciano v. York University* (2000), O.J. No.183 Court File No. 97-CU-122189, paras. 15–17.

34. The president of York University, referring to tuition indexation, was quoted by the CUPE 3903 Negotiating Team Members as saying, "We have to get rid of it." Author's personal conversation with team members, January 2001.

35. The rules and regulations governing the proceedings of class action law, while too detailed and involved to summarize here, have provided a further regulatory system for consumers, allowing individuals to collectively sue institutions and individuals who are believed to be in breach of contract. For an analysis of the rules and regulations governing the *Ontario Class Proceedings Act 1992*, see Paul Martin, "Class Action Certification: The Growing Uncertainty," in *Class Action Proceedings* (Toronto: Fasken Martineau DuMoulin LLP, February 2001), A1–24.

CHAPTER 13

LIVING ON CAMPUS: REFRAMING THE RESIDENCE AS A CORPORATE BUSINESS

Elizabeth Blaney & Judy Piers-Kavanaugh

MUCH OF THE RESEARCH ON WOMEN'S WORK and the corporatization of the university has focused on the exploitation of academics. While some publications have discussed the effects of corporatization on students' lives, such as increased tuition fees and poorly paid graduate students with teaching responsibilites,[1] an analysis of the residence system and how it is being reshaped is missing. In this chapter, we argue that corporatization permeates all of the nooks and crannies of the university — including the spaces where we live on campus. Specifically, we expose the realities that we both experienced when we were working in university residences as graduate students.[2] This is our story — it is about power and how it works discursively and materially. It is about how we experienced the residence system as it was being redesigned according to a corporate discourse whose goal is to see education "produced, packaged, advertised, sold and consumed."[3] It is a story of how our feminist consciousness and our concern for issues of equality and justice came into direct conflict with this discourse.

We use the term "discourse" to refer to the relationship between language and people's social reality. According to Norma Jean Profitt, discourse can be defined as a "regulated system of statements and set of assumptions, socially shared, often unconscious and reflected in language, that position people who speak within it and delimit what can be said by framing knowledge within certain bounds."[4] We examine the different discourses that circulated in and around the university residences where we worked and lived. Our intention is to "deconstruct and demystify" the "jargon and terminology"[5] of corporatization that attempt to frame the residence experience as a beneficial one while disguising the degree of exploitation that is actually taking place.

We are aware that our own theorizing is problematic. In different places and in many conversations across campus, a discourse of "corporate control over Canadian higher education"[6] is being invoked in order to construct an argument that vilifies corporatization while romanticizing the past and its relations. While being mindful of our own complicity — how we were able/willing or unable/unwilling to take up our positions to frame or reframe the story of our residence experience — we want to present our story as a reflective conversation. Alongside our personal narratives, we look at arguments that support and contest the corporate discourse so we can better examine our resistance and our complicity in the production and performance of our "labour of identity"[7] — that is, the identities available to and performed by us through the terms and conditions of our work as dons.

Our experiences suggest that the exploitation of staff in the campus residence is on the rise and that many of us are expected to do more for less in the race to the meet the "capitalist patriarchal bottom line of cost efficiency."[8] In the meantime, the reorganization of the residence — or what the university calls the "renewal" strategy — is taking place on the backs of women. We begin by talking about how power shapes the telling of our story.

FEAR OF WRITING

While I embrace the idea of this politics as emancipatory, the actual doing of it is not an easy prospect. As I made my decision to attempt the, as it turned out, difficult yet necessary project of drawing on my own experience as the ground of my analysis, I continually weighed the personal impact against the political possibilities of the text.

— Magda Gere Lewis, *Without a Word*[9]

JUDY: I was and still am afraid to share my criticism of the university because in exchange for my blood, sweat and tears, the university provides an apartment that helps me to continue my doctoral studies. As a working-class student, completing a doctorate is difficult. I was also convinced that the sharing of my personal experiences did not an academic paper make. Even though my personal experience *is* political, as Lorri Neilsen expressed, incidents at the university continue to teach me that "androcentric values of the academy resist notions of the political."[10]

ELIZABETH: I am also a working-class woman. For me it comes down to a working-class fear of personal scrutiny with real consequences — in other words, that I would be called a liar and dismissed. Because I was forced out of residence for not "being trainable" — in their words, "maybe residence living isn't for you," in mine because I didn't co-operate or silence myself — I wonder if the act of writing this chapter is going to bring further scrutiny and repercussions. Magda Lewis says it well:

> It is precisely because of the power of the personal that, traditionally, the academy has encouraged us to believe that knowledge is possible only if we set our looking outside of the context of our lived realities. Contained by the blinders of "objectivity" our peripheral vision has been limited by those restrictive codes which forbid personal discourse. In this context, telling the "truths" we have lived is both difficult and risky; more so for those in positions of subordination — as women are.[11]

Setting Ourselves Up

ELIZABETH: Prior to my doctoral studies, work was sporadic and provided nothing in the way of savings that I might use to support myself while doing graduate work. A previous dean of residence, who was committed to feminist social justice, encouraged me to become a don within my residence. The don supervises the students as a live-in mentor. She encouraged me to do this because living in residence would help me to finance my doctorate. I mention she was dean because when I agreed to take on the job, she had been replaced by a "director of residence." This shift has been referred to in university documents as a "philosophical reorientation."[12] As we argue here, the residence system is shifting towards a more corporate orientation, and residence staff, like the dean and the dons, are being reconstructed to fit into a capitalist paradigm whose objective is an increasingly managed workplace.[13] Despite this, I thought I would still be able to apply my feminist principles and ideas to my work in the residence.

In lieu of monetary compensation, I received a large apartment complete with furniture and janitorial services and a meal plan. Hence, it was not easy to leave residence. Nor was it easy to speak out or to avoid participating in residence life.

JUDY: I became a don about a year after you had left residence. My partner attended the information session sponsored by the university and came home reciting what the residence's work environment would look like. In brief, it was presented as a collaborative work culture with team building, mentoring, mutual commitment and trust, visions and values, community and the opportunity for professional development — these were a few of the clever terms that were used. Coming from a twenty-three-year career in banking, I have to admit I wanted to believe there was a place like this. So, as a "family" we saw this as an "opportunity," and my partner and I decided that I would apply for the position.

ELIZABETH: Historically, the residence system has been based on a model known as the Presidential College System, which was designed to accommodate faculty by offering them an opportunity to live on campus. Within the residence, a faculty member was hired to be a mentor for students and was known as the "don." Assuming this responsibility looked good on their academic record. The expectation was "Do your best while recognizing others' endeavours."[14] Faculty are still recruited as dons but in increasingly smaller numbers; at the time of writing this chapter, only two of seventeen dons in the university are faculty members. Increasingly, more graduate students are being hired for this position. A former don described the shift in terms of it being easier to "control" student dons than tenured faculty. Positions for dons are now advertised as part-time, meaning being on twenty-four-hour call in exchange for room and board. However, this "discourse of opportunity," as Mary Beth Krouse argues, is invoked to justify the below-poverty wages.[15] Furthermore, dons are encouraged to give both residence and academic commitments equal priority. Yet this distorts the reality of present-day graduate-student dons whose residence workloads have increased and who are now required to be on-call twenty-four hours a day, seven days a week.

JUDY: What is interesting are the types of faculty who are deemed "acceptable" dons. There are two faculty who currently live and work in residence. One has been dubbed "the quintessential Renaissance man." The other don is a new faculty member who, in the words of residence administration, is "a woman with a young family." She was given the assurance that her experience in residence would work favourably towards a tenured appointment. Furthermore, while there may be some gender balance, both are white — so while white students see themselves reflected in their "mentors," students of colour are not represented. Who is acceptable and who is not is not necessarily an outcome of corporatization. It is historical.

While I mention there is some semblance of "gender balance" in the male–female ratio, the shift towards a more corporate orientation hasn't shifted gender relations. Dons can live with their partners in residence, but there is an unwritten expectation that both partners must contribute to running the residence. However, while male partners receive accolades for their involvement, which can be as minimal as sitting down to have a beer with the male students during a football game, women (both dons and partners of dons) work unceasingly and are not shown the same appreciation.

THE CORPORATIZATION OF OUR VOCABULARY

In this section, we examine the key discourses that we and the university used to frame our experiences and to construct our understanding of what was going on around us. The discourses helped us to shape our resistance to the corporatization of our own vocabulary[16] as well as to the changes the residence administration was trying to introduce. The elements integral to these discourses include the culture of change; community relations (and its relationship to violence against women); managing diversity; individual psychology; adaptability, trainability and flexibility; accountability; partner collaboration and marketability; and political correctness.

The Culture of Change

ELIZABETH: Camille Natale argues that in the "culture of change," the construction of a "leaner and meaner market based system" is pivotal to business success.[17] Restructuring of the residence involved a number of changes. This included increasing the levels of bureaucracy by adding another layer of reporting responsibilities, which was introduced as a means with which to centralize residence responsibilities, that is, to relieve dons of paperwork so that they might spend more time mentoring students. It also included reorganizing the responsibilities of residence administration away from day-to-day disciplinary issues, for instance, towards more global student concerns. However, the creation of a new level of bureaucracy eroded the dons' authority. It also increased our workloads; dons were expected to attend numerous meetings, sometimes seeming to be little more than policing opportunities.

In a residence document, a discourse of change was invoked to defend restructuring. Specifically, it was recommended that residence could "maximize their educational potential, generate greater revenue ... [and] ... become an important public relations feature for the institution ... a philosophical reorientation."[18] While told that I was an important part of the process, I was never quite sure of what part I played, other than the part of subject without a voice. Resisting seemed futile. My requests for a philosophical discussion, while recognized, were never taken seriously by residence administration. For instance, upon resisting a new level of bureaucracy I was met with blank stares. From my experience, the "culture of change" seemed carefully sheltered. As Maude Barlow and Heather-jane Robertson argue, "[T]he right to participate in decision making is rationed and carefully guarded from those who are most affected by the decisions of those who hold the most power."[19]

Still, I wanted to participate in the restructuring process, especially when the changes affected women's safety in the residence. And when I did have a chance to voice my opinion, I found that I often contradicted myself. At times I would speak out against what I saw as the normalization of violence against women in the residence — for example, when I questioned postering of woman-demeaning advertisements for local bars, censorship was invoked. At other times, I caught myself speaking of change that, now on reflection, was contrary to critical feminist action and a long way from what I envisioned to be a safe residence for women. The unspoken words of "status quo good, change bad" worked to dismiss my concerns and effectively blocked constructive dialogue between myself and other dons and residence administration, especially when it came to women's issues. In fact, for a long time, I could not make sense of what was actually going on in the residence.

What was confusing was that we were told that the changes would benefit us all — both dons and students. This was not the case. The changes actually increased the violence against women in residence. For instance, instead of increasing outside lighting, women who were leery of walking through a dark parking lot were told that they could instead try to find someone willing to let them walk through a neighbouring new co-ed house. Similarly, the creation of a new level of bureaucracy fragmented the dons' responsibilities and authority in ways that increased women's vulnerability to violence. For instance, when a female student disclosed to me that she was being stalked by a male student who was scheduled to move into our residence, I had to attend numerous meetings to try and convince several levels of the new residence bureaucracy of the danger of this move. My attempts were blocked. Instead, the student had to sign a document stating her claims. Residence administration also wanted me and the other residence administration to meet with the male student and his don so that he could defend himself against the claims. This would have been a decision I could have made on my own as a don of the house before the restructuring.

Margaret Somers and Gloria Gibson call this kind of mental confusion "political emotion."[20] Confusion does not come from an inability to name what is happening. We become confused when we cannot place the instance into a historical context and relate it to ourselves and what is going on around us. Indeed, duplicity framed the residence restructuring process — on the one hand, I was told that my input in the change process was important, while on the other hand, any hopes of my being taken seriously were dashed. For example, in the Director's Discussion Paper on the vision of the residence system, the director referred to the restructuring as a "process of renewal and renewing." Dons were told to

> accept [and] participate in [maximizing] the residential experience, work collaboratively ... enhance the developmental opportunities, and optimize the economic potential of the residence ... strive to be part of an organizational culture which values each student, recognizes the input of every staff member, and acknowledges each contribution to the overall residence community.[21]

Yet while "consensus" was articulated within these documents as being the backbone of the process, discussions went flat when substantive consensus was insisted upon. Dons were pushed away from philosophical questions and asked to undertake the "fine tuning and editing." The language of consensus was used to move the renewal processes forward while disguising the corporate goal of creating hierarchical business-like relationships.

Community Relations (and the Issue of Violence against Women)

JUDY: A former staff of my university residence told me that in the university documents relating to residence restructuring she read, the number of times the language of community was used felt to her like violence — that community or some form of community was being forced upon us, as a way to dismiss or downplay the reality of violence against women.[22] In these documents, a community model of residence living was proposed that focused on teams, families and positive living environments, using already established institutional norms and traditions — norms and traditions that are not conducive to women's safety. The "oppressive and abusive relational structure"[23] of this community took many forms, and the concept of community was appropriated by the administration, so too the historical contexts in which these structures exist.

While I was writing this chapter, a security officer suggested to me that the university prides itself on the fact that there have not been any violent attacks (as in murder) committed against women compared with other campuses. In addition to this comment, the officer indicated that the university was enhancing its image as a secure campus. It would seem that his comments are supported by a recent promotional brochure in which the university presents itself as a "safe place to work, study, learn and grow," yet the reality is that the university is proposing cutbacks to security,[24] and the same officer admitted that there have been a number of rapes on campus. These often take place during the first few weeks of the academic year outside of residence on the campus grounds, and are kept quiet by the administration. However, several sexual assaults that occurred in the past academic year have been revealed and a possible cover-up has been exposed. This sexual violence is clearly omitted in the university's electronic monthly newsletter in which security issues focus on vandalism, theft, lost-and-found and parking. The reality is that in residence and elsewhere on campus, violence against women is taking place — it is not decreasing; it is hidden, covered up, individualized, dismissed and explained away by the administration.

Acts of violence against women occur at all levels of the residence system. We know of countless acts of violence against female students — male residence administration against female student; male don against female student; male don against female don; male residence staff against female residence staff; and male residence staff against female students. Yet the discourse of psychology is used to excuse these incidents. Seen as an act of youthful male aggression, violence against women is normalized, constructed as an isolated instance, and the aggressor's behaviour is managed through performance surveillance mechanisms such as "performance bonds." He is successfully rehabilitated into the residence community. Dismissing violence against women is common practice, as is constructing women as being responsible for avoiding it in the first place. In a recent open letter to the university community, the president expressed her "concern" about such "incidents," yet she went on to provide "tips" on how "personal safety," which is "the responsibility of us all," could be ensured.

ELIZABETH: An example of the university's contradictory concern for personal safety happened during my first year as don. In fact, my first action was to push for increased outside lighting. This came about from the physical restructuring that had been done on the women's residences, which resulted in slicing our residence in half to create a more fiscally attractive co-ed residence. In the process, women students were rerouted from a well-lit to a poorly lit entrance, obscured by shadows and surrounded by woods. When I requested immediate action to improve the lighting, I was told that the entrance was "safe enough."

The corporate university once saw community as a threat, but now it sees community as a way to fulfill its agenda of surveillance and control over our environment. Nonetheless, at times, I sometimes embraced the institution's discourse. I wanted to believe that the university's discourse of change and community involved commitments to women's safety and so I heard myself, unproblematically, speak through them, but I was consenting to my own subordination. I failed to push for clearer, less opaque interpretations. While I believe that it is our relationship to community that determines how we tell our own story,[25] it was the telling of my story of community that resulted in my removal. I refused to embrace the "den mother" metaphor of women residence dons, expected of me by both students and residence administration. I insisted that residents view me as an advisor. I questioned residence readings of "house" issues and problems, and I refused to be available for twenty-four-hour surveillance of students. When I sought support from residence administration, I found it used against me.

For example, posters advocating sexual assault and depicting women as sexual predators have been permitted within a discourse of censorship and given further institutional support in public forums. For instance, prior to speaking at a residence event, an ex-don postered my residence and other houses with signs that read When No Means Yes. When I challenged the appropriateness of his topic, I was told that he, the speaker, was "just being controversial." While there may be forums for these kinds of discussions, such as the classroom, debating the question "was it rape or just kinky sex?" in a residential setting seems problematic. There was no analysis of violence against women and what this might mean in a residence context. It was seen as an intellectual exercise devoid of the political. When I pursued the issue and sought support from feminist academics, not only was anti-censorship invoked but so was a discourse of academic freedom — I was charged with violating the speaker's "academic freedom." Yet no one in the residence community referred to my academic freedom and my right to raise my concerns.

JUDY: What you've said about the construction of community is exactly what I fell into. When I came into residence, I wanted to think of community as some untouched perfect place. I forgot that everything is embodied with power. Those in power defined the terms of my employment and how I was positioned as a woman don. This positioning started at our first house meeting where I was introduced to the students as "the mom of the house." The male associate don was not introduced as "the dad of the house." Adrienne Rich sharply distinguishes between motherhood as "the *potential relationship* of any woman to her powers of reproduction and to children" and to motherhood as "the *institution,* which aims at ensuring that that potential — and all women — shall remain under male control."[26]

One evening in the dining hall one of the students turned to me and said, "So what do you do all day?" Over and over again, the way in which I was being constructed meant "there was no place for a 'subject', no place to be human."[27] I recognized that not being a subject meant being the "other." As Angela McBride says, " [T]he other's role is to offer devotion, comfort, constancy, and admiration so that I can be …"[28] In the beginning, each time one of the students would refer to me as their mom, I would correct them. Over time, I began to see that it did not matter how I wanted to be identified — my labour of identity was naturalized into a gendered performance of being don of the house. According to Linda Neilsen, "[T]he master narratives continued to hold sway; they were simply more palatable ones."[29] I have to admit I got tired. I gave in. Angela McBride describes my feelings perfectly, "I [would] sometimes catch myself playing MOTHER to the hilt as if some emcee were about to open an envelope and say, now for the best performance in the role of mother the winner is ..."[30]

At the conclusion of the year, I received a ROLA (Residence Outstanding Leadership Award). I was told that one of the students had commented, "She is always there for us, twenty-four hours a day; she puts our needs ahead of her own." I felt completely co-opted into an institutional agenda where the promise was community but the reality was violence. As Alison Bartlett reminds us, "[T]he persistence of the asexual mother-figure does serve specific institutional purposes in continuing to deny the impact of embodied knowledge through an (apparently benign parental role)."[31]

ELIZABETH: Unlike your experience, I was constructed as the don who would bring issues of difference and violence forward, until I sought professional support from administration for female student leaders. And then things changed. When I approached administration, I was told to bring in a non-Aboriginal man to facilitate a Talking Circle (the current trend in solving disputes is drawing from Aboriginal healing circles, of which this is one). I expressed a problem with this suggestion. Refusing to participate in another co-optation of Aboriginal culture, I also argued that feminist practice was better suited to the situation. I came up with an alternative with which the administration agreed, or so I thought. Instead of hiring the man, I hired a feminist counsellor to help the women work through their difficulties. When it became clear that one session alone would not suffice, I was told to bring in the man who would host the Talking Circle. Upon refusal this time, I was given an on-the-spot evaluation and disciplined for challenging sexist and racist practices.

Managing Diversity

JUDY: Working hand in hand with the discourse of community is the discourse of diversity. By using education as the mechanism through which issues of difference and diversity, specifically issues of race and sexuality, are resolved has only increased the tensions around these issues in the residence. As Susan Chase asks, "What kinds of public dialogue do we have — or fail to have — about various kinds of diversity?" Likewise, "What is the effect of our dialogue or silence on the personal identities that students — and for that matter, faculty and other employees — can comfortably develop?"[32] In my residence, diversity was used to apply sexual and racial differences. Sexuality was talked about in terms of lifestyle and racism as a need for multicultural sensitivity, both of which effectively discouraged constructive dialogue. As one of the dons exclaimed, "It is great what we do for the international students when it comes to diversity. We put them all in [name of particular residence] so that 'they' will be more comfortable."[33]

The corporate agenda appropriates equity and, in doing so, avoids any meaningful action that can achieve equity. Underlying the discourse of the "residence experience" is an assumption that all foreign students are the same and is used as a way to avoid addressing racial equity. The "university student recruitment and integrated marketing brochure" puts it this way: "Living in residence is the definitive university experience." This apparently translates into treating every student the same and ensures that all students — no matter their racial/cultural background — will have the same residence experience and be treated in the same manner. This approach fails to acknowledge systemic violence and action on sexism, racism and homophobia.

When students apply for residence, they choose a particular "lifestyle choice." In other words, students choose whether to live in a co-ed or single-sex residence. Once in residence, if a student finds that she/he would prefer a change in lifestyle choice, she/he has to apply for a change, which is easily facilitated. However, on at least two occasions two transgendered students challenged the institutional discourse. In both cases, the students were living their lives as women but were not accepted as women when they applied to live in an all-female house. When one of the students requested a move from one co-ed house to another, several meetings and phone calls took place before the move was allowed. However, the don of the new house actively resisted the transfer, which resulted in the student being forced to change her mind and staying in her original residence. The administration intended to address the don's discomfort and promised to provide sensitivity training on transgender issues for dons in the following year. In the meantime, however, the student left residence.

Dealing with Change: Adaptability, Trainability and Flexibility

JUDY: Training and education have become a means of helping dons and most residence staff deal with problems. Through a discourse of adaptability, trainability and flexibility, we were brought "onboard" and "onside." At the beginning and throughout the academic year, our training emphasized that it was crucial for dons to model a willingness to embrace change for the good of their student leaders. Part of being adaptable was to be flexible. My experience with flexibility was to be all things to all people. For me, the new changes meant that I was no longer solely a mentor but also a mother, counsellor, programmer, social monitor and caretaker. However, my associate don, a man, escaped many of the duties imposed on me. He was considered to be a true mentor and students hesitated to disturb him because he was "too busy."

ELIZABETH: And those of us who were labelled "untrainable" and "inflexible" were asked to leave residence because we were not doing as we were told. As it was put to me at the time, "Maybe residence isn't a place for you."

JUDY: I was considered trainable. When offered the don position, I was told that because of my "age and life experiences" I was a perfect fit for a large house of primarily new students. What I heard was I was to be the perfect mother to these students. I've often thought that if I had constructed myself differently, I could have avoided what happened — becoming the Other. The students refused to construct me in any other way than "mother." Seeing me as the mother of my own children, seemed to enable them to transfer their mother onto my being. The men of the house came to my apartment asking me to iron their clothes or sew for them. They expected me to always be available. I was considered approachable, getting more knocks on my door than the male don of the same house who was a part-time single student. In one instance, in an effort to redistribute the work, a student requested my assistance and I referred her to the other don. Upon which she claimed, "He already has a lot to do."

But during the writing of this chapter, I remembered that I had constructed myself differently. Throughout my residence experience, I continually tried to make the point that I was more than "mother." For instance, during my interview I stated that mothers are leaders and that my skills and experiences as a mother would benefit me as a don. While I saw myself as someone who fosters independence, I was assured at the end of the interview that a "naive" mother, such as myself, may not be able to function, in other words, be "tough" in order to "discipline" students in residence. I immediately responded by stating that I did not intend to "mother" students in residence. Although throughout the two years that I was don I resisted the construction of mother and students accepted me as leader of the house, they nevertheless fell back on the previous construction of me as mother. Every time students introduced me they called me the "mother of the house." This one part of me was continually pulled out — the part of me that would serve the interests of the institution.

Accountability or Silence

JUDY: Another discourse that helped frame our realties was that of accountability. As incoming dons, we received documentation outlining how the needs of students have changed. More to the point, it was the needs of the institution that had changed. For instance, one of the words I read over and over during the course of the two years I was a don was "accountability." I found myself questioning whether I was accountable to the students or to the institution, whose needs I should put forward and what would happen as a result. While trying to be accountable to both the institution and the students, I ended up working a double shift. It soon became obvious to me that to be accountable to the institution, I did not really need to worry about the students — until it was their turn to evaluate me.

The residence's evaluation process requires residence staff to review one another's job performance on a yearly basis. Recent changes call for more frequent evaluations. I suspect that this is to ensure that staff adhere to the mandate of the institution. In a letter from the director, we were told that our "behaviour will be scrutinized on a regular basis and you will be expected to demonstrate conduct that comes from being in a leadership role."[34] This effectively silenced my voice. I engaged in self-surveillance. I buried the feminist. I said to myself, Shut up now. I felt like a prisoner housed in a brick building. Some of the student leaders I worked with told me they felt like they were always being watched.

We assumed that they were. It seemed to me that this pressure of being watched at all times resulted in student leaders "turning on one another." I found myself weighing every word. I felt eyes always upon me.

ELIZABETH: I know what you're saying. I discouraged the students in my house from turning on one another, insisting that no one in the house was disposable. In the end, I was.

Partner Collaboration and Marketability

JUDY: In one strategic document, the director was quoted as saying, "We must foster a climate of service and be prepared to meet the needs of our partners and customers. We must also be fiscally responsible, innovative ... and ready to meet the challenges of a sophisticated and diverse residential community."[35] It is not indicated just who these partners were. I suspect that in order to achieve fiscal responsibility, partnership discourses determine how much gets done to address problems that arise as a result of partners' marketing strategies; strategies such as Pub Crawls, Mystery Tours and House Wars. Nor is it clear who the "customers" were, what their needs were and what kind of checklist would be used to determine if these needs were being met. According to K. Brookland, the "university formula" results in "student = client = business = money = profit motive = silence."[36]

ELIZABETH: In demanding unquestioned and unremitting loyalty, residence administration emphasized the importance of maintaining a positive attitude. In order to keep a positive attitude, the residence's guiding principles invoked other psychological discourses of the individual — balance, wellness and self-care. Couched in terms of "for our own good" and "for the good of the students," these discourses individualized and constructed those who were not acquiescent to the corporate mandate as individuals with problems. Most of those constructed as individuals with problems were women. In the last two years, four women dons have been forced out of residence, all having committed the offence of questioning the strategies being imposed to improve our attitudes. These include on-the-spot evaluations, public rewards for exhibitions of positive attitudes and team-building workshops. Those with negative attitudes are required to work with those with positive attitudes — for example, dons were told to "behave positively" when speaking to those dons who were seen as negative about restructuring.

Or, as another example, while I tried to bring a critical feminist analysis to "positive" residence living by focusing on women's experiences of violence, the concept was soon co-opted and "positive living" became a mantra for silencing feminist concerns. What administration seems to overlook is that that those of us with negative attitudes might just raise the consciousness of our "more positive" colleagues.

JUDY: In being told to maintain a proper attitude, dons were asked to reframe "challenges" as "opportunities to be embraced and innovatively overcome." After a year as a don, I saw that the challenge was to conceal what was actually taking place. By using a discourse of collaboration, residence staff were encouraged to think and act as a "united front." Student leaders, including those of us who did not take an approach not endorsed by the team, risked discipline, ostracization and being talked about as unwilling to collaborate. As a result, many of us silenced our own dissenting voices. More than one team learned to bully, gossip, threaten and discard one another, creating expendable subjects — modelled on the practices of residence administration. The work culture was also collaborative in the sense that I was told that there would be regular consultations between the residence system and the dons. Consultations usually took the form of e-mails in which administration asked for "feedback" or "input." There was no chance for dialogue, unless the click-clack of computer keys counted. I saw it as an opportunity for residence administration to manage my thinking, perspectives and practice, checking in to see if I was still onboard. When I did raise questions, I was told that I was too deliberative and strident.

ELIZABETH: Returning to my experience around campus lighting, I was shocked when men and women dons worked to convince me that it was safe for the women in my house to walk to their classes across a poorly lit parking lot. I gave into the argument when a token gesture was made to "allow" the women, under strict rules set by the co-ed don, and myself to enter our building through a side entrance. In the end, I grew tired of fighting, so I compromised, which for me was collaboration.

ELIZABETH: Another form of partnership and marketability was the introduction of the "employability skills profile," which was offered to students working in residence. Known as the "Student Development Record" (SDR), the profile falls within the psychological discourse of development; attendance at training sessions formed the basis of the SDR. Administration convinced students that it would increase their marketability upon graduation. In my house I saw it used to police students — each time that a student attended a training session, she/he had to sign-in with both student ID and a personal signature. If the student failed to sign-in, she/he stood to lose a student leadership position if she/he could not provide adequate proof of attendance. It was also a means of constructing us as particular kinds of residence staff with particular kinds of skills and knowledge: few opportunities existed for students to increase their knowledge on issues such as violence against women, heterosexism and homophobia and racism.

JUDY: Prior to the inception of the SDR, student leaders received a room and a portion of their meals in exchange for their student leadership work in residence. However, now students are encouraged to surrender monetary support for promises of marketability. For instance, students leaders are told that the SDR is a "good résumé builder" and a desired vehicle for future employment. At the same time, students are now required to pay the full cost of their meals and some money towards their room.

THE CONSTRUCTION OF WOMEN'S COMPLICITY IN THEIR OWN SURVEILLANCE

JUDY: In the residence system women have been historically constructed in very particular ways. For example, the language of "den mother" used to refer to women dons. Of course, a mother is attached to a man making her legitimate.

ELIZABETH: Because I wasn't attached to a man, I stood to be ridiculed and all sorts of suggestions were made that would enhance my profile. For example, I was often pressured by the women residents in my house to ask one of the assumingly unattached heterosexual residence administration men to accompany me to events. Across residence houses, unattached women's sexuality was often a point of conversation and women dons were constructed as asexualized, desexualized, problematically sexualized — as mothers, whores and lesbians. For instance, during my first term as don in the women's residence, students told me that, in his classes, the male faculty who was don before me would refer to the "sluts" who lived in his residence.

We were told that we, as residence dons, were living in a "fish bowl," meaning that our lives were public. For the first year and half that I lived in residence, I kept my relationship secret, for fear of having my sexuality and relationship scrutinized. I desexualized myself and worked hard at making myself into a certain kind of woman, in order to demonstrate to the women in my residence that a woman's value is not only in relation to someone else. Perhaps that made people even more curious. For upon having my partner spend the night in my apartment, the residence system was informed that someone was sleeping in my bed. The only way that anyone would have known this was if they had entered my apartment without my permission.

JUDY: I understand what you mean. As I mentioned earlier, we received a letter from the director that said, "Your behaviour will be scrutinized on a regular basis and you will be expected to demonstrate conduct that comes from being in a leadership role." However, I also understood that the level of scrutiny that you were forced to endure was different. I was scrutinized, but it was more about whether I was "doing maternal authority" that had been outlined for me from the very beginning. I was also engaging in self-surveillance and silencing myself. While I knew that I was "safely" constructed in the "family" context, I was disappointed when I found myself weighing every word. I felt that eyes were always upon me. There were other moments of self-surveillance that were different than the forms of maternal performance/regulation that I have described earlier. Sexuality and its possible enactment became a site of my complicity in the regulation of other women. For instance, one of the women dons was told that if she continued to date a student, who was also living in residence and who happened to be her own age, she would lose her job. Upon complaining that the same restrictions were not required of a senior male administrator, she was told that his situation was none of her business and that it did not relate to her particular situation. It seemed that after this happened, her life was under a microscope. As a feminist, I wanted to lend my support, but I did not pick up the phone.

ELIZABETH: Interestingly, male dons continue to move in with women students who work in the residences. This is granted legitimacy through future marriage announcements. I have never heard of one of these men being fired. The only time I heard of a male having left residence because of his relations with a female student was when a female don's male partner was found to be harassing women students. He was told to leave the residence and if he refused, she — the don — would have to leave. She left. Thus another woman was dismissed and the issue along with her. Overall, it is difficult not to feel guilty. No matter how hard we try — the two of us, as well as other women dons who have left residence — it's a struggle not to blame ourselves for failing one another as well as the women in our residences. As Mary Beth Krouse so eloquently puts it:

> It is this mind-set that turns "others," as well as ourselves, into objects — the fundamental move of oppression. From this perspective, there is no time to step out of the logic of the system to connect with one another and to see and feel experiences of oppression — our own and one another's. Therefore, we are divided from one another, from ourselves, and from a larger more critical view.[37]

*

So how are things framed in a university residence to ensure that we are, to use Miriam Henry's words, "too busy, burned out …or simply too powerless to exercise a countervailing vigilance"?[38] The parameters of this framework — the attitudes, cultures, visions, profiles, boundaries, constructs and assurances — increasingly promote compliance of the corporate model. Our experiences demonstrate that this model steals what is necessary to achieve its goals. Severed from its social and historical contexts, power, "located in the cultural practice of enframing,"[39] positions itself onto the lives of women. Likewise, the labour of identity is performed and scrutinized to promote compliance through discursive practices of vision statements, programming, profiling, development plans, evaluation, accountability and marketability. We are all implicated. In and of itself, the corporate sector is not the "bad guy." Patriarchy, racism, classism, heterosexism, ableism and elitism are still very much in place. The problem, as we see it, is that feminist analysis and sociopolitically grounded change is further undermined through corporatism's appropriation of these same discourses, turning them and us on our heads in the race to the bottom line.

> It is the strength of those shared stories, however tenuously they may cross, that resistance to everyday begins … This is not mere information; these are experiences that matter, that bring us to our senses. These are the "stones in our shoe."[40]

NOTES

1. See, for example, Neil Tudiver, *Universities for Sale: Resisting Corporate Control over Canadian Higher Education* (Toronto: James Lorimer, 1999); Mary Beth Krouse, "Women and the University as Corporation," in Somer Brodribb, ed., *Reclaiming the Future: Women's Strategies for the Twenty-first Century* (Charlottetown, PEI: Gynergy Books, 1999); and Gordon Lafer, "Graduate Student Unions Fight the Corporate University," *DISSENT* 48 (2001), 63 –70.

2. An earlier version of this chapter was presented at the COOSH Annual Symposium on Women in the Academy: Humanities and Social Sciences Federation of Canada, Women's Issues Network Program, "The Roles of Women Intellectuals in Society: Paid, Unpaid, and Underpaid," Quebec City, May 2001. One of the comments made at the conclusion of the presentation suggested that we need to be conscious of the fact that corporatization inundates the university. The speaker said that while she was aware that corporatization had affected the university, she had not considered how it was also affecting the residence system. In her words, "It was one area which I had completely forgotten about."

3. Krouse, "Women and the University as Corporation," 223.

4. Norma Jean Profitt, *Women Survivors, Psychological Trauma, and the Politics of Resistance* (New York: Haworth Press, 2000), 4–5.

5. Camille Natale, "Eduspeak: A Teachers Guide to the Orwellian Language of the 'Ministry for the Culture of Change,'" *OurSchools/OurSelves* 7, no. 4 (1996), 35–57.

6. Tudiver, *Universities for Sale*, iii.

7. Lisa Adkins and Celia Lury, "The Labour of Identity: Performing Identities, Performing Economics," *Economy and Society* 28, no. 4 (1999), 598.

8. Krouse, "Women and the University as Corporation," 215.

9. Magda Gere Lewis, *Without a Word: Teaching Beyond Women's Silence* (New York: Routledge, 1993), 7.

10. Linda Neilsen, *Knowing Her Place: Research Literacies and Feminist Occasions* (Halifax: Backalong Books, 1998), 150.

11. Lewis, *Without a Word*, 5.

12. Document not cited for reasons of anonymity.

13. James Paul Gee, "Foreward: A Discourse Approach to Language and Literacy," in Colin Lankshear, ed., *Changing Literacies* (Philadelphia: Open University Press, 1997), 84.

14. A remark made by residence administration at an information session for incoming dons, explaining the expectations of the residence office and how these have shifted through a reconfiguration of the don position.

15. Krouse, "Women and the University as Corporation," 218.

16. See Natale, "Eduspeak."

17. Ibid., 41.

18. Document not cited for reasons of anonymity.

19. Maude Barlow and Heather-jane Robertson, *Class Warfare: The Assault on Canada's Schools* (Toronto: Key Porter Books, 1994), 125.

20. Margaret Somers and Gloria Gibson, "Reclaiming the Epistemological 'Other': Narrative and the Social Construction of Identity," in Craig Calhoun, ed., *Social Theory and the Politics of Identity* (Oxford: Blackwell, 1994), 59.

21. Document not cited for reasons of anonymity.

22. Anonymous, personal communication with author, 1998.

23. Marilyn Friedman, "Feminism and Modern Friendship: Dislocating the Community," in Eve Browning Cole and Susan Coultrap-McQuin, eds., *Explorations in Feminist Ethics: Theory and Practice* (Bloomington: Indiana University Press, 1992), 95.

24. Anonymous, personal communication with author, 2001.

25. See, for example, Rina Benmayor, "Testimony, Action Research and Empowerment: Puerto Rican Women and Popular Education," in Sherna Berger Gluck and Daphne Patai, eds., *Women's Words: The Feminist Practice of Oral History* (New York: Routledge, 1991), 167.

26. Adrienne Rich, *Of Woman Born*, quoted in Rosemarie Tong, *Feminist Thought* (San Francisco: Westview Press, 1989), 87. Italics in Tong.

27. Jane Gallop, *The Daughter's Seduction: Feminism and Psychoanalysis* (Ithaca, NY: Cornell University Press, 1982), 12.

28. Angela Barron McBride, *Living with Contradiction* (New York: Harper Colophon, 1979), 57.

29. Neilsen, *Knowing Her Place*, 106.

30. McBride, *Living with Contradiction*, 93.

31. Alison Bartlett, "A Passionate Subject: Representations of Desire in Feminist Pedagogy," *Gender and Education* 10, no. 1 (1998), 88.

32. Susan Chase, "Universities as a Discursive Environment for Sexual Identity Construction," in Jaber Gubrium and James Holstein, eds., *Institutional Selves: Troubled Identities in a Postmodern World* (New York: Oxford, 2001), 142.

33. Monthly meeting of the Board of Dons, April 2002.

34. Document not cited for reasons of anonymity.

35. Document not cited for reasons of anonymity.

36. K. Brookland, "University Formula," *The Brunswickan*, 25 January 2002, 4.

37. Krouse, "Women and the University as Corporation," 232.

38. Miriam Henry, "Globalisation and the Politics of Accountability: Issues and Dilemmas for Gender Equity in Education," *Gender and Education* 13, no. 1 (2001), 92.

39. Ibid.

40. Neilsen, *Knowing Her Place*, 119.

CHAPTER 14

CONTROL, ALT, DELETE? FEMINIST PEDAGOGY AND THE DIGITAL ACADEMY

Cynthia Jacqueline Alexander

The enormous expansion of ICT ... throughout the 1990s began to change both the world economy and the place of higher education institutions in that economy. Debates on borderless universities, e-learning and the expanding global reach of higher education remains ungendered.
— Louise Morley et al., "Sounds and Silences"[1]

IN THE KNOWLEDGE-BASED ECONOMY, computer mediated technologies (CMCs), or information and communication technologies (ITCs) as they are sometimes referred to, are key elements in the transformation of higher education. From the concept of the academic community to the nature of academic work to the meaning of academic literacy, institutions of higher learning are in a period of profound — and felt — transition. Discussions about the role of universities in the twenty-first century, and about the teaching and learning processes within academe, have tended to ignore the value-laden choices that accompany the adoption of computer-based learning networks. Indeed, technological systems tend to be introduced on university campuses as if they were value-neutral; not surprisingly, then, the questions, challenges and opportunities related to gender and technological innovation on campuses largely remain unidentified, let alone broached.

Computer-based learning models are being introduced in a period when commitments to academic freedom, tenure and other hard-won professional entitlements are being threatened. The time required to "alt"er traditional learning models using new media resources may be compelling for constructivist feminist pedagogues, but such activity involves a degree of professional risk, including foregone research and publishing opportunities. Indeed, innovation initiatives, as exciting and rewarding as they might be, are sometimes too professionally and personally costly, leading to a decision to reverse or "delete" their innovations in the classroom. Simply stated, it may be much easier, more pragmatic and far safer to stay the course within the prevailing academic system and forego opportunities to introduce technological innovation in the classroom. This is particularly true for women. Jon Carroll's observation of the academic classroom makes this clear: "It's a place of ancient grievances and little charity. It is a place with rules of combat codified two hundred years ago on the Continent. And it is definitely a place where women are always held to a higher standard."[2]

Academe is "a political playground in which teaching, curriculum development, assessment and educational policy formation are value-laden political acts that operate with historically constructed relations of power."[3] Successful technological innovation in any complex organization depends on leaders who champion change, who introduce processes to manage change, who allocate adequate resources (including time) and, most importantly, who bring a willingness to re-evaluate current power relations, dominant values and prevailing cultures within the learning environment. If technology is overlayed on top of existing structures and processes (including tenure and promotion processes), it tends to exacerbate rather than alleviate existing problems (including learning challenges), and deepen rather than close existing cleavages (including gender). Given that technological systems are not neutral artifacts but are embedded with values, then we must not perceive the introduction of educational technology as existing "free from the environmental limits and social logics that constrain the rest of the world."[4] As feminist academics, this recognition should give us reason enough to examine critically the new digital environments in our midst and on the horizon. Given that we "are, in universities, caught up in a vast episte-mological re-negotiation," then what opportunities exist to advance feminist pedagogy in the new technological frontier?[5] Indeed, what are the stakes and implications for those who seek to advance feminist pedagogy using new media technologies? This chapter explores the cre-ation of new feminist technological designs and the professional opportunities — and negative implications — of doing so.

GENDER DISCREPANCY IN COMPUTING SCIENCE

A 2002 Pew Internet and American Life Project study found that American college students are early adopters and heavy users of the Internet, with one-fifth (20 percent) of college students in the United States initiating their use of computers between the ages of five and eight. While the Pew study informs us that almost half of all college stu-dents (48 percent) are required to use the Internet to contact other students in at least some of their classes, and offers us important insights into how college students use the Internet socially and academically, there is no gender analysis.[6] Similarly, there is no gender analysis in Acadia University's annual computer-use survey of students and faculty at the university (an IBM ThinkPad campus similar to the approxi-mately thirty other campuses in North America in which IBM laptop computers are available to every student and faculty member).[7] In the midst of the sea-changes that are accompanying technological change, the gender dimensions of the computer revolution should *not* be over-looked. Although the number of women enrolled in university-level computer science was growing in the 1980s, in the 1990s their numbers plummeted. Technological systems, including hardware and software, are not value-free. Instead, they reflect the values, assumptions, choices and objectives of those who design and implement them. The gender discrepancy in computing science across North America is appalling:

> [B]y almost any measure we might choose, men dominate the computer world through sheer numbers. Eighty-seven percent of all doctorates in computer science go to men (and two-thirds of all bachelors degrees); 92% of all computer science faculties are male (and 97% of all tenured faculty). These numbers suggest that those who are designing hardware, software, and networks, supporting and servicing them, and teaching about them are most likely to be men.[8]

A landmark 1999 report by a Massachusetts Institute of Technology committee on how its female science faculty had been systematically discriminated against for decades shook institutions of higher learning in the United States and Canada: "The report acted as a call to arms for many female faculty members across the country displeased with the conditions under which female professors were often forced to work."[9] By January 2001, presidents, chancellors, provosts and twenty-five women professors of nine top research universities in the U.S. held an all-day meeting at MIT in an unprecedented dialogue on equitable treatment of women faculty in science and technology based on the recognition that "'barriers still exist' for women faculty."[10] Monique Frize, the NSERC/Nortel Joint Chair for Women in Science and Engineering (Ontario), reflects on the need to remedy the crisis in engineering:

> There is no question that Faculties of Science and Engineering need to have a higher number of women faculty. Having women with varying attributes, styles, and attitudes would be helpful on many counts: first, their presence in the classroom and in the laboratory demonstrates that women are competent and that they belong.[11]

A 1995 University of Washington study found that the highest drop-out rate for females in engineering is right after the freshman year and that the reasons women drop out include "feelings of isolation, experiencing a chilly campus climate, and the lack of role models, but not poor grades."[12] It says a lot about the computer revolution that gender inequity on university campuses is profoundly and appallingly evident in the discipline of engineering.

Men and women use computer technology differently, as computer anthropologists Sherry Turkle and Dale Spender have informed us. In May 2000, the Pew Internet and American Life Project published its study "Tracking Online Life: How Women Use the Internet to Cultivate Relationships with Family and Friends," in which some interesting gender differences in the use of the Web were identified. More than men, women seek out health information, search for religious or spiritual information, find job information and, surprisingly, play on-line games. The study found that the "most conspicuous thing about online women is that they become attached to email early in their online life."[13] Like earlier technologies, such as television and video cameras, computer technologies have great educative and democratic potential. However, like other technologies, their democratizing potential can be lost or abandoned or perverted to meet petty ends. Consider, for example, the number one activity on the Internet of "linking cyberdiscourses to worlds offscreen, we see the vicious traffic in women that has been given new life by the Internet, a traffic that affects women of all races."[14] Technology tends to take the path of least resistance, reinforcing dominant power bases, exacerbating existing cleavages and reflecting prevailing values and assumptions.

What are the implications of a technology of "command and control" on the lives of women in university and college communities? Tara Brabazon suggests that "[t]echnology is driven by the competitive business sector … In this environment, a teacher's behavior has to be controlled, scrutinized and evaluated. Radical ideas and expansive research are crushed into modules, criteria and bullet points, being rendered consistent and predictable."[15] Consideration of the new roles for twenty-first-century universities leads James Duderstadt to caution, "The market forces unleashed by technology and driven by increasing demand for higher education are powerful. If they are allowed to dominate and reshape the higher education enterprise, we could well find ourselves facing a brave new world in which some of the most important values and traditions of the university fall by the wayside."[16] There are four special interest groups that have a stake in e-learning: (1) vendors of computer software and hardware; (2) corporate training advocates who view training from an economical high speed, highly specialized perspective; (3) university administrators who wish to be considered up to date with the most modern educational systems; and (4) technological "zealots" who view computers as the solution to every problem and simply enjoy working with them.[17]

For Randall Engle, the "frenzy to infuse corporate management models into intellectual, academic settings not only represents a threat to long-standing academic traditions such as open intellectual discourse, debate, and critical analysis, but also documents the determination of corporate technocrats and managers to become prominent players and decision-makers in all aspects of the ever-expanding educational marketplace."[18] The resistance to these corporate initiatives was aptly demonstrated at two Canadian universities. In February 1998, 91 percent of Acadia faculty voted to strike. In an "Open Letter to Our Students," the Acadia University Faculty Association stated: "For

Faculty, the real issues are those of traditional academic principles and practices. These include ... [a]cademic freedom — the right of professors to decide how and what to teach, within the agreed guidelines of traditional curriculum development."[19] At York University, Canada's third largest institution of higher learning, full-time faculty ended a two-month strike in response to unilateral administrative initiatives to implement instructional technology. Among the initiatives was an official solicitation to private corporations inviting them to place their logo permanently on a university on-line course in return for a $10,000 contribution to courseware development. The contract realized a historic first: that all decisions regarding the use of technology as a supplement to classroom instruction or as a means of alternative delivery

> "shall be consistent with the pedagogic and academic judgements and principles of the faculty member employee as to the appropriateness of the use of technology in the circumstances." ... Thus, the York faculty will be able to ensure that the new technology, if and when used, will contribute to a genuine enhancement rather than a degradation of the quality of education, while at the same time preserving their positions, their autonomy, and their academic freedom. The battle is far from won, but it is a start.[20]

In the past decade, health and education have been the last professional domains that the informatics sector has fought hard to infiltrate. As in the health sector, the informatics industry is promising to realize "substantial efficiencies" in education, as David Noble describes:

> Educom, the academic-corporate consortium, has recently established their Learning Infrastructure Initiative which includes the detailed study of what professors do, breaking the faculty job down in classic Tayloristic fashion into discrete tasks, and determining what parts can be automated or outsourced. Educom believes that course design, lectures, and even evaluations can all be standardized, mechanized, and consigned to outside commercial vendors.[21]

The potential exists for the same kind and degree of administrative surveillance and supervision, regimentation, discipline and even censorship that have been apparent in other professional fields, especially those dominated by women such as nursing and social work. Those who herald CMCs in higher education point to their ability to enable universities to compete "effectively for additional students while maintaining the same or smaller faculty."[22] Significantly, in a knowledge-based economy that privileges the hard sciences and undervalues the arts, especially the humanities where women are the majority of faculty members, the gender implications of such developments are serious. As Jill Arnold and Hugh Miller astutely observe, "Academia is also a place that often seems to be trying to turn itself into a market place and the output of student endeavours (and our own) are commodified ... there are plenty of issues left for us [as feminists] to tackle as we gain territories in cyberspace too."[23]

FROM STUDENT TO CONSUMER

The transformation of students into "clients" has pushed academic institutions to serve their "consumers" who are seeking to optimize their educational dollar in ways that increase their competitiveness in the knowledge economy. David Whittle, an IBM executive and cultural commentator, has stated that "over the years, I've learned far more online about how things really work than I learned about how things should work in theory in six years of higher education as an undergraduate and graduate student."[24] Whittle's comment aside, we need to ask what it means to be literate in the technological age. How can students' use of CMCs enable them to become deeper thinkers, effective learners and astute problem solvers? There is no turning the clock back to a time before the Internet. Instead, there is a need to "begin to understand what appropriate educational implementation of these new tools might be, and more importantly, that we might begin to take seriously what it could mean to see and better imagine the ways in which new technologies have already altered, and will continue to alter, what it is we know and how we know it."[25] Technology tends to reinforce existing power bases, organizational processes, cultures and systems. "The possibilities offered by the web to enable academics to construct a cyberculture free from traditional, cultural, sexual political baggage are offset by continuing ambivalence about visual representations and the ongoing vulnerabilities of women academics to issues of status equality."[26]

Rather than privileging dominant ways of knowing and communicating, technological systems can be designed that support multiple learning methodologies. Rather than supporting passive-based learning methodologies that have tended to accompany the old "chalk and talk" information-sharing model, students can become producers of information, creating "knowledge as they are making meaning of information and its relationships to their day-to-day lives."[27] Computer-mediated communication technologies can support humanist pedagogies; for example, "online discussions may be one tool to help students collaboratively construct a better understanding of course material and examine the ways that their newly-constructed knowledge intersects their day-to-day activities. As a result, students become more fully engaged in the educational process, and thus more fully human. Isn't that one of the points of a liberal arts education?"[28]

In 2001, when the 120 participants of the Fourteenth Annual Cross Faculty Teaching Forum on the Future of Educational Technology were asked to envision what a course at Queen's University in Kingston would look like in five years' time, they expressed the following commonly held visions about technology: (1) it can be used to disseminate basic knowledge, which frees classroom time for discussion and other interactive activities; (2) it can enhance interactivity between students and between students and instructors; (3) it provides greater flexibility about when and what students learn, including catering to students with disabilities; (4) it increases access to knowledge worldwide; and (5) technology should not diminish Queen's role as a residential university and should be recognized by the institution as having the potential to contribute significantly to teaching and learning. Interestingly, in its report, the Learning Technology Faculty Associates included a section on pedagogical and technical support but failed to include any gender considerations.[29] This is not surprising, given that universities, like governments and other organizations, still vastly underestimate, or ignore altogether, the full costs of innovation. For example, technological innovation within institutions of higher learning necessitates a time commitment from faculty that diverts their attention away from other scholarly pursuits or from scarce personal time and resources. Yet at Acadia University, for example, no course-relief time to develop new computer-mediated pedagogies and course material was built into their IBM ThinkPad campus initiative. With students arriving on campus in 1998 to enjoy the benefits of the "Acadia Advantage," the pressure was on faculty to discover or develop new ways to realize the potential of ICTs to enhance the learning process.

For women, the implications of allocating time to pedagogical and technological innovation are serious, as Tara Kuther illustrates: "Academic careers pose tripartite demands of research, teaching and service; at many institutions — perhaps the majority — professors find that campus time is taken up mostly by the latter two, leaving research and writing for evenings and weekends — time that women need to keep up their homes and raise their families."[30] When software design, curriculum development, Web design and maintenance, e-mail interaction and new media student course material to evaluate are added to the responsibilities of the academic innovator, something has got to give, personally or professionally. Academic workloads increase. The challenge and the opportunities technology proffers may drive innovation, may fuel inspiration among the faculty member and her students and may successfully realize new pedagogical objectives. However, at some point, unless administrative and cultural transformations have accompanied the introduction of hardware and software, the harsh reality is that time would have been better spent on research and publishing.

Even when a campus-wide model of computing is introduced, it cannot be assumed that its administration alone will pose the greatest challenge to individual academic innovators. In our Information Society, the term information "have-nots" is immediately recognizable. What innovators in laptop campuses need to worry about are not the "have-nots" but the computer "will-nots." Just as confounding and interesting as the strong personal relationship humans build with particular software (such as WordPerfect versus Word) or hardware (IBM versus Macintosh), so too are personalities and politics mixed up with campus computing initiatives. Innovators may be resented, viewed as superficial, crude and rude peddlers of computer-based pedagogies, perceived as practitioners of academic neo-sophistry or, at best, gadget-wielding, naive techno-enthusiasts.

Often academic innovators are wooed by the administration. For example, first-wave faculty at Acadia University received an e-mail inviting them to pick-up a package the first Christmas following their technological efforts. In a world without bonuses and few accolades for teaching innovation, finding yellow ski-jackets emblazoned with the IBM logo was met first with surprise and perhaps some hidden glee about the acknowledgement of their hard work. However, being marked as an innovator by virtue of a jacket in addition to the deed meant that few faculty members wore their coats on the small campus, and some tried to scratch out or embroider over the IBM logo. The coats were not worn because they were not necessarily perceived as a badge of service but as a mark of complicity in senior management's technological scheme. The implications of using, if not buying into, the administration's technological initiative presented some serious implications for workplace collegiality. There was no evident comprehensive change of management strategy at Acadia, beyond the phasing in of faculty and students over several years and a competition for allocating meagre "innovation funds."

While roundtables for first-wave faculty offered a chance to share successes and frustrations, faculty's recommendations to enhance the innovation process were not followed up on and few bridges were built between first-wavers and the rest of the campus. The small size of the campus community of 3,700 students meant that the gulf between the technological innovators and technological will-nots was quite marked and, in some cases, it was not very subtle. Interestingly, but not surprisingly, old cleavages within small departments, based on ancient history and personalities, were compounded by choices about whether or not to embrace technological change. Structured or reasoned discourse about the value dimensions involved, gender relations, pedagogical alternatives, technological choices, strategic departmental visions and objectives were neither encouraged nor resourced, although some departments independently identified and took up the opportunity to strategize or collaborate. Timetables, course credits and other institutional frameworks were not reconsidered. Instead, at Acadia as elsewhere, technology was overlaid on top of the existing, and some would say, archaic university infrastructure. The focus was on getting the technological hardware and software in place and selling the new computer-mediated learning environment to prospective students. A comprehensive ICT strategy must be based on critical thinking not only about technological choices and fiscal realities but also about the relationship between technology and institutional patterns of racism, sexism and poverty issues.

There is much to be learned from early campus adopters of computer technology. The Acadia Institute for Teaching Technology (AITT) undertakes an annual faculty computing survey, although gender analyses have yet to be undertaken. In December 2002, the AITT Faculty Survey received a 100 percent response rate from faculty, with 39 percent of respondents having taught more than ten years. One faculty member stated: "I need creative solutions to help me guide [students] away from simply looking up a topic online and in 5 minutes, thinking they are experts, and to guide them towards critical thinking and analysis. In the early days, I thought use of the laptops would encourage critical thinking but sadly, it doesn't."[31]

Embedded in this statement is the assumption that somehow, the mere possession and use of a laptop would inspire and enlighten the student who used it. At Acadia and elsewhere, the faculty "we are talking about are process changers ... Innovative faculty appear to be constantly pushing the edge of the problem, and as soon as it gets close to being solved, they reformulate the whole thing and start again."[32] Hence, the buzz of activity that technological innovation introduces can shake up the institution in unexpected ways.

Although there certainly is a need for including the experiences and interests of female faculty, students and staff, the computer use surveys and studies at Acadia have not done so. For example, during the transition to the Acadia Advantage (AA), when students in the Faculty of Arts were allowed to voluntarily opt into the AA, there were courses that included both students who possessed a laptop and those who did not. In those early years, it was female students without laptops who needed extra attention in the after-class computer labs. It was fascinating to watch their body language change when they sat in front of the screen to learn how to use PowerPoint. At first, they were terribly fearful and hesitant that their actions would somehow break the system. By the end of the session, their feelings of empowerment were clearly evident as they enjoyed their newly acquired ability. More recently, in my Fall 2002/Winter 2003 courses, I introduced my students to digital video equipment. Most of the young women were fearful about using the technology as "producers" as opposed to consumers of new digital information. Indeed, at first they were angry that I would ask them to bother to learn how to use this new communication resource. Within one learning session, they were clearly empowered, so much so that some of the women volunteered in subsequent classes to work with the technology.

One might overlook such technology as superfluous in a university classroom — particularly a political science classroom — but learning to use the technology as an information and communication resource is an academic experience not to be overlooked in the knowledge economy. Furthermore, for my international students of colour, adding new media technologies to their Web design and building experience connected

them in important ways to their communities at home. Indeed, technological resources can serve as tools for building bridges between different
communities of interest in the classroom as well as off-campus. One of
the challenges in pursuing such endeavours is that

> [w]hen students have the additional task of acquiring computer skills in
> their courses, less time is available for development of these missing com-
> ponents. Many professors are concerned that classroom listening and
> note taking skills may be decreasing as students depend more on
> PowerPoint presentation outlines and upload notes. The number of dis-
> tractions available in the form of email, ICQ, and the internet has also
> increased.[33]

Clearly, the introduction of laptop computers into a traditional learning
environment poses significant challenges, not the least of which are the
distractions available to every connected student. A *New York Times* article in 2003 illustrates the magnitude and breadth of the challenge:

> "This is an addictive thing that hurts the students themselves," says Ian
> Ayres, a professor at the Yale Law School who opposes much of the
> Internet's entry into the classroom, saying that computer use is rude and
> that other students are "demoralized" by seeing their peers attention wan-
> der. "When you see 25 percent of the screens playing solitaire, besides its
> being distracting, you feel like a sucker for paying attention," Professor
> Ayres said.[34]

Among the observations of new faculty's involvement in the Acadia
Advantage, the Centre for Organizational Research and Development
(COR&D) study found that their actual experience of teaching with
technology meant that "the instructor was on call 24 hours per day.
There was frustration when students expected new faculty to know how
to deal with problems with equipment and student laptops. Faculty
learned as they went along, but this meant extra preparation time, especially when discovering what technological tools work effectively.
Faculty members estimate that this process increased prep time 4 to 10
fold."[35] The expectations and assumptions of students have to be considered when one considers whether or not to introduce innovative
computer-mediated pedagogies, particularly when some students might
be uncomfortable or ill-prepared to participate in a new learning environment. Women faculty who are thinking about accepting the risks
that accompany innovation of any kind should consider the implications of innovation in the classroom, given the growing emphasis on

"client" satisfaction and the influence of students' course evaluations on annual assessments of faculty performance. As students' ideas of what constitutes a good education shift and as they adopt the consumer mentality, the pressure to pander to student expectations can become intense and irresistible.[36]

There is a need to examine the frustrations and burn-out that may arise in this period of technological innovation in university environments. The pressure to introduce technological teaching innovations is increasing at the same time that faculty are being expected to, among other things, compete for scarce research funding and publish as much or more than was expected in previous decades. Both the research and teaching environments have changed markedly in the past decade. The "halo effect" of technology, or what we might call the presumption that learning becomes a "point and click" endeavour, glosses over the complex process of learning. The ability to produce clean, glossy and well-designed (if not well-conceived or well-composed) essays can blind a student to the need to commit to the hard work of reading, assessing, interpreting and communicating complex information effectively. The transition from a print-based culture to a media-saturated "jolts per minute" culture means that students take less care in the tasks involved in preparing an assignment.

The challenge is to ensure that the pursuit of knowledge is not transformed into attainment of mere competence. What are the implications for the knowledge economy of such change? In male-dominated disciplines, the implications of consumer-based evaluations for innovation designed to promote feminist pedagogy are serious. Given that feminist pedagogy is rooted in social change, the learning environment may not be easy or emotionally uplifting; the challenge, then, is that with the shift in pedagogical authority, students' *re-definitions of themselves as consumers reinforce, in turn, teacher strategies to produce satisfied and entertained consumers.*[37] In this context, it is a lot easier and there is less at stake professionally to define innovation by virtue of providing lecture notes that have been converted into PowerPoint presentations, computer-generated quizzes and computer-mediated seminars.

FEMINIST INNOVATIONS

In 2001, taking up the opportunity and the challenge to be an innovator, I co-designed the Digital Agora information and communication resource. In a nutshell, the objectives that I wanted the technology to serve included providing opportunities for collaborative learning; developing lateral and linear thought processes; and encouraging consideration of multiple perspectives on any given subject or issue. On the Digital Agora Web site students could find everything they needed for the course, including their course syllabi; additional resources to consult; digital video tapes of the research being undertaken by key political scientists in Canada; lateral maps for lectures; a gender-friendly and ethnically diverse symbol bank that students could use to make their own lateral maps (sometimes referred to as idea maps); and an on-line tutorial.

The software was designed by Carolyn Watters (the only full-time female computer science professor in Nova Scotia at the time) along with several undergraduate computer science students. Our team included Watters, Marshall Conley, myself and a group of primarily undergraduate women. With funding from Acadia University and a SSHRC President's Grant for Innovation, the Digital Agora became one of the showpieces of the Acadia Advantage. The objectives, the design process and the application of the system were founded on the principles of feminist pedagogy.

The classroom's wall expanded when junior class assignments were shared with and commented on by students in senior classes at Acadia, and when Acadia students held on-line discussions on political issues with their counterparts at Lethbridge one year and with students at the Hebrew University in Jerusalem another year. We found that when students shared their work with their peers, via the on-line newspaper, their interest levels and aspirations increased. In subsequent years, I became more innovative. When the Fall 2000 federal election was called, I challenged the students in my Introduction to Law, Politics and Government course to build a Web site for national consumption that would inform and engage Canadians about an issue that was not receiving adequate attention. The result of their efforts was the comprehensive site CanWIN e-2000 (Canadian Women's Issues Network for Election 2000), which included gender-related political and policy facts and information they researched; interviews with candidates, fellow students and local community residents; gender-based assessments of media coverage; and moderation of an on-line national (and international) dialogue about gender issues in the election. The feedback that students received from activists like Judy Rebick and from interested Canadians inspired them to go well beyond what is typically expected in an introductory course. Their collaborative work ultimately earned them an invitation to participate in the first Election Town Hall hosted by *CBC National.*

Several years later, the innovation continued. Students in my Gender and Politics class were invited in Winter 2003 to identify an issue that they would like to research together and a community that they would like to serve in the course of their research collaboration. They chose to focus on their own backyard, after initial research indicated that sexual assault and sexual harassment on campuses in North America were important issues that were not receiving the attention they merited. Working in partnership with the equity officer at Acadia and with other stakeholder communities, their collaborative research and writing project culminated in the creation of a new Healthy Relationships Web site for Acadia University. Their interest in and knowledge of the subject matter far surpassed anything that mere reading of a textbook or writing a paper could achieve. In the fall 2003, students in my Politics of Identity class worked in partnership with diverse communities of interest to produce two major reports: (1) a comprehensive Task Force Report on Cross-Cultural Relations at Acadia, and (2) a major funding proposal to create an African-Canadian Youth Network national Web site and a summer ICT Learning Institute for African-Canadian youth and community leaders. Students involved in community-based learning initiatives gained a whole set of aptitudes and attitudes that would never be broached in a traditional classroom. Furthermore, their productive capacity served the needs and interests of under-resourced community stakeholders.

This experience in innovative pedagogies, which harness the power of ICTs to realize greater equity in the classroom and in the service of diverse community stakeholders, indicates that the role of the university in the knowledge-based economy and in society can change quite radically. That is, just as national granting councils like SSHRC are asking academics to achieve new levels of public outreach, the university can ask students to share their work with the community. As Cathy Davidson agrees:

> Educational technologies might also be used to help close the "digital divide" that separates social "haves" and "have-nots." As in the past, the

creation of a new technology tends to highlight the gap between the affluent and the impoverished — whether within a nation or between rich and poor nations. Reconceiving the campus could help here. Mentorships between college students and children from disadvantaged backgrounds could become a service component in courses from math to sociology. Technology could facilitate these interactions, which would have a variety of social and educational goals. We also know that there is a technology gender gap. Similar mentoring relationships between female college students and young girls could help here, too.[38]

In my senior Public Administration class — a subject typically regarded as terribly boring — my students agreed to work together to investigate, from the perspectives of youth, the evolution and direction of e-government as realized by the Canadian federal government. They worked hard at their project, and the final product was a collaboratively designed Web site that offered their assessments; they knew that the site's content would be reviewed by senior officials in the federal government. Their final class involved a teleconference with senior federal government policy officials. No such study has ever before been undertaken by a team of students. They felt and knew that they were offering input into the policy-making process and were given feedback by Privy Council Office officials that their assessments were accurate and their insights were valuable.

These examples are indicative of how technology can reshape learning relationships and engage and inform students effectively and meaningfully. In such a deeply collaborative learning environment, anything less than coming to class prepared affects the whole class and the community stakeholders who are the partners in the classroom. The sense of responsibility for learning moves beyond the individual or the student–faculty relationship into the classroom as a shared endeavour. Indeed, the responsibility moves beyond the student's obligation to herself, to her professor or to her peers to include the communities that the class chooses to serve, from the nation of voters, to their fellow university community, to the African-Canadian communities, to policy officials influencing and citizens affected by e-government initiatives. Those changed relationships, facilitated by technology, are what moves learning into the twenty-first century. Such relationships become truly meaningful knowledge networks.

The opportunity exists to encourage students to become knowledge producers. The Canadian Network of Federalism Studies, for example, invites both undergraduate and graduate students to submit their essays for publication in the network's two electronic journals.[39] And Dave Knowlton suggests

> online discussions may be one tool to help students collaboratively construct a better understanding of course material and examine the ways that their newly-constructed knowledge intersects their day-to-day activities. As a result, students become more fully engaged in the educational process, and thus more fully human. Isn't that one of the points of a liberal arts education? ... In fact, the information age has changed the very nature of what counts as valid knowledge. Valid knowledge is not discrete bits of information that exist in textbooks; instead, students create knowledge as they make meaning of information and its relationships to their day-to-day lives.[40]

Is it this shift from instructor as sole purveyor of knowledge in the classroom that contributes to the resistance of the "will nots"? Certainly the time involved for faculty and students alike to participate in innovative learning processes is daunting and the rewards of doing so within traditional institutional frameworks need to be extended for both faculty (e.g., recognition in tenure and promotion processes) and students (e.g., additional course or lab credit). The institutional routines have not been altered in ways that acknowledge and reward the additional work that is required of participants in such learning initiatives. Indeed, the innovation courses are often self-selected; students must have a keen interest in learning since, undoubtedly, their participation in such a course demands an inevitable extension of their working time and intensifies their work experience. Students in these classes not only have to ensure that they are on top of the traditional reading material, but they also have to stay on top of the technology, given that they are asked to learn new media technology skills that go far, far beyond using the Internet. They, themselves, have to become innovators, with all the additional time and energy that such action demands.

*

While universities may be seeking ways to harness ICTs to increase their market share, the opportunity exists to refocus the application of technological resources. The "will-nots" in our community should have the academic freedom not to employ technological resources, but in doing so, they should not constrain the imagination of those who seek opportunities to create or apply existing technological designs in ways that serve to engage and nurture students as learners. The transformative potential of ICTs in higher education is as much constrained by the fears, interests, values and preferences of academics as it is by market preferences. If we seek to enhance civic competence and inspire citizen engagement, technological resources can support that vision. Similarly, if we seek a knowledge-based economy and society, then the onus is indeed on universities to invite and sustain an open, community-based dialogue about teaching and learning. What is "on the line" are not questions about technology per se, but rather questions about authority and power relations at all levels, including the relationship between the university and society. A discussion about the transition from dependent to interdependent learners throws light on the power relationships that are involved in traditional modes of learning.

Campbell observes that the challenge for feminist pedagogical innovators lies in "confronting and reconciling their own values and practices, associated with teaching and assessment, with those of the patriarchal institution and with the expectations of learners who are acculturated to the implied power structures."[41] In a period of crisis and change within the academy, the very identification of the gendered nature of society and its institutions threatens it. Technological resources can support the social construction of new pedagogical communities. Students become agenda setters, problem identifiers and sometimes, through their individual and collective efforts, they may serve to ameliorate or address socio-political and other problems in valuable ways. Although we are only at the very early stages of exploring and understanding the potential of ICTs to facilitate profound pedagogical shifts, it is clear that technological resources can enable students to develop their own research communities, with results that can serve diverse communities of interest.

Fear of and resistance to technology in academe may be rooted in the recognition that we can choose to embed equity-seeking values and objectives in the new technological Trojan horse. However, responses to technological innovation reflect a myriad of fears, opposing interests and diverse values. Fundamentally, the issue is not technological change itself but the profound and long overdue *social change* within institutions of higher learning that can be facilitated by powerful new technological resources. In this period of transition, an unprecedented opportunity exists to challenge the market-driven technological imperative and to destabilize inequitable gender relations on university campuses by designing and applying computer-mediated feminist pedagogical resources. We can imagine a "control, alt, delete" scenario in which our technological future is characterized by the further loss of control over our feminist-based intellectual activities, the inability to imagine and realize alternative gender relations in our classrooms and in our work-place and, indeed, the deletion of those who are most vulnerable within the academic system.

Or we can imagine a "control, alt, delete" scenario in which women and other marginalized communities of interest within the academy gain control over their own intellectual paths, in which alternative gender relationships are realized and valued, and in which persistent, inegalitarian, gendered power relations within the academy are identified and deleted. Support, and perhaps even the impetus to advance this second vision, may come from outside the academy. That is, I expect that an important source for change in academe is likely to come from savvy incoming students who have already experienced the democratic communicative potential of technology. Those students will be dissatisfied with traditional pedagogical approaches and will seek out the kind of intellectual engagement that feminist pedagogical technological designs proffer.[42]

NOTES

1. Louise Morley et al., "Sounds and Silences: Gendered Change in Higher Education Institutions in the Commonwealth" (paper presented to the 8th International Interdisciplinary Congress on Women, Women's World 2002, July 2002, Makerere University, Kampala, Uganda), 1. Available on-line from <http://www. makerere.ac.ug/womenstudies/full%20papers/morley.htm>.

2. Jon Carroll, "The Glass Ceiling as Signifier," *SFGATE,* 12 February 2001. Available on-line from <http:// www.sfgate.com/chronicle/archive/2001/02/12/ DD192690.DTL>.

3. Katy Campbell, "Power, Voice and Democratization: Feminist Pedagogy and Assessment in CMC," *Educational Technology and Society* 5, no. 3 (2002), 29.

4. V. Reed, "Cyberspace(s), Critical Gazes," 5. Retrieved from <http://epsilon3. georgetown.edu/~coventrm/asa2000/panel4/reed.html>. January 1, 2004.

5. David Beckett, "Disembodied Learning: How Flexible Delivery Shoots Higher Education in the Foot: Well, Sort of," *EJS* 3, no. 3. (1998), 2. Available on-line from <http://www. sociology.org/vol003.003/beckett.article.1998.html>.

6. Steven Jones, "The Internet Goes to College." Pew Internet and American Life Project (15 September 2002). Retrieved from <http://www. pewinternet.org/reports/toc.asp?Report=73>. January 2, 2004.

7. George Kontos, "The Laptop University: A Faculty Perspective." *Educational Technology Review* 9, no. 1 (2001), 5–6. Available on-line from <http://wwww.aace.org/pubs/etr/issue1/kontos.cfm>.

8. Laurie Finke, "Women: Lost in Cyberspace?" Retrieved from <http://www.enhanced-learning.org/prox/paper5.htm>. January 2, 2004.

9. Mary Anne Feeney, "Women in College: Blatant Lack of Faculty Equality, Female Profs Say," *Virtually Advising*, 21 August 2000, 3. Retrieved from <http://www.virtuallyadvising.com/content/wic/03faculty.shtml>. January 2, 2004.

10. "Leaders of 9 Universities and 25 Women Faculty Meet at MIT, Agree to Equity Reviews," *MIT News*, 30 January 2001. Retrieved from <http://www.web.mit.edu/newsoffice /nr/2001/gender.html>. January 2, 2004.

11. Monique Frize, NSERC/Nortel Joint Chair for Women in Science and Engineering (Ontario), Presentation to the HSSFC's Women's Issues Network Symposia, Ottawa, 2000. Available on-line from <http://www.hssfc.ca/english/policyandadvocacy/win/ivorytworfrize.cfm>.

12. Vera Dordick, "RPI Program Encourages, Supports Women Who Choose to be Engineers," *The Business Review*, 19 October 2001, 2. Available on-line from <http://albany.bizjournals.com/albany/stories/2001/10/22/focus6.html>.

13. "Tracking Online Life: How Women Use the Internet to Cultivate Relationships with Family and Friends." The Pew Internet and American Life Project (10 May 2000), 7. Available on-line from <http://www.pewinternet.org>.

14. Reed, "Cyberspace(s), Critical Gazes," 3. See also Kathleen Korgen, Patricia Odell and Phyllis Schumacher, "Internet Use Among College Students: Are There Difference by Race/Ethnicity?" *Electronic Journal of Sociology* (2001), 7. Available on-line from <http://www. sociology.org/content/vol1005.003/korgen.html>.

15. Tara Brabazon, "Internet Teaching and the Administration of Knowledge," *First Monday: Peer-Reviewed Journal on the Internet* 6, no. 6 (June 2001), 3. Available on-line from <http://www.firstmonday.dk/issues/issue6_6/ brabazon/index.html>.

16. James J. Duderstadt, "New Roles for the Twenty-first Century University," *Issues in Science and Technology Online* (Winter 1999), 11. Available on-line from <http://www.nap.edu/issues/16.2/duderstadt.htm>.

17. Theodore Panitz, "Re-organizing Knowledge: Trans-forming Institutions and the University in the Twenty-first Century" (position paper presented at the International Conference of the University of Massachusetts, September 17–19, 1999). Available on-line from <http://www.capecod.net/~tpanitz/tedspage/tedsarticles/teaching.htm>.

18. Randall K. Engle, "The Neo Sophists: Intellectual Integrity in the Information

Age," *First Monday: Peer-Reviewed Journal on the Internet* 6, no. 8 (August 2001), 13. Available on-line from <http://www.firstmonday.dk/issues/issue6_8/engle/index.html>.

19. Acadia University Faculty Association, "Open Letter to Students" (n.d.). Retrieved from <http://www3.ns.sympatico.ca/aufa/negotiations/openlet.htm>.

20. David F. Noble, "Digital Diploma Mills: The Automation of Higher Education," *First Monday: Peer-Reviewed Journal on the Internet*, 10. Available on-line from <http://www.firstmonday.dk/issues/issue3_1/noble/index.html >.

21. Ibid., 9.

22. Brabazon, "Internet Teaching and the Administration of Knowledge," 4.

23. Jill Arnold and Hugh Miller, "Same Old Gender Plot? Women Academics' Identities on the Web" (paper presented at the Cultural Diversities in/and Cyberspace Conference, University of Maryland, May 2000), 10. Available on-line from <http://www.ess.ntu.ac.uk/miller/cyberpsych/gendplot.htm>.

24. Brabazon, "Internet Teaching and the Administration of Knowledge," 3.

25. Suzanne de Castell, Mary Bryson and Jennifer Jenson, "Object Lessons: Towards an Educational Theory of Technology," in *First Monday: Peer-Reviewed Journal on the Internet* (January 2002), 11–12. Available on-line at <http://www.firstmonday.dk/issues/issue7_1/castell/index.html>.

26. Jill Arnold and Hugh Miller, "Breaking Away from Home? Cyberculture and Gendered Academic Identities on the Web" (paper presented at Constructing Cybercultures: Performance, Pedagogy and Politics in Online Spaces Conference, University of Maryland, April 6–7, 2001). Available on-line from <http://www.ess.ntu.ac.uk/miller/cyberpsych/maryland.htm>.

27. Dave S. Knowlton, "Promoting Liberal Arts Thinking through Online Discussion: A Practical Application and its Theoretical Basis," *Educational Technology and Sociology* 5, no. 3 (2002), 192.

28. Ibid., 193.

29. "Faculty Involvement with Educational Technology at Queen's." A Report Prepared by the Learning Technology Faculty Associates (7 March 2001). Available on-line from <http://www.its/queensu.ca/ltfa/report/ETAC.shtml>.

30. Tara Kuther, "Gender, Work, Stress, and Health." *What You Need To Know about Graduate School.* Retrieved from <http://gradschool.about. com/library/weekly/aa012603a.htm>. See also George Kontos, "The Laptop University: A Faculty Perspective," *Educational Technology Review* 9, no. 1 (2001). Available on-line from <http://www.aace.org/pubs/etr/issue1/kontos.cfm>.

31. The Acadia Institute for Teaching and Technology, *Faculty Survey 2002*. Retrieved from <http://www.acadiau.ca/research/research.html>. January 2, 2004.

32. Michele Jacobsen, "Excellent Teaching and Early Adopters of Instructional Technology" (paper submitted to Ed-Media 2000, Montreal, June 26–July 1, 2000). Available on-line from <http://www.ucalgary.ca/!mjacobs/edmedia/edmedia2000_proposal.html>.

33. ICQ refers to the "I See You" chat software that students love to use. Centre for Organizational Research and Development (COR&D), *2000 Survey of Acadia Faculty* (Wolfville, NS: COR&D, 2000), 11.

34. John Schwartz, "Professors Vie With Web for Class's Attention," *The New York Times Online* (January 2003). Available from <http://www.austcolpsych.org /newsroom/sources/blackboard.html>.

35. COR&D, *2000 Survey of Acadia Faculty*, 5.

36. Mike Sosteric, Mike Gismondi and Gina Ratkovic, "The University, Accountability, and Market Discipline in the Late 1990s," *Electronic Journal of Sociology* (1998). Available on-line from <http://www.sociology.org/content/ vol003.003/sosteric.html>.

37. Ibid., 9. Emphasis added.

38. Cathy N. Davidson, "Teaching the Promise: The Research University in the Information Age," 6. Availble on-line from <http://www.digitalpromise.org/about/digital_gift/index.asp>.

39. "The Canadian Network of Federalism Studies." Available on-line from <http://www.cnfs-recef.net>. This is a university-based "virtual network" that promotes the study of federalism among undergraduate and graduate students.

40. Knowlton, "Promoting Liberal Arts Thinking through Online Discussion," 193.

41. Campbell, "Power, Voice and Democratization," 36.

42. See, for example, the Bridges of Understanding Initiative at <http://www. bridgesweb.org> or the Aboriginal Youth Network at <http://www.ayn.ca>.

CONTRIBUTORS

CAROL AGOCS is a Professor in the Department of Political Science and Director of the Local Government Program at the University of Western Ontario. Her publications include *Workplace Equality: International Perspectives on Legislation, Policy and Practice* and *Employment Equity: Cooperative Strategies for Organizational Change*, as well as a number of articles and chapters on discrimination in employment and on equality policy and its implementation.

CYNTHIA JACQUELINE ALEXANDER is an Associate Professor of Political Science at Acadia University. She has been investigating the adoption of computer technologies by the Canadian government since the mid-1980s, paying particular attention to how new media technologies can meet the policy needs and interests of marginalized communities. She is the co-author of *A Stake In the Future: Redefining the Canadian Mineral Industry*, the co-editor of *Digital Democracy: Policy and Politics in the Wired World* and has had numerous articles published in academic journals. She is currently co-investigating with a small research team whether and how "youth at risk" in Nova Scotia and Nunavut are acquiring the literacy skills they need to participate in the digital world.

REEM KHALIL ATTIEH is a PhD candidate at York University. She is currently living in Ramallah, Occupied Territories, and working at Birzeit University in the Information Technology Department as a researcher, where she is part of a team examining the feasibility of developing and delivering on-line courses in the Occupied Territories and the Arab world. Her work is also part of her preliminary research for her dissertation, which will focus on Israel's construction of the wall and its impact on people living in the Hebron region.

ELIZABETH BLANEY is a PhD candidate in the Faculty of Education, University of New Brunswick. She is also a research co-ordinator for the Muriel McQueen Fergusson Centre for Family Violence Research. She teaches Women's Studies, violence in society and personal and social issues and education. Her research interests include critical feminist theory, class and gender in education and violence against girls and women in rural communities.

ILYA BLUM is Associate Professor of Mathematics at Mount Saint Vincent University. In addition to his work in mathematics, he frequently uses his statistical and analytical expertise in collaboration with colleagues in other disciplines. Recent journal publications include "Selection Theorems and Real Compactness," *Pacific Journal of Mathematics;* "A Watershed Level Analysis of the Lakeshore Plant

Community," *Canadian Journal of Botany*; and "Entrepreneurship of University Dietetic Program Graduates," *Canadian Journal of Dietetic Practice and Research* (forthcoming). He actively uses his expertise in his work with the Faculty Association on issues of salary and benefits.

ELIZABETH BRULÉ is a doctoral student in the Faculty of Sociology and Equity Studies at the Ontario Institute for Studies in Education/University of Toronto. Her research interests include education policy, feminist and anti-racist pedagogy, the social organization of knowledge and contractual law. For the past ten years she has taught courses in the Faculty of Social Science, Atkinson College, York University.

A. MARGUERITE CASSIN is a specialist in public sector management and gender, work and organization. She is the author of numerous papers and monographs on the topics of work, pay, management, gender and organization. In the early part of her career, Dr. Cassin spent ten years working in policy, planning and management for the federal government and for the provincial governments of Manitoba and British Columbia. Since joining the university she has consulted governments and organizations on matters of policy, gender, governance, amalgamation and organizational development. She has appeared as an expert witness on matters of organization and gender equality before provincial human rights commissions, boards of inquiry and provincial courts.

MARTIN COOKE is a PhD candidate in the Department of Sociology at the University of Western Ontario, where he holds a SSHRC Doctoral Fellowship. He is a winner of the Policy Research Initiative's 2000 Policy Research Awards graduate prize, and has interests in the welfare state and social inequality as well as the social demography of Aboriginal peoples. He is currently working with the Workforce and Ageing in the New Economy project at Western.

LINDA EYRE is Professor in the Faculty of Education, University of New Brunswick, where she teaches courses in critical studies, feminist theory and critical/feminist approaches to health education. Her recent publications include "No Strings Attached? Corporate Involvement in Curriculum," "Gender Equity and Education Policy in Canada, 1970-2000," "The Discursive Framing of Sexual Harassment in a University Community" and "Re-forming (Hetero)sexuality Education."

JANE GORDON is Professor of Sociology at Mount Saint Vincent University. Her scholarly interests focus on undervalued and invisible work. Recent publications include the journal articles "Fieldwork among Friends" and "Women as Voluntary Board Members," *Resources for Feminist Research;* "Scholarship: The New Dimension to Equity Issues for Academic Women," *Women's Studies International Forum;* and "Dancing the Road to Success: Metro Dance and Women" in the collection *Feminist Success Stories/Celebrons Nos Reussites Féministes.* She is the co-ordinator of the graduate program in Women's Studies at Mount Saint Vincent and continues to be involved in equity work through her faculty association and other committees. Her latest passion is learning to play piano music by Canadian women composers.

ELLA HALEY is an Assistant Professor in Sociology in the Centre for Global and Social Analysis at Athabasca University, and an Adjunct Professor in Sociology at the University of Alberta. Her research interests include the deconstruction of environmental inquiries, the sociology of science, environmental health, community organizing around rural industrial pollution issues and the examination of environmental pollution as corporate crime.

JENNIE HORNOSTY is a Professor of Sociology and Women's Studies at the University of New Brunswick. She has been involved for many years with women's issues and the faculty union. Her major research interests are wife abuse in farm and rural communities, issues of equity and the changing nature of academe. Her published anthology articles include "Academic Freedom in Social Context" in *Academic Freedom and the Inclusive University;* "Balancing Child Care and Work" in *The Illusion of Inclusion;* and "Responding to Wife Abuse in Farm and Rural Communities" in *The Trajectories of Rural Life.*

DIANE MEAGHAN is a Professor of Sociology and Women's Studies at Seneca College in Toronto. She has been a visiting scholar in the Centre for Women's Studies at the Ontario Institute for Studies in Education/University of Toronto and is currently on the External Research Funding Committee for the Status of Women Canada and is a consultant for the National Film Board on women's issues. Her numerous chapters in texts and journal articles pertain to issues involving international sex trade work, women's labour, standardized testing as well as equity and restructuring post-secondary education — the later topic is also the focus of a recent SSHRC grant.

LINDA JOAN PAUL is an instructor in the Department of Geography at the University of Regina. Her research interests are related to geography and gender, Aboriginal people and geography and women and travel. She was a member of the CAUT Status of Women Committee for two terms. Along with Swani Vethamany-Globus and Elena Hannah, she co-edited *Women in the Canadian Academic Tundra: Challenging the Chill.*

JUDY PIERS-KAVANAUGH is a PhD candidate in the Faculty of Education, University of New Brunswick. During her time at UNB, she has been a teaching assistant in the Department of Political Science and has taught Personal and Social Issues and Education. Currently, she teaches Political Science and World Issues at a local high school. Her research interests include teacher activism, the experiences of gay youth in school, women and work in teaching and critical feminist theory.

CLAIRE POLSTER is an Associate Professor in the Department of Sociology and Social Studies at the University of Regina. Her research focuses on the ongoing transformation of higher education and university research, particularly in Canada, and its implications for the public interest. She has published articles on a variety of related topics, including government policy and policy-making for higher education and academic research, intellectual property, academic authority and competition within and between universities.

MARILEE REIMER is an Associate Professor at St. Thomas University in Fredericton, New Brunswick, in the Sociology Department. Her research has focused on equity issues for women in both public sector office work and the corporate university. Her published articles include "The New Rule/s, the University and the Consequences for Women" in *Ivory Towers, Feminist Issues: Selected Papers from the WIN Symposia, 2000-2001*; "Searching for Gender Neutrality: A Preliminary Analysis of Gender Neutrality in the Universal Classification Standard," *Optimum: The Journal of Public Sector Management;* "Downgrading Clerical Work in a Textually Mediated Labour Process" in *Knowledge, Experience and Ruling: Studies in the Social Organization of Knowledge;* and "Women's 'Invisible Skills' and Gender Segregation in the Clerical-Administrative Sector," *Optimum: The Journal of Public Sector Management.* She has been involved in establishing the Women's Studies and Gender Studies program at St. Thomas University.

DOROTHY E. SMITH is Professor Emerita in the Department of Sociology and Equity Studies in Education of the University of Toronto and Adjunct Professor, Department of Sociology, University of Victoria. Her published books include *Feminism and Marxism: A Place To Begin, A Way To Go; The Everyday World As Problematic: A Feminist Sociology; The Conceptual Practices of Power: A Feminist Sociology of Knowledge; Texts, Facts, and Femininity: Exploring The Relations of Ruling;* co-edited with Susan Turner, *Doing It the Hard Way: Investigations of Gender and Technology* (Sally Hacker's Collected Papers); *Writing the Social: Critique, Theory and Investigations;* and with Alison Griffith, *Mother's Work for Schools* (forthcoming 2005). She is currently at work on *Institutional Ethnography: A Sociology for People* (forthcoming).